CAMPAIGNS OF THE EASTERN ASSOCIATION

The Rise of Oliver Cromwell, 1642-1645

Laurence Spring

'This is the Century of the Soldier', Fulvio Testi, Poet, 1641

HELION & COMPANY

Helion & Company Limited
Unit 8 Amherst Business Centre
Budbrooke Road
Warwick
CV34 5WE
England
Tel. 01926 499 619
Email: info@helion.co.uk
Website: www.helion.co.uk
Twitter: @helionbooks
Visit our blog http://blog.helion.co.uk/

Published by Helion & Company 2022
Designed and typeset by Mary Woolley, Battlefield Design (www.battlefield-design.co.uk)
Cover designed by Paul Hewitt, Battlefield Design (www.battlefield-design.co.uk)

Text © Laurence Spring 2022
Illustrations as individually credited © Helion & Company 2022
Front colour artwork by Giorgio Albertini © Helion & Company 2022
Maps by George Anderson © Helion & Company 2022

ISBN 978-1-915113-98-6

British Library Cataloguing-in-Publication Data.
A catalogue record for this book is available from the British Library.

For details of other military history titles published by Helion & Company Limited
contact the above address or visit our website: http://www.helion.co.uk.

We always welcome receiving book proposals from prospective authors.

Contents

Acknowledgements iv
Introduction v

1 First Campaigns 8
2 Manchester Takes Command 37
3 Newark 57
4 Siege of York 70
5 Marston Moor 89
6 Crawford's Campaign 127
7 Manchester's Campaign 134
8 Newbury Campaign 146
9 The Winter of Discontent 165
10 Last Campaigns 179
Conclusion 190

Notes and Observations of the Eastern Association Cornets 197
Colour Plate Commentaries 199

Appendices:
I Organisation 208
II Journal of Colonel Montagu's Regiment 228
III Captured Regimental Colours 232

Bibliography 234

Acknowledgements

I would like to thank the staff of The National Archives, the British Library, the Bodleian Library, the Parliamentary Archives, Essex Record Office, Hampshire Record Office, Hertfordshire Record Office, Norfolk Record Office, Somerset Heritage Centre, the Suffolk Record Office, West Yorkshire History Centre and the team that are responsible for the Civil War Petitions website, without whom this book would not be possible.

The Series Editor would like to thank Serena Jones for her work on this manuscript and Stephen Ede-Borrett for his contribution of illustrations and notes on the colours and cornets of the Eastern Association Army.

Introduction

The army of the Eastern Association has two claims to fame, the first is that Oliver Cromwell served in the army and the second is that thanks to him the Parliamentarians won the battle of Marston Moor. True, Cromwell did play a major role in the war and the army, but he has overshadowed many who also deserve recognition for the parts they played. Cromwell largely contributed to this since he often wrote the accounts of battle himself which were published in the various Parliamentarian newspapers of the time, with his actions overshadowing others. Even at the time he was accused of climbing to the top on the backs of others. Today, even people who know very little about the Civil War have heard of him and he came third in the 'Greatest Britain' TV series. When writing his article for the *Dictionary of National Biography* John Morrill identified over 160 biographies and 1,000 publications dedicated to Cromwell alone and there is no doubt that this number has increased considerably since then. He has also appears in the 1970 film bearing his name, with various other cameo performances in films and television programmes. Therefore I hope in the following pages to give a more balanced view of the events of the Eastern Association during 1643 to 1645.

Although Lord Grey of Warke and the Earl of Manchester have their own entries in the *Dictionary of National Biography*, little else has been written about them. The Victorian historian Samuel Rawson Gardiner compared Manchester with Cromwell, by stating that Manchester, 'often acknowledged, he was a civilian, not a soldier, and he was not, as Cromwell had been two years before, a civilian with the making of a soldier in him.'[1] The Royalist Sir Philip Warwick judged Manchester to be a 'gentleman of very good parts … but very facile or changeable.'[2] Whereas a letter written to Manchester's wife, Essex, during the siege of York in June 1644 records that, 'My Lord of Manchester's health doth very well agree with a soldier's life and suffers without distemper.'[3] True the letter writer could have been just humouring his wife, Essex, who was the daughter of Sir Thomas Cheke of Pirgo in

---

1   S. R. Gardiner, *The History of the Great Civil War* (London: Longmans, Green & Co., 1893), vol. II, p.49.

2   Sir Philip Warwick, *Memoirs of the Reign of King Charles the First* (Edinburgh: John Ballantyne and Co., 1813) pp.272–273.

3   Parliamentary Archives (PA): Wil/2/43.

Essex. Her grandfather was the Robert Rich, Earl of Holland and 1st Earl of Warwick.[4] In all Manchester would have five wives.

Like all of the armies of the Civil War the Eastern Association never had enough money to pay and equip its soldiers, despite the heavy burden of taxation on the local inhabitants. As Professor Ronald Hutton rightly points out:

> There is a story, very popular in recent decades, of a farmer on Marston Moor, who was working in a field in July 1644, when the armies arrived to fight the biggest battle of the English Civil War. On being told that the quarrel was between king and parliament, he replied, 'what, has they two fallen out again?' Unfortunately, the incident is not recorded in any contemporary source. The Civil War was just not that sort of war. For almost two years our farmer would have had to send money and supplies to a garrison at York, seven miles away. Soldiers would continually have crossed his lands. For the past two months he would have been forced to give money and food to a huge army besieging York. His horses would probably have been taken too, and he would have been lucky if his cottage had not been plundered bare. This was, in brief, not a conflict that anybody could either not know about or could ignore. In fact, it was because the people were dragged reluctantly into it and loathed it, that it was eventually halted.[5]

When it comes to the second battle of Newbury, for those who have read my book on *Campaigns of Sir William Waller*, I hope you will excuse that I have repeated several eyewitness accounts, but this cannot be helped since they are necessary to explain the narrative of the battle.

Although Lord Grey of Warke had to rely on the trained bands of the counties which made up the Eastern Association so that he could take the field, Manchester was luckier since his army was strong enough to dispense with these regiments, although they were still used for local actions.

The same cannot be said of the armies of the Earl of Essex and Sir William Waller, who had to rely on the London Trained Bands to bring their armies up to strength. However, this strategic reserve was a double-edged sword: on the one hand Essex and Waller needed them to take the field, but on the other they were reluctant to serve for long periods. For example the gains of Waller's victory at the battle of Cheriton (29 March 1644) were lost within a month because his London Brigade wanted to go home, and likewise it was not Waller's defeat at the battle of Cropredy Bridge (29 June 1644) which made his army disintegrate, but the loss of the Trained Bands for the same reason. Moreover Essex and Waller hated each other, and were unwilling to work with each other, but Manchester's army was different in that it was divided through faction fighting within its ranks. According to Robert Baillie:

> Our greatest fear is, that the forces we have to oppose the King are full of jealousies and malice one against another. The most of the officers in the General's [Essex]

---

4   *Dictionary of National Biography.* This was his third wife, who died 28 September 1658.
5   Ronald Hutton, 'For King and County', in *The Making of Britain: the Age of Expansion*, ed. Lesley Smith (London: Macmillan, 1986), p.67.

and Waller's army is open and known quarrels. Manchester's army is more pitifully divided: it is like to divide us all incontinent. Manchester himself is a sweet meek man, permitted his Lieutenant General Cromwell to guide all his army at his pleasure: the man is a very wise and active head, universally well beloved, as religious and stout; being a known Independent, the most of the soldiers who loved new ways put themselves under his command.[6]

Moreover the counties which made up the Eastern Association are seen as staunch supporters of the Parliamentarian cause, but this is also not true. On 8 August 1642 John Merrill at Huntingdon wrote to Manchester (at that time still styled as Lord Mandeville), 'Ordinances of Parliament are little regarded', and said that those who supported Parliament – the 'good people', as Merrill calls them – were 'openly reviled and threatened'. The King's lifeguard and the regiment of foot commanded by Charles' Lord General, the Earl of Lindsey, were both originally raised in Lincolnshire. Throughout the war the Eastern Association's war efforts would be continually threatened by Royalist sympathisers who lived on its borders. In February 1646 it would take 30 troopers and 60 dragoons to escort 296 recruits to their rendezvous and in 1648 during the Second Civil War, Essex would be in open revolt against Parliament.[7]

6   Robert Baillie, *Letters and Journals of Robert Baillie*, ed. D. Laing (Edinburgh: 1841), p.229.
7   HMC: Appendix to 8th Report, p.59; British Library (BL): Stowe, MS 164 f.63–64; Peter Young, *Edgehill: The Campaign and the Battle* (Kineton: The Roundwood Press, 1967), p.255.

1

First Campaigns

On 22 August 1642 when the King raised the royal standard at Nottingham many believed that there would not be a war since Charles would not have enough supporters to fight it. Even the trained bands who had been embodied for the occasion soon went home and when the standard blew down that evening it was seen as a bad omen. However, in September Charles had gathered enough soldiers to fight. During these months the counties which would make up the Eastern Association were wavering in their support for King or Parliament, with Lincolnshire raising two regiments for Charles' field army and the universities of Cambridge sending him their plate and other riches for his cause.

While the gentry were raising their regiments they could summon their county's militia or trained bands, which on paper formed a considerable force. On 9 February 1637 the trained bands in England mustered a total of 93,718 infantry and 5,239 cavalry of which 4,030 infantry and 250 horse came from Essex: 1,800 infantry and 230 cavalry from Lincolnshire; 5,317 infantry and 400 cavalry from Norfolk; 1,500 infantry and 80 cavalry from Hertfordshire, and 4,148 infantry and 129 cavalry from Suffolk, a total of 16,795 infantry and 1,089 cavalry.[1] However, these were designed for defence of their own county and were only willing to serve for short periods of time, so were unsuitable for a lengthy campaign. Furthermore, despite Charles I's best efforts to modernise the trained bands and keep them well trained by introducing drill sergeants, these reforms had little to no success. Some counties, such as Essex and Hertfordshire, even included some lancers which had long since gone out of fashion in Europe. Also a militiaman could hire a substitute to go in his place, who probably had little to no training. Even so the trained bands still had a strategic place in the war because the side who could secure a county's militia not only deprive the other sides of this force, but also their weapons could be 'borrowed' to arm other regiments who were willing to serve for a longer period of time.

Among those commissions issued by Parliament in August was one appointing Oliver Cromwell a captain of a troop of horse. One early

---

1   TNA: SP 16/381/143, 'The Trained Bands of the Several Counties of England and Wales', collected 9 February 1637.

biographer states that his troop was raised at his own expense, but warrants issued at the time clearly show that this was not the case since he received £1,104 plus the arms and armour were supplied centrally.[2] With this troop he prevented the universities at Cambridge from donating more money and plate to the Royalist cause, but on 13 September he was ordered to join the Earl of Essex who was gathering his army at Northampton. Cromwell's troop was listed in Essex's own regiment of horse.

Among the regiments which also joined Essex was that of Edward, Lord Mandeville (later Earl of Manchester) who had raised a regiment of foot, but at the battle of Edgehill on 23 October it was one of the first regiments of Colonel Charles Essex's brigade to run away. Although Essex's regiment of horse was present and was one of the few cavalry units to distinguish itself that day, Cromwell appears to have arrived late on the scene. Denzil Holles, whose regiment also distinguished itself during the battle, was all too ready to accuse his political opponents of cowardice: he records that Cromwell dallied during the battle, and claimed that 'the day after, that he had been all that day been seeking the army and place of [the] fight, although his quarters were but at a village near [to] hand, whence he could not find his way, nor be directed by his ear, when the ordnance was heard, as I have been credibly informed, 20 or 30 miles off'.[3]

No doubt Cromwell's troop accompanied Essex's army on its march to London, probably along with other troops commanded by Lord Grey of Warke, Captain Valentine Walton and Henry Ireton, who would have key roles in the future Eastern Association, while the remnants of Mandeville's Regiment were disbanded. Fortunately for the Parliamentarian cause Essex's army arrived first at the outskirts of London, Charles having refused to allow Prince Rupert with a flying column of Royalists to race ahead and seize the

Oliver Cromwell (Public Domain)

---

2   Charles H. Firth and Godfrey Davis, *The Regimental History of Cromwell's Army* (Oxford: Clarendon Press, 1940), vol. I. p.1.
3   Denzil Holles, *Memoirs of Denzil, Lord Holles* (1699), p.17.

capital, fearing that he might leave a trail of plundered towns and villages behind him.

On 12 November both sides faced each other at Turnham Green, but there would be no battle and later that day being greatly outnumbered the King retreated to Oxford, which would be his capital for the rest of the war. By now it was obvious the war would go on and preparations were made on both sides for 1643. On 26 November 1642 Parliament ordered that the gentlemen of Norfolk, Suffolk and Essex meet to consider an association of these counties for their mutual defence. Two days later it was proposed that Cambridgeshire, Hertfordshire and the city of Norwich should also join this association, but the final decision was not made until the Commons had spoken with the Earl of Warwick.[4] On 15 December the associating of these counties was voted upon in the Commons and then sent to the Lord for consent.[5] Even so it was not until 9 February that the various county leaders agreed to implement Parliament's ordinance associating their counties; but who was to command the army of the Eastern Association? Originally it was planned that the Earl of Warwick should take command. He was the Lord Lieutenant of the county of Essex, but had been appointed to command another army, which was later reduced into the Earl of Essex's army. By then he had been promoted to admiral of Parliament's navy, so the command fell to Lord Grey of Warke, who was appointed Major General of the Eastern Association. By this time King's Lynn had already been fortified, since it was considered so important that it had two companies of trained bands, who were ordered not to leave the town except by order of the mayor and aldermen. A plan of King's Lynn by Wenceslaus Hollar shows that the town was encompassed on three sides by fortifications with 10 bastions of various sizes, the fourth side being protected by the River Ouse.[6]

At the beginning of the war Queen Henrietta Maria went to Europe with the royal jewels to sell for the Royalist cause, and rumours quickly spread that she had raised an army of 13,000 Catholics to fight for cause. Therefore large parts of East Anglia were put on alert for fear of the forthcoming invasion. On 5 November 1642 several officials of King's Lynn were ordered to attend a meeting 'for consulting and considering of some speedy course to be taken for the trained bands of horse and foot to be fitted in a readiness to oppose [the] foreign forces much feared to be suddenly landed in some part of the coast of Norfolk, Suffolk and Essex.'[7] While on 8 December 1642 the Committee of Cambridge wrote to the Deputy Lieutenants of Norfolk to muster the trained bands:

> to be in readiness to answer any alarm that shall be given upon the coasts and to draw down the said forces to oppose the landings of any enemies in performance

4   *Journal of the House of Commons*, vol. II, pp.865, 867.
5   *Journal of the House of Commons*, vol. II, pp.865, 867, 889.
6   HMC: 11th Report Appendix 3, 'the manuscripts of the Corporations of Southampton and King's Lynn' (London: HMSO, 1887), pp.178–179.
7   HMC: 11th Report Appendix 3, 'The Manuscripts of the Corporations of Southampton and King's Lynn' (London: HMSO, 1887), p.178.

of which command and performance of that duty we owe to our country, we have thought fit to desire and require you that you forthwith put your band or company in such a posture as that they be ready to march to such rendezvous as shall be appointed by us in an hour's warning and that you cause every musketeer presently to provide himself of two pounds of powder, four pounds of bullets and one pound of match and for the present defence of themselves, their wives, children religion and country.[8]

No such invasion came, but it shows that many feared that Charles would stoop so low as to hire foreign mercenaries to impose his will on the people. When the Irish Rebellion had broken out in October 1641, Lucy Hutchinson wrote, 'long was he [Charles] before he could proclaim these murderers rebels'.[9] Everyone saw that an army was needed to put down this uprising, but many did not trust Charles, whose situation was made worst by the Irish Catholics actually claiming that they had a royal warrant to carry out their actions. Although the warrant was almost certainly a fake, it did not stop the propagandists declaring that 200,000 Protestants had been slain by the Catholics, and many refugees who fled from Ireland, appeared to prove the atrocities which were happening in Ireland and caused various 'Catholic panics' throughout England of a similar uprising. Later in the war Charles would indeed bring over the regiments which formed the English army in Ireland and later detachments of Irish soldiers. However, it was when Charles' correspondence was captured after the battle of Naseby in June 1645, which revealed that these fears with correct, albeit several years too early. His 'cabinet' revealed that since January 1645 Charles had been not only negotiating with the Irish Confederates to bring over their army, which was estimated to be about 10,000 strong men from Ireland, but also a similar size army commanded by Duke Charles of Lorraine, whose army was renowned for its ill discipline. Although neither armies appeared in the English theatre of war the very thought horrified both Parliamentarians and Royalists alike.[10]

On 27 February Parliamentarian forces under the command of Lord Willoughby of Parham, who commanded the Parliamentarian forces in Lincolnshire, marched out of Lincoln and were joined by other detachments from the county as well as from Derbyshire under Sir John Gell and laid siege to Newark. The Lincolnshire infantry seems to have been mainly from the county's trained bands and volunteers who were 'armed with such weapons they can procure'.[11] The siege appears to have gone badly from the start, although Gell managed to gain part of the town, but the Lincolnshire trained bands failed to support him and even the Parliamentarian newspaper *The Kingdomes Weekly Intelligencer* records that they 'ran away like cowards'. Without their support Gell was soon driven out of the town with four of

---

8   Bodleian Library (Bod Lib): Tanner, MS 64 f.117.
9   Lucy Hutchinson, *Memoirs of the Life of Colonel Hutchinson* (London: Henry and Bohn, 1846), p.94.
10   *King's Cabinet Opened or certain packets of secret letters and papers written with the King's own hand, and taken in his cabinet at Naseby field, 14 June 1645* pp.17–18, 21–23, 31–32.
11   *A Perfect Diurnall.*

N

● Pontefract

Hull ●

River Trent

● Gainsborough

● Winceby

River Witham

● Bolinbroke

Newark ●

● Sleaford

Boston ●

● Belton

Nottingham ●

● Grantham

King's Lynn ●

● Crowland

River Wellard

● Wisbech

● Leicester

River Nene

● Ely

Huntingdon ●

Cambridge ●

Northampton ●

| 0 | 5 | 10 | 15 | 20 | 25 miles |

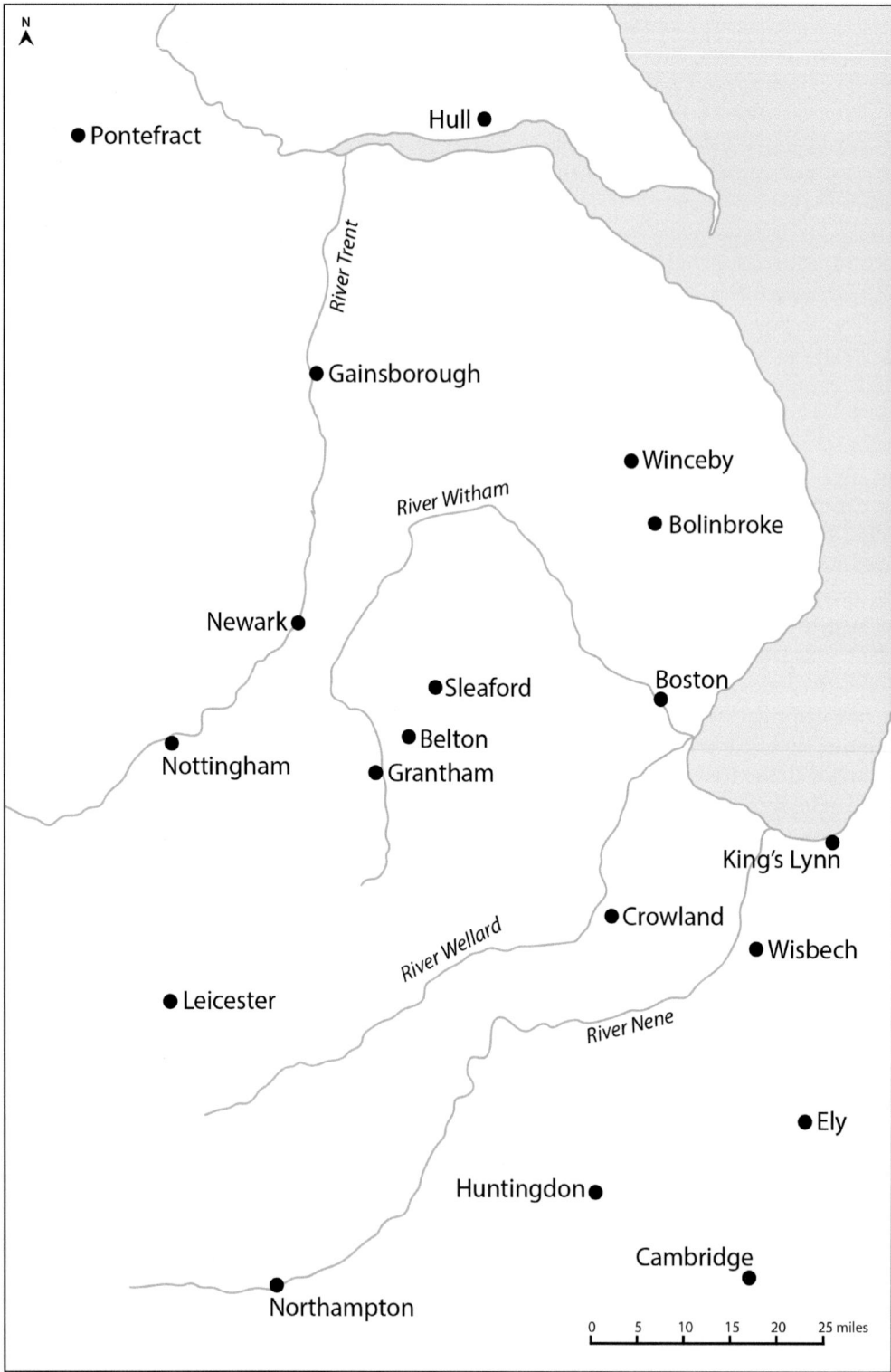

Campaigns of 1643

their 10 pieces of ordnance being captured.[12] Had the Lincolnshire trained bands supported Gell and captured Newark, then the Civil War in East Anglia would have been very different because the town would be a thorn in the Parliamentarians' side throughout the war, only surrendering in 1646 when ordered to do so by Charles I himself. But now with a secure base, the garrison of Newark would raid the counties of the Eastern Association. The Lincolnshire trained bands were not the only county militia to be assembled: those of Suffolk secured the town of Ipswich for Parliament, who also had Royalist sympathisers and searched their houses for weapons.

Having been commissioned as Major General of the Eastern Association, Grey set about raising regiments for his army. He raised a regiment of horse using the troop he had commanded in 1642 as a nucleus, and also a regiment of foot. To add to this force on 25 March Thomas Ayloffe received a commission to raise a regiment of foot in Huntingdonshire, while the three Essex trained band regiments of Sir Thomas Barrington, the Earl of Warwick and Thomas Honeywood, were also allocated to join his army. Sir John Palgrave and Sir John Wittrough were also commissioned to raise a regiment of foot in Norfolk and Hertfordshire respectively. Norfolk raised another regiment of foot under the command of Sir Miles Hobart, which captured Wisbech and afterwards garrisoned the town.

The recruiting of volunteers soon gave way to 'impressment' or conscription, who usually came from the poorest in a parish, the so called 'masterless men' who were a burden to the parish in that they claimed poor relief, but gradually as the war progressed more and more men from a parish would be forced into the army. In Essex (and probably the other counties), the prescribed method of conscription was as follows:

List at least 12 score of men well affected, being nearest together.

Let them be called together unto a communal place and when they are so listed apart [from] all those who in regard of ages, infirmity and public employment the rest of that company left be agreed upon.

The half of that company must go and half stay at home.

Those whose lot it is to stay at home shall advance so much money as it shall be thought reasonable they will spend, in case their lot should be to go and that money to be for their uses thereafter agreed.

Then let them be papers equally cut and half marked and half not; here do many as there is in the company and being well mixed and put into a bag after Sessions commending the business of God everyone draw his lot, if a blank he stay if a marked paper to go.

Then let those whose lot it is to go together and choose their captains and also those that are to stay do the like and the captains, their officers and when 10 companies of each sort are thus gathered then that those captains choose their colonel.[13]

12   *The Kingdomes Weekly Intelligencer; Mercurius Aulicus* 3 March 1643.
13   BL: Egerton, MS 2651.

However, there were exemptions to those who could be impressed, those who belonged to the clergy or were students of 'any universities … or any [of] the trained bands in any county, city or place'. Those wealthy enough to pay the taxes imposed by Parliament or 'any person of the rank or degree of an esquire or upwards, or the son of any such person'.[14] Recruits choosing which officers they were to serve under was quickly stopped and they had officers imposed on them.

There was also corruption by the constables of a parish, who were responsible for raising recruits. On 9 May 1643 Thomas Jeake of Upminster in Essex was fined £2 because he discharged two recruits who had been impressed and went to Colonel Walden's house, 'in a very malicious way and at midnight', where he intended 'to press two of his ploughmen' as substitutes. Jeake did not record why he released the two men – presumably a sum of money changed hands – but he had to pay his fine within a fortnight, or it would be increased to £5. On 3 September 1644 William Wood, a servant of Edward Godsall was ordered to be released from military service because he was under 18, the military age being between 18 and 50. The constables of Brentwood, where Wood lived, were ordered to find a replacement.[15] The men would be gathered together and marched off to the appointed rendezvous, where they would either be formed into a company or reinforce an already existing one. Since they were impressed against their will they often made poor soldiers and sought to desert at the first opportunity.

Among those who were to assist Grey was Oliver Cromwell, who was now commissioned to raise a regiment of horse, which mustered just five troops in April. However, Cromwell was a two edged sword to the Eastern Association: on the one hand he was a very capable cavalry officer rising to become a lieutenant general and his religious fervour was a driving force within the army, but it also brought about divisions particularly when his Independent faction clashed with the Presbyterian faction within the army. To help Cromwell defend the counties of the Eastern Association on 17 February 1643, a warrant ordered the delivery of 10 'sakers of brass or iron or such other guns as may best be spared, along with 10 field carriages … 10 barrels of gunpowder of the best [type], 20 hundred [weight] of match, 500 of iron shot fit for the guns'.[16] On 14 March 1643 Cromwell scored an early success at Lowestoft when he surprised a party of Royalists within the town, who surrendered with little or no resistance.

While Grey was organising his own army he was suddenly ordered to join the Earl of Essex's army. He ordered most of his army to rendezvous at Cambridge where the Committee of the Eastern Association would meet throughout the war, and on 7 April 1643 he marched out of the city with 5,000 horse and foot to join Essex, leaving Cromwell behind to defend the

---

14   C. H. Firth and R. S. Rait, *Acts and Ordinances of the Interregnum 1642–1660* (London: 1911), pp.650–651.
15   BL: Add MS 37,491 ff8, 20. Although, some sources state that the military age was between 16 and 60.
16   TNA: WO 55/457 f.36.

heartland of the Eastern Association.[17] At the beginning of April 1643 plans had been drawn up to capture Reading, which had been a thorn in the side of Parliament, and so on 13 April Essex marched out of Windsor, and according to the Earl of Clarendon, 'The Earl had never before been in the head of so gallant an army, which consisted of 16,000 foot and 3,000 horse, in as good equipage, and supply with all things necessary for a siege.' However, a modern estimate states that Essex's army was more likely 12,000 strong.[18] According to Clarendon the town's governor, Sir Arthur Aston, had received orders to abandon it and join Charles at Oxford. The garrison had just 40 barrels of gunpowder, which according to Clarendon, 'would not have held a brisk and a daring enemy four hours', although they were 'abundantly stored' with provisions.[19]

On 15 April Essex arrived at Reading and summoned the garrison to surrender or if Sir Arthur Aston refused then to send out the women and children.[20] To this Aston is quoted as saying that he would not deliver the town until wheat was worth 40 shillings a bushel and that the women and children should 'all die with him'. Whether he actually said this is open to debate since this is taken from a Parliamentarian newsletter which compared it to a 'cruelty unheard of amongst the savages in America, much less among Christians'.[21] Whatever was said, Aston did refuse Essex's summons and the Earl of Clarendon would later record:

> The soldiers without [i.e. the Parliamentarians] were for the most part newly levied, and few of the officers acquainted with the way and order of assaulting towns ... Upon the first sitting down before it, after they had taken a full view of the ground, their general advised with his council of war in what manner he should proceed, whether by assault or approach; in which there was great diversity of opinions. After arguments and debates (in which all the reasons were considered on both sides) the major part of the council inclined – and with that the General complied – to pursue the business of approach.[22]

That night the Parliamentarians began erecting batteries for their artillery and earthworks, as Clarendon continues; 'The approaches advanced very

---

17   Clive Holmes, *The Eastern Association in the English Civil War* (Cambridge University Press, 1974), p.69.

18   Chris Scott and Alan Turton, *Hey for Old Robin, the campaigns and armies of the Earl of Essex during the First Civil War, 1642–1646* (Solihull: Helion and Co., 2017), p.70.

19   Earl of Clarendon *The History of the Great Rebellion*, ed. Roger Lockyer (Oxford University Press, 1967), p.110.

20   According to a book of provisions for Essex's army, reference TNA: SP 28/136 part 56, Colonels Harry Barclay's, Lord Peterborough's, Sir William Constable's, Sir John Meldum's and Lord Roberts' regiments of foot received provisions on 17 April; while Colonel Thomas Ballard's, George Langham's, and James Holborne's regiment first received their provisions the following day. Essex's own regiment on 19 April along with the train of artillery and Philip Skippon's on the 20th; Sir Henry Cholmley's on 21st and Lord Rochford's on 22 April. No cavalry regiments are mentioned.

21   *Certaine Informations.*

22   Clarendon, *The History of the Great Rebellion*, p.111.

fast, the ground being in all places as fit for that work as could be'.[23] The garrison tried to prevent the Parliamentarians digging by opening fire upon them, which according to Sir Samuel Luke's siege diary 'we answering in the like kind'.

Meanwhile Grey's force had reached Watford on 17 April, where the parson, a Mr C. Burgess, saw one of Grey's regiments marching through the town and wrote to the Deputy Lieutenants of Essex:

> to see such a regiment of gallant men come out of your county [Essex] for the public cause. I have presumed to give you some private advertisements of what I observed among the soldiery here, submitting all to your wisdom to make what use thereof you please. The officers they [are] almost out of patience that they be not in action and by their example many of their soldiers stand alike affected, but I find among the bulk of the common soldiers not only murmuring for want of a surgeon, ammunition, wagons, to carry it, and especially an able preacher, but professed resolutions taken up that they will not march beyond this county … without these supplies. And if these be not speedily provided I am confident they will most of them disband.[24]

A Royalist account agreed with Mr Burgess stating that they were, 'all raw and unexperienced men and very ill armed, food for powder only'.[25]

On the 18 or 19 April Grey finally arrived on the outskirts of Reading. Sir Samuel Luke recalls:

> By this time, the Lord Grey appeared before the town, with three regiments of foot; two consisting of 700 a piece, and one of 1700; six troops of horse, of 80 a piece; two troops of dragoons; and three pieces of ordnance; which begirt the enemy round from Sonning to Caversham, northward and southward, being outreached with as much as nature could afford us; the Thames, Kennett, and the Hallowed Brook with many little rivers issuing out of them.[26]

The three regiments of foot probably belonged to the Essex trained bands and the large regiment was possibly Grey's regiments of foot and horse. Luke's enthusiasm for Grey's arrival was short lived because on 21 April while Essex's army was battering Reading with its artillery, Grey's quarters kept 'themselves very quiet'.[27]

Since, as Luke calls them, they were 'freshwater soldiers', two regiments of foot from Essex's army under Colonel Bulstrode and five troops of horse under Major Gunter of Essex's own regiment of horse were allocated to reinforce Grey's men, and 'that night they made their approaches to the town, and planted their ordnance'.[28] In his diary Jeremy Baines, who was

23   Ibid.
24   Quoted in M. C. Barres-Baker, *The Siege of Reading* (Ottowa: ebooksLib, 2004), p.98.
25   Ibid.
26   Luke's siege diary printed in Coates, *History and Antiquities of Reading*, p.33.
27   Ibid.
28   Ibid.

the major of Colonel Melve's regiment, jotted down various tips to remind himself of military matters, and recalls that a corps du garde would be sent 30 or 40 yards in front of the army and if a sentinel heard someone approach he challenges them, 'who goes there?' If the person says friend then he calls for the corporal who is the only one who knows the password, if not then the alarm is sounded.[29]

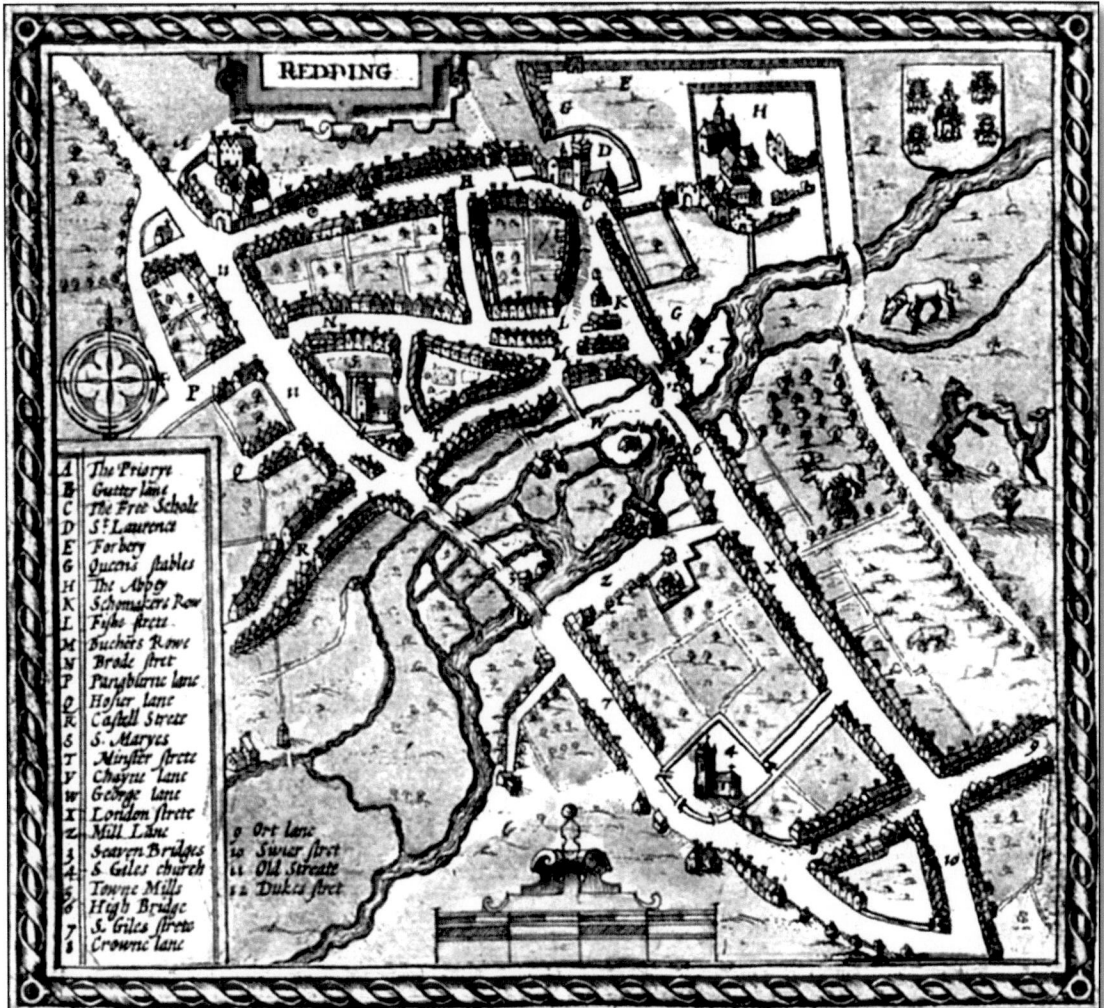

The town of Reading, c.1611

In their book on sieges during the Civil War, Brigadier Peter Young and Wilfred Emberton believed that the Eastern Association's quarters were north of the River Thames between Caversham and Sonning. However, this position is rejected by M.C. Barres-Baker; instead he places them 'in the area north-east of Reading, stretching southward from the Thames towards the present London Road. Warke's lines would thus have extended both north

---

29 BL: Add MS 32477 Diary of Jeremy Baines. He also records that the password for 18 April was 'Lichfield', the 19th 'Coventry', 20th 'Brainford', 21st 'Newbury', 22nd 'Coventry' and 23rd 'Lincoln'.

and south of the River Kennet, placing Caversham Bridge to his right and Sonning behind him'. Since Grey was reinforced by some of Essex's regiments, this meant that he had to extend his lines further south until his force was facing the eastern defences of the city near to Harrison's Barn.[30]

With both Essex's and Grey's soldiers encompassing Reading, Sir Edward Nicholas wrote to Colonel Henry Hastings on 19 April from Oxford, 'We have news that the Lord Grey's forces being joined with the Earl of Essex's, they have begirt Reading so as no man can come forth, or go in; that Sir Arthur Aston is dangerously hurt and that if Prince Rupert come not instantly Reading will be lost'.[31] According to John Gwyn, 'a cannon shot came through the guard house and … [a tile] fell upon his [Aston's] head and sunk him almost to the ground before Colonel [Henry] Lunsford and another officer caught him by both arms, [and] held him up'. He was taken to his house and 'during the rest of the siege' Gwyn continues, 'he was speechless'.[32] The defence of the town now fell upon the deputy governor, Colonel Richard Fielding.

By 19 April it was said that Essex had 'come within musket shot of the town, and have gotten some of the enemy's outworks, and they have strongly entrenched themselves about it'. The newspaper continued, that Essex had not bombarded the town, 'in compassion to the women and children'.[33] However, as Hastings and Gwyn show this was clearly not the case, but the Parliamentarian newspaper *Certaine Informations* was trying to demonise Aston and his Royalists to its readers whereas Essex and his Parliamentarians were shown as civilised in their war effort. This is not to say that the Royalist press was always reliable since on 21 April *Mercurius Aulicus* reported that 500 Parliamentarian soldiers had deserted and 1,000 had been killed, including Lieutenant General Sir Edward Peyto, who commanded Essex's artillery and Colonel John Dalbier, a German engineer; but it would not be until 21 September 1643 that Peyto died and 1648 that Dalbier was killed having changed sides during the Second Civil War. Although, events were not going all the besiegers' way either: in his letter of 19 April Sir Edward Nicholas had also written:

> the Earl of Essex hath not gotten a foot of ground upon Sir Arthur Ashton at Reading, but we have there from the town killed 700 of their men, and broken thereby their two of their best regiments of blue and red coats. If we had here all our forces together it is conceived we might make a very fair opportunity to destroy their army[34]

The redcoats are probably those belonging to Lord Robartes' regiment, which are known to have worn redcoats at this time and was referred to in

---

30   Barres-Baker, pp.98–99.
31   HMC: Report on the Manuscripts of the late Reginald Rawdon Hastings (London: HMSO, 1930), p.98.
32   John Gwyn, Military Memoirs, in *Military Memoirs, The Civil War, Richard Atkins and John Gwyn* (Longmans, Green and Co. Ltd, 1967), ed. Brigadier Peter Young and Norman Tucker, p.48.
33   *Certaine Informations.*
34   HMC: Report Hastings, p.98.

Mercurius Aulicus, which reported that the Earl of Essex's first attack had been repulsed, so a second attack was made, which stormed one of the town's outworks, but:

> was no sooner done by the Lord Robartes, his regiment, (on whom that honour was bestowed) but they [the garrison] fell upon them from the town, being yet unsettled and disordered, repulsed them with the loss of 160 of their men which they left behind them, besides many others which they lost before they could recover their trenches and get out of gun shot [range].[35]

However, other sources record a much lower death toll and that Essex had been advancing his siege lines towards Reading and in some instances had gotten to within musket, or even pistol, shot of the Royalists' defences. On the other hand Nicholas' letter cannot be entirely dismissed as propaganda because the Venetian ambassador, Gerolamo Agostini, wrote about the siege:

> The Parliamentarian soldiers suffer severely from the sword and from the severe weather, which is colder than the winter, and by the lack of food, all of which has to be brought from this city, and is mostly asked in alms, The hospitals are already full of wounded and sick and never a day passes that a considerable number does not arrive, to the universal horror, as the people here are quite unaccustomed to the horrible aspects of war.[36]

According to Clarendon, the Parliamentarians had to hide the large number of casualties, 'who were sent to hospitals near London. Those that were sent to London (as many cart loads were) were brought in the night, and disposed with great secrecy, that the citizens might take no notice of it'.[37] Certainly disease is known to have been ravaging Essex's ranks even before he left Windsor, and what with the cold weather and lack of tents and provisions, so typhus and exposure almost certainly added to the Parliamentarians' casualty figures.

By 21 April two great pieces of artillery had arrived at the siege: according to *Mercurius Aulicus* they were called 'Roaring Meg' and that 'one of them was discharged so often that it had no leisure to cool and so broke in pieces killing the cannoneer, besides divers others'.

At 2:00 a.m. on the 23 April about 2,200 Royalist cavalry and 300 dragoons under Patrick Ruthven, advanced on Reading, hoping to surprise the besiegers. Their aim was to supply the garrison with powder and ammunition, but they were intercepted by two troops of Parliamentarian cavalry who after charging the Royalists fell back to where Colonel Harry Barclay's regiment of foot were, which had been drawn over Caversham Bridge to meet this new threat. They were supported by musketeers of Colonel John Holborne's regiment, which also belonged to Essex's army. With the firepower of both

---

35   *Mercurius Aulicus*, 17 April 1643.
36   Allen B. Hinds, *Calendar of State papers relating to English Affairs in the Archives of Venice, 1643–1643* (London: HMSO, 1925), Geolamo Agostini, to the Doge and Senate. 8 May 1643.
37   Clarendon, pp.111–112.

Barclay's and Holborne's regiments, the Royalists could not cross Caversham Bridge and so drew off. Essex chose Colonels Middleton and Meldrum's regiments of horse and Colonel Melve's regiment of dragoons to pursue them, which at 11:00 p.m. caught up with them at Dorchester and beat up their quarters, but they saw an opportunity to plunder the town rather than continue their pursuit of the Royalists.[38]

Meanwhile, the Royalists were gathering a relieving force at Wallingford. The forlorn hope consisting of 160 horse was commanded by Captain Richard Atkins, which set out at 8:00 or 9:00 a.m. on 25 April. On their arrival they found the Parliamentarians arrayed in battle order ready to meet them. They took up position between the river Thames and Harrison's Barn, 'within musket shot of both', records Atkins, but 'they sent no party out to fight us'. About an hour later the King's main force arrived and drew up on a hill about a mile from Atkin's forlorn hope. To cross the River Thames, the Royalists had to seize Caversham Bridge, but the Parliamentarian picquets seem to have been unaware of their advance because Sir Samuel Luke records:

> Under the Caversham Hill, unexpected to us, came His Majesty's forces, under the command of General Ruthven and Prince Rupert, consisting of about 40 colours of horse, and nine regiments of foot, with ordnance and other ammunition: fell upon a loose regiment that lay there to keep the bridge, gave them a furious assault both with their ordnance and men … This was answered with our muskets, and made the hill so hot for them that they were forced to retreat.[39]

Colonel Harry Barclay's regiment of foot held this area for the Parliamentarians, and they put up a stiff resistance. Lord Robertes' regiment arrived soon afterwards to support Barclay's as well as other regiments which were probably filtered into the fray as the day went on; Atkins continues:

> The Cannon played upon us, but did us no harm; we killed some and took some prisoners, they mistaking us for their own party: between 12 and 1 of the clock, the king sent down several regiments to storm the barn; without the taking of which, we could not have access to the body of their army, which lay mostly between the barn and the bridge … the barn was as good a bulwark as art could invent … for they had made loopholes through the walls, that they had the full bodies of the assailants for their mark, as they came down a plain field: but the assailants saw nothing to shoot at but mud walls, and must hit them in the eye, or lose their shot. Upon this disadvantage I need not tell you what men we lost; about three of the clock, my party was relieved for half an hour, and then the party that relieved us was drawn off again.[40]

---

38   Anon., *Journal of the House of Lords*, vol. 6 p.17, the Earl of Essex to the Speaker of the House of Lords, 25 April 1643.

39   Luke's siege diary, p.35.

40   Richard Atkins, *The Vindication of Richard Atkins* (ed.) Brigadier Peter Young in *Military Memoirs, the Civil War* ed. Peter Young and Norman Tucker (London: Longmans, Green and Co Ltd, 1967), pp.10–11.

Clarendon states that the King:

> was encountered by a party of the enemy which defended their post, and being
> quickly seconded by supplies of horse and foot from all their quarters, after a
> very sharp conflict in which many fell on both sides, the king's party commanded
> by the Earl of Forth [Ruthven] himself, and consisting of near 1,000 musketeers
> – was forced to retire their body. This they did the sooner, because those of the
> town made no semblance of endeavouring to join them, which was what they
> principally relied up.[41]

Atkins confirmed that the Royalists came under a heavy fire, describing how, 'Twould grieve one's heart, to see men drop liked fruit in a strong wind'.[42] On the hand John Vicars describes the Royalists fell, 'like so many leaves from a tree in Autumn, or acorns beaten from an oak to feed hogs'. The total number of casualties varies enormously depending on the source, but was between seven to 300 killed and 100 to 400 wounded. Among this attacking force was Christopher Wilson who was a soldier in Colonel Blagge's regiment of foot, who had served the King since he raised the standard at Nottingham, and 'lost one eye at the relieving of Reading'. Despite this he continued to serve in the Royalist army until 1646 when Oxford surrendered, and it would not be until 1674 that he applied for a petition in place of William Hollings who was 'safely dead'.[43] The Parliamentarians claimed just three to six killed and three to 10 wounded.[44]

What part the soldiers of Eastern Association played in this engagement is not recorded, even though according to Luke's siege diary on the previous day they had planted 'their ordnance [to] within pistol of the place called Harrison's Barn, ready to shoot'.[45] Having made no headway against the Parliamentarians the Royalists withdrew, although according to Atkins they had managed to send some ammunition into the town. By now it was evening, and Atkins' small band had been left alone:

> the danger was not small, for two or three hundred musketeers had lined the
> hedge by this time, within half musket shot of us and began to play one the one
> side, a regiment of foot and cannon about musket shot fronted us, and a strong
> party of horse on the other side; so I had much ado to keep them from running …
> we stuck together more like a flock of sheep, than a party of horse.[46]

Fortunately for Atkins, Prince Rupert sent an order for him to retire which he did under cover of darkness which hampered the Parliamentarian pursuit. Clarendon would later claim that this battle was not so much to break the siege, since the Royalists were not strong enough for that, but to

---

41 Clarendon, p.116.
42 Atkins, *The Vindication* pp.10–11.
43 West Yorkshire History Centre (WYHC): QS1/13/4/6/5, Petition of Christopher Wilson of Reedness, West Riding, 28 April 1674. Civil War Petitions website.
44 Barres-Baker, p.144.
45 Luke's siege diary, p.35.
46 Atkins, *The Vindication*, p.11.

open a corridor so that the garrison could evacuate the town. If this is so then no one appears to have told Fielding, because at about 9:00 a.m. that morning, according to Luke, Reading had shown a white flag, a sign that they wanted to negotiate, and hostages were exchanged. Therefore, 'while the fighting was going on at Caversham', according to Gwyn, Fielding 'was no more concerned at it than if he had been a neuter to look on and see them fight; and … he would not stir, nor consent to make any opposition against them [the Parliamentarians]'.[47] Fielding would not break a truce that he had negotiated with Essex and Grey, since it was against his honour, even though the other colonels of the garrison demanded it. For his treachery he was court martialled and condemned to death. Clarendon suggests that the King had wanted to abandon Reading anyway, a point he raised at his trial, and that Aston had known about his negotiations, but it was no use and Fielding was sentenced to be beheaded, the usual method for a gentleman to be executed. Fortunately for him, this sentence was never carried out and he was allowed to re-join the Royalist army.

For Essex's and Grey's armies the joy of the surrender of Reading was short lived because instead of being allowed to plunder the town they were informed that they would each receive 12s instead, despite their pay being in arrears. Sickness within Essex's army was further increased by the 'great mortality' within the town which quickly spread to the Parliamentarians, and the misery of the soldiers was made worse by the unseasonable weather, so that many deserted their regiment. The Parliamentarian armies dispersed to fresher quarters within Berkshire and Surrey, 460 men of Sir Henry Cholmeley's regiment of foot were sent to Kingston on Thames along with 70 sick and lame soldiers from Lord Robartes' regiment. No doubt the sickness spread to the regiments of the Eastern Association also.

By 13 May 1643 Lord Grey was at Sunning when he wrote to Sir Thomas Barrington;

The bearer can best inform you of the state of your regiment, the men are so mutinous that unless they may have after the rate of twelve pence a day as was conditional with them by their masters. They will stay no longer the payers have prevailed and at them to be satisfied with 8 pence a day until Wednesday. If you can advise upon some way how they may be paid hereafter … your presence one day would persuade and carry some authority … now Major Harper has gone back they have no officer amongst them that they respect. [Lieutenant Colonel] Skipworth [of Barrington's regiment] is not worth your owning and has no reputation amongst the soldiers here. I have prevailed with mine own regiment in the same condition, if this is not dealt with all effectually it will infect others.[48]

On 26 May the county of Huntingdon was added to the Eastern Association and then on 20 September Lincolnshire, even though Lord Willoughby of

---

47 John Gwyn, 'The military Memoir of John Gwyn' (ed.) Norman Tucker in *Military Memoirs, the Civil War* (ed.) Peter Young and Norman Tucker (London: Longmans, Green and Co Ltd, 1967), p.49.
48 BL: Egerton, ms 2646.

Parham had a commission from the Earl of Essex to command all the forces within that county.

On 7 June 1643 Lord Grey wrote to Sir Thomas Barrington about the Earl of Warwick's regiment of the Essex trained bands were quartered in Ash, near Farnham in Surrey;

> The Essex regiment conducted by [Major] Dawkins, hath much discredited their county and much wronged the service although I blame him more than them for when I urged him to march with his men to Caversham[?] he pressed, and urged with great earnestness to return to Maidenhead, which I utterly denied he poured[?] from my Lord General a warrant, under pretence of leading away two colours and carried away eight colours the whole regiment indeed. I think him to be an unfit man to march those men any more, the captains seem to be honest men and I have given them leave to go back; who promises to make up their companies and return to the Army.[49]

The same day Grey also wrote to the House of Lords from his quarters at Nettlebed, near Henley upon Thames in Oxfordshire, 'I am confident the forces under my command would dissolve in [a] very few days; of what ill consequence that might be'.[50] Parliament was eager for Essex to march on Oxford and so at the beginning of June he set up his headquarters at Thame, in Oxfordshire. It was about this time that a Colonel in Essex's army, John Urry, changed sides and gave the Royalists detailed information as to where the Parliamentarians were quartered and news of a convoy bringing £21,000 to pay the army. This was too tempting a target for Prince Rupert, and although he failed to capture the convoy on 18 June he fell on part of Essex's Army at Chalgrove Field. This action would just be remembered as a skirmish if it had not been for the death of Colonel John Hampden, who was one of the five MPs Charles had tried to arrest in the Commons on 4 January 1642. By the end of June, Grey's artillery was also at Thame and Grey's force would remain with the Earl of Essex until July 1643.

On 22 June Lord Grey was summoned to Parliament believing it was something to do with his army, but he was informed that he had been chosen as a member of a committee which was to be sent to Scotland. At first Grey claimed ill health and then he refused altogether, so on 18 July he was ordered to be imprisoned in the Tower of London for the 'great contempt' shown to the House of Lords. It was also ordered that he should be dismissed from the command of the Eastern Association.[51]

---

49 Ibid.
50 Anon., *Journal of the House of Lords* vol. 6, p.86.
51 Anon., *Journal of the House of Lords* vol. 6, pp.104, 134, 135.

Cromwell

On 23 March, even before Grey had marched to the siege of Reading, Colonel Charles Cavendish from Newark captured Grantham in Lincolnshire, who was followed two days later by another party from Newark, which was supported by local Royalists, seizing Crowland (or Croyland) Abbey. The town of Stamford, and then Peterborough, also fell to them. With these places in Royalist hands the rest of Lincolnshire and even the other counties of East Anglia were open to invasion, which the Earl of Newcastle, who commanded the Royalist army in the north, lost no time in taking advantage of. On 1 April his army was reported to be marching towards King's Lynn, with no other forces able to confront him, apart from Major Livewell Sherwood's company, which mustered about 100 volunteers, who were sent to reinforce the garrison, while Major Knight with a further 100 soldiers were sent to Wisbech.

On 11 April Lord Willoughby and his Lincolnshire forces was defeated at Ancaster Heath, but Peterborough was soon retaken by Cromwell, and then the Parliamentarians looked to recapture Crowland, which was described by John Vicars as a 'most malignant town, but a place of great consequence.'[52] It is situated on a gravel peninsular within the fens near to the river Welland, with the ruins of an old 13th century Benedictine abbey which is situated on the south east edge of the old town, close to which is a medieval church and its churchyard, which had been fortified by a series of banks and ditches with bastions. The garrison are said to have raided parts of the Association, as well as the neighbouring counties, which 'were subject to their daily plunderings and pillagings.'[53]

On the 25 April the town was assaulted on three sides by detachments of Colonels Sir Miles Hobart, Sir Anthony Irby and Cromwell. At one point the Royalists are said to have brought a Robert Ram, who was the minister of the town and supporter of Parliament, to the north bulwark and pinned him down for five hours on the wet ground to prevent the attack on that quarter. According to the Parliamentarian newspaper *Special Passages*, Ram was not the only one to be used as a human shield, the Parliamentarians, 'perceiving their enemies place a minister and divers other friends in that place where they were to shoot, [who] did at first forbear to shoot'. After a while the besiegers decided that they had no option but to open fire, but when the cannon burst its barrel they considered it a bad omen, so decided 'not to attempt that way, but try some other way; but that not being agreed to, they came back.'[54]

---

52 John Vicars, *Gods Ark Overtopping the Worlds waves, or the third part of the Parliamentarian Chronicle*, p.203.

53 *A Catalogue of Remarkable Mercies conferred upon the Seven Associated Counties* (April, 1644), p.2.

54 BL: TT E 104/34, *Divers Remarkable Passages of God's Good Providence in the wonderful preservation and deliverance of John Harington, Mr Robert Ram ... who were taken prisoners by the Cavaliers of Croyland*; TT E 91/21 *Special Passages*, 18–25, April 1643.

The *Divers Remarkable Passages* also mentions the following about the siege:

> That Tuesday proved a very wet and windy day, and so continued till Thursday morning, that most of our companies were forced to quit their moorish [boggy] rotten quarters and retreat, only some small parties on the west and south held them in exercise day and night most part of that time, though the weather was very extreme and they had no shelter to defend themselves from it. On Thursday in the afternoon all the companies were drawn down upon the three approaches or banks by which the town only is accessible by land, who so plied the Croylanders upon every quarter that their hearts began to fail, divers of them stealing away into the coverts and moorish grounds on the east side of the town … and many more that night followed their fellows.[55]

According to *Certaine Informations* it was Cromwell who captured Crowland, but according to an opponent of Cromwell, who is believed to be a Captain William Dodson, it was due to him that the town surrendered. How true Dodson's claim is cannot be proven, but Cromwell was accused of taking the credit of other people's actions, or as Dodson puts it, 'yet that service, and all others done by me and others, must go in his name or else all is not well'.[56]

The following morning there were few of the Royalist garrison left and when the Parliamentarians attacked again they met little opposition:

> Of our men were killed five and some eighteen or twenty wounded, whereof some are since dead, their wounds being incurable by reason of their [the Royalists'] poisoned bullets. Ten champed bullets were found in one man's pocket, some of their muskets being drawn by our men had such bullets in them, and abundance of the same sort found by our soldiers.[57]

Whether the musket balls were poisoned or the wounded soldiers died due to infection cannot be verified, but the pamphlet's aim was to stir up hatred of the Royalists since it also accused them of ripping pages of the Bible to light their pipes.

One person who did not support Cromwell's attack on Crowland was Lord Grey of Groby, who commanded the forces of the Midland Association which had been formed at the same time as the Eastern Association. This was not the only time that Groby's force did not support Cromwell, because on 3 May 1643 he complained to the Committee at Lincolnshire:

> My Lord Grey hath now again failed me of the rendezvous at Stamford, notwithstanding that both he and I received letters from his Excellency commanding us both to meet, and together with Sir John Gell and the Nottingham forces to join with you. My Lord Grey sent Sir Edward Hartop to me, to let me

55 BL: TT E 104/34.
56 Printed in John Bruce and David Masson, *The Quarrell between the Earl of Manchester and Cromwell* (London: Camden Society, 1875), p.73.
57 BL: TT E 104/34.

Ruins of Crowland Abbey
(Public Domain)

know he could not meet me at Stamford according to our agreement; fearing the exposing of Leicester to the forces of Mr Hastings and some other troops drawing that way.[58]

Cromwell goes on to suggest that 'Sir John Gell and the other forces' should meet him at Grantham adding 'Our Norfolk forces, which will not prove so many as you may imagine by six or seven hundred men will lie conveniently at Spalding and, I am confident, be ready to meet at Grantham at the general rendezvous'.[59] What Cromwell did not realise was that Groby was correct in his assumption that his absence would leave Leicestershire open to attack,

---

58 Thomas Carlyle et al., *The Letters and Speeches of Oliver Cromwell*, pp.131–133 (London: Methuen & Co, 1904)

59 Ibid.

since on 20 April Prince Rupert and Henry Hastings captured Lichfield after a short siege and the Parliamentarians did not know where they would strike next. Nevertheless, Cromwell's actions had pushed the Royalists back over the River Nene.

On 9 May Cromwell met with the Lincolnshire forces under Lord Willoughby and the forces of Sir John Hotham at Sleaford with the aim to summon Newark, but first they decided to seize Grantham, which they did on 11 May and stayed for two days. The Royalists at Newark had intelligence of this and Colonels Charles Cavendish and Henderson set out to intercept them. Accounts vary as to the size of Cavendish's force, which state that he had between 16 and 21 troops, which would have put his force to be about 1,120 to 1,470 strong, but it is unlikely that these troops were at full strength and by stating the number of troops rather than men the Parliamentarian newsletters made Cavendish's force sound stronger than it really was. On the morning of 13 May Cavendish defeated a party of Parliamentarians at Belton, near Grantham. The Parliamentarian newsletter *Remarkable Passages* recorded that Cavendish, 'fell upon the troop of Captain Rey and a Dutchman's troop and forced them out of their quarters, but Colonel Cromwell having thereby the alarm advanced against them and routed them, following the flight almost to Newark'.[60]

In a letter to Sir Miles Hobart, Cromwell states:

It was late in the evening when we drew out; they came and faced us within two miles of the town. So soon as we had the alarm, we drew out our forces, consisting of about twelve troops, whereof some of them so poor and broken, that you shall seldom see worse: with this handful it pleased God to cast the scale. For after we had stood a little above musket-shot the one body from the other and the dragoons had fired on both sides for the space of half an hour or more, they not advancing towards us, we agreed to charge them. And, advancing the body after many shots on both sides, we came on with our troops a pretty round trot, they standing firm to receive us: and our men charging fiercely upon them, by God's providence they were immediately routed, and ran all away, and we had the execution of them two or three miles.

I believe some of our soldiers did kill two or three men apiece in the pursuit; but what the number of dead is we are not certain. We took forty-five prisoners, besides divers of their horse and arms, and rescued many prisoners whom they had lately taken of ours; and we took four or five of their colours.[61]

This letter was printed in the Parliamentarian newsletter, which included another letter which gives a slightly different account:

---

60   *Continuation of Certain Remarkable Passages from Both Houses of Parliament* (London: Cole and Leach, 11–18 May 1643). The Belton parish register records the burial of three soldiers killed in this fight.

61   Anon., *A true Victory of a great victory obtained by the Parliament forces in Lincolnshire, under the command of the Lord Willoughby, Colonel Hobart, Colonel Cromwell, Lieutenant General Hotham. Declared in several letters one from Colonel Cromwell to Colonel Hobart, dated from Shasten. And another from Master Bridge a minister to a friend in London ...* (London: William Bridge, 1643), p.1.

> Lieutenant General Hotham, the Lord Willoughby and Colonel Cromwell lay with divers troops of horse ... the enemy was upon his march towards us with some thousands of horse and foot ... At about 8 o'clock in the evening our men all mounted in a short time and drew out into the field, the commander in chief commanded our men that they should not give fire till they came within half pistol shot of the enemy, which being done, it was so dreadful a charge that the enemy were immediately routed and fled for their lives.[62]

Here we see that it was not Cromwell who commanded the Parliamentarians this day, but Sir John Hotham, even so by the time this incident was reported in the *Remarkable Passages* only Cromwell is mentioned, further adding to Cromwell's fame. Nevertheless, Grantham is seen as Cromwell's baptism of fire since he had missed Edgehill and up to now he had only seen little in the way of fighting. It is clear from these accounts that the cavalry of both sides employed the 'caracole', or firing their pistols and carbines before they came into contact with each other, a tactic usually associated with the Parliamentarian cavalry rather than the Royalists. It would not be the last time that the Royalist cavalry would use this tactic rather than galloping straight at their opponents as is believed was often the case.

Fernando Lord Fairfax, commander of the Northern Association (Public Domain)

After Grantham it was agreed that Cromwell's force, with Lord Grey of Groby's Midlands Association and those of Sir John Gell, should support Lord Fairfax's Northern Association. Lucy Hutchinson, whose husband was the governor of Nottingham, records that Cromwell, Grey and Gell met at Nottingham, along with Hotham who 'brought some more rude troops out of Yorkshire', and that they were 'the scum of mankind'.[63]

However rather than supporting Fairfax, they decided to prevent the Queen, who had recently landed with a large quantity of arms and ammunition, from joining the King in Oxford and also to guard those parts from the Royalists. Hutchinson continues; 'The forces now united at Nottingham were about five or six thousand, my Lord Grey being commander in chief'.[64] Being ordered to take Wiverton House, this force reluctantly marched out of Nottingham, but the attempt was at best half hearted and after facing the house they withdrew to Nottingham once more. Then:

---

62 Ibid., p.3.
63 Ibid., p152.
64 Lucy Hutchinson, *Memoirs of the Life of Colonel Hutchinson, written by his widow* (London: Henry G. Bohn, 1846), p151.

Two or three days after the enemy's horse faced them; but they would not be prevailed upon to go out, though they were not inferior to them … Nottingham was more sadly distressed by their friends than their enemies; for Hotham and Gell's men not only lay upon free quarter, as all the rest did, but made such a havoc and plunder of friend and foe, that it was a sad thing for anyone that had a generous heart to behold it.[65]

Hotham had been in contact with Newcastle for some months and had begun negotiating with the Queen to change sides, which being brought to the attention of Cromwell and Colonel John Hutchinson complained to Parliament. Unfortunately the letter does not appear to have survived, but it was acknowledged as having been received on 21 June and a week later Hotham and his father were arrested but managed to escape while travelling to London under escort.[66] With this turn of events the Earl of Essex appointed the experienced Scottish commander Sir John Meldrum to command Hotham's men.

On 28 May Cromwell was still at Nottingham when he wrote to the Mayor of Colchester asking for reinforcements 'for this great service', adding:

My Lord Newcastle is near six-thousand foot, and about sixty troops of horse; my Lord Fairfax is about three-thousand foot, and nine troops of horse; and we have about twenty-four troops of horse and dragoons. The enemy draws more to the Lord Fairfax: our motion and yours must be exceedingly speedy, or else it will do you no good at all … I beseech you hasten the supply to us: forget not money. I press not hard; though I do so need that, I assure you, the foot and dragoons are ready to mutiny.[67]

About the 8 June Cromwell was at Boston, no doubt to rendezvous with any soldiers raised in Essex and other counties of the Association, proceeding to Newark where he arrived on 11 June and faced the town the following day, before retiring to Nottingham once more on 13 June where he remained until 16 July. In July 1643 Lord Willoughby had captured Gainsborough, but the town was quickly besieged by an element of Newcastle's army under Colonel Charles Cavendish. Gainsborough was strategically important because, along with Newark, it was a main crossing over the River Trent. On 22 July Torrell Jocelyn from the fort of the Hermitage in the Isle of Ely wrote to William Lenthall, the Speaker of the House of Commons:

there are daily alarms given to Wisbech; the well affected there do much fear the fidelity of that Norfolk regiment under the command of Sir John Palgrave, from divers of which regiment they daily receive threats and disgraces, and do think themselves in less danger without them, than with them. But there is very lately

65   Ibid.
66   Anon., *Journal of the House of Commons,* vol. III p.138.
67   Carlyle, *The Letters and Speeches of Oliver Cromwell*, pp.136–139.

four under of Sir John Holland's Regiment of whom they hope well, unless the town of Wisbech in time may corrupt them.[68]

Even the regiment's Lieutenant Colonel, Sir Edward Astley, did not think highly of Palgrave's regiment, writing to his wife 'the condition of our regiment, which is very ill [disciplined] at the present, the soldiers doing what they list [like], having the power in their own hands'.[69] Adrian Parmenter also wrote about the regiment, that many of its soldiers 'to their great infamy, ran away, and the truth is that Colonel Palgrave hath not the courageous spirit of a brave commander, but is very timorous'.[70]

On 24 July the Commons resolved to write a letter to the Committee of Cambridge to send all the men they could spare to assist with the relief of Gainsborough, and they ordered Sir John Palgrave to go into Norfolk to assist the Deputy Lieutenants of the county in securing the county while his regiment under Lieutenant Colonel Astley was to march to Gainsborough.[71] However, before Cromwell relieved the town, he wanted to capture Burleigh (or Burghley) House, which is said to have been situated in a large park surrounded by a stone wall. Cromwell's force, which included Palgrave's and Hobart's regiments and some ordnance arrived at the house at 3:00 a.m. on 9 July, and set up batteries of his ordnance. What calibre these guns were is not recorded but they are said to have fired for two or three hours to little effect. According to John Vicars, Cromwell then summoned the garrison to surrender, but this was rejected with the Royalists declaring that 'they would neither take nor give quarter'.[72] Lieutenant Colonel Astley confirms that if the garrison refused then they could 'expect no mercy but to be put all unto the sword. They answered us again that they would fight it out unto the last man before they would yield up the place'.[73] Although, he places this summons as taking place before the bombardment of the house began. Another account which corroborates Astley is a letter written to the Committee of Huntingdon which states that 'At the first sitting down, Cromwell sent a trumpet to summon the cavaliers, this being refused Cromwell caused the ordnance to play upon the house, but after a few hours proved no good would be done that way. Whereupon our colonel caused their musketeers in three squadrons to draw up to the house'.[74]

Astley continues:

About 12 o'clock we approached upon them in several places, and our men assaulted them with such courage that by 3 o'clock in the afternoon they sounded a parley and after some consultation our trumpet answered them with the like, but such was the madness of our soldiers for pillage that they broke in upon them and

68   Bod Lib: Tanner, MS 62 f.181.
69   Quoted in R. W. Ketton-Cremer, *Norfolk in the Civil War* (London: Faber and Faber, 1969), p.199.
70   BL: Add MS 22,619 f.80, 'Adrian Parmenter to the Mayor of Norwich', July 1643.
71   *Journal of the House of Commons*, vol. III p.180.
72   Vicars, *Gods Ark*, p.7.
73   Edward Astley to his wife, 29 July 1643, Ketton-Cremer, *Norfolk in the Civil War*, pp.202–203.
74   BL: Egerton, MSs 2647 f.61.

fell a plundering. We took 300 prisoners whereof 40 were officers, the commander in chief Colonel Welby … we lost not above four men, but we have some 20 or 30 sore wounded, and we cannot hear of many killed of theirs.[75]

Vicars' version of events is that after the summons was refused Cromwell gave the order to:

storm and assault it [Burleigh House] with his musketeers, whereupon the fight grew very hot and was bravely performed on both sides for a while, and with much difficulty and danger on ours, the enemy being very active and confident; and thus the assault continued divers hours, till at last the cavaliers courage began to fail, ours pressing on them very fiercely and furiously so that they sounded a parley.[76]

The Parliamentarians are said to have captured two colonels, six or seven captains, 300–400 foot, and about 150–200 horse and all their arms and ammunition. According to Vicars despite the length of the fighting only 'six or seven were killed (though many were hurt)'.[77] Despite the reservations of his lieutenant colonel, Palgrave's men seems to have particularly distinguished themselves. Among the wounded was Sergeant William Burnham of Steeple Bumpstead in Essex who served in Captain Thomas Smith's company who 'utterly lost the use of his right hand'. He was awarded a pension of £4 having a wife and 'five poor small children'. When he died in 1653 his widow Mary petitioned for a pension 'having not anything in the world left for their relief, but are in exceeding[ly in] great want'.[78]

Hearing that there was a relieving force of about 400 men approaching, Cromwell sent out three troops of horse under Captains Dobson, Walton and Disborough to intercept them. Captain Dobson was the first to charge the Royalists, but he was wounded and beaten off his horse. Walton managed to rescue him and the Parliamentarians attacked once more, defeating the Royalists and, it was said, killing about 50 of them.[79] On 27 July the Committee of Cambridge wrote:

Colonel Cromwell having sent about 200 Cavaliers unto Cambridge, taken at Burleigh House we thought fit to send them to London to be disposed of by your approbation and wisdom unto you. That the town of Cambridge is malignant enough and we fear the sickness is much dispersed about the Spittle House end. And our garrison [is] weak. So as to continue them here would be both [a] danger and charge to the town and consequently to the whole Association … we crave

75   Edward Astley to his wife, 29 July 1643, quoted in Ketton-Cremer R.W. *Norfolk in the Civil War* (London: Faber and Faber, 1969), pp.202–203

76   Vicars, *Gods Ark*, pp.7–8.

77   Ibid., p.8.

78   Essex Record Office (ERO): Q/BSa2/82, Unfortunately which regiment he served with is not known.

79   BL: Egerton, MS 2647 f.61.

your directions how you will have them disposed of and we shall carefully keep them in the meantime.[80]

After the surrender of Burleigh House, Cromwell then proceeded to Gainsborough. At Grantham he met with 300 horse and dragoons from Nottingham, then at North Scarle a contingent from Lincolnshire, which is about 10 miles from Gainsborough. It was at the latter place where he decided to refresh his men before proceeding to Gainsborough during the early hours of 28 July. In his report to the Committees of Suffolk and Cambridge, Cromwell writes:

> About a mile and a half from the town, we met a forlorn hope of the enemy of near 100 horse. Our dragoons laboured to beat them back; but not alighting off their horses, the enemy charged them, and beat some four or five of them off their horses: our horse charged them, and made them retire unto their main body. We advanced, and came to the bottom of a steep hill, upon which the enemy stood; we could not well get up but by some tracts, which our men assaying to do, a body of the enemy endeavoured to hinder; wherein we prevailed, and got the top of the hill. This was done by the Lincolners, who had the vanguard.[81]

When the Parliamentarians gained the top of the hill they:

> saw a great body of the enemy's horse facing of us, at about musket-shot or less distance; and a good reserve of a full regiment of horse behind it. We endeavoured to put our men into as good order as we could, the enemy in the meantime advancing towards us, to take us at a disadvantage; but in such order as we were, we charged their great body, I having the right wing; we came up horse to horse, where we disputed it with our swords and pistols a pretty time; all keeping close order, so that one could not break the other.[82]

Finally the Royalists began to give way, which turned into a rout, with the Parliamentarians pursuing them 'about five or six miles'. However not all the Royalists fled as Cromwell continues:

> I, perceiving this body which was the reserve standing still unbroken, kept back my Major, Whalley, from the chase, and with my own troop and one other of my regiment, in all being three troops, we got into a body. In this reserve stood General Cavendish; who one while faced me, another while faced four of the Lincoln troops, which were all of ours that stood upon the place, the rest being engaged in the chase. At last the General charged the Lincolners, and routed them. I immediately fell on his rear with my three troops, which did so astonish him, that he gave over the chase, and would fain have delivered himself from me, but I pressing on forced them down a hill, having good execution of them, and below the hill, drove the General with some of his soldiers into a quagmire, where

---

80   BodLib: Tanner, MS 62 f.182.
81   Carlyle, pp.140–144.
82   Ibid.

my Captain-lieutenant slew him with a thrust under his short ribs. The rest of the body was wholly routed, not one man staying upon the place.[83]

It is in the pursuit of a broken enemy when most of the casualties occur, but the fight was still not over because there were still six troops of horse and 300 foot on the other side of Gainsborough:

> we desired some foot of my Lord Willoughby's, about 400; and, with our horse and these foot, marched towards them: when we came towards the place where their horse stood, we beat back with my troops about two or three troops of the enemy, who retired into a small village at the bottom of the hill. When we recovered the hill, we saw in the bottom, about a quarter of a mile from us, a regiment of foot; after that another; after that Newcastle's own regiment, consisting in all of about 50 foot colours, and a great body of horse; which indeed was Newcastle's Army.[84]

Cromwell and Lord Willoughby quickly held a council of war to discuss what to do next, but with the 400 infantry retiring in disorder and his cavalry 'wearied' from its exertions of the day they decided to withdraw. 'Our horse', recalls Cromwell, 'came off with some trouble, being wearied with this long fight, and their horses tired; yet faced the enemy's fresh horses, and by several removes got off without the loss of one man'.[85] It is usually held as an example of the discipline of Cromwell's regiment that it managed to withdraw by divisions, but only four troops belonged to his regiment, the additional four troops had been raised in Lincolnshire and were under the command of Captain Ayscough:

> They with this handful faced the enemy, and dared them to the teeth in, at the least, eight or nine several removes, the enemy following at their heels; and they, though their horses were exceedingly tired, retreating in order near carbine shot of the enemy, who thus followed them, firing upon them; Colonel Cromwell gathering up the main body and facing them behind those two lesser bodies.[86]

Gainsborough has been seen as a success for the Parliamentarians, especially for Cromwell, but they failed in their aim of relieving the town, and on the following day, faced with Newcastle's entire army, Willoughby sounded a parley; the Royalist newspaper, *Mercurius Aulicus* for 3 August takes up the narrative:

> it was advertised this day that Gainsborough was yielded to the Earl of Newcastle; on whose first coming before the town, with the rest of his forces, the Lord Willoughby and other of the rebels in it desire a parley, which being granted upon Saturday night last, July 29, the Commissioners for both parts did agree, in the next morning early (that is to say, about two of the clock), that the town should be

---

83 Ibid.
84 Ibid.
85 Ibid.
86 Ibid.

delivered, by five of the clock that morning, to such as his Excellency the Earl of Newcastle should appoint to receive it for his Majesty; the Lord Willoughby and other officers of the rebels to go away, worth such arms as they brought into the town; no common soldier to go forth with any arms at all, not with more baggage than he brought thither with him; neither the officers nor soldiers to take with them any colours of horse or foot; no ordnance, nor any kind of ammunition, to be carried out of the town or destroyed in it, nor any part of the town or the goods thereof to be burnt or hurt. All prisoners belonging to the army of the Earl of Newcastle, or which were there when the Lord Willoughby first entered, to be left behind; and finally, no townsman to go out of the town under pretence of being soldiers.

Willoughby marched to Lincoln and then to Boston, from where on 5 August he wrote to Cromwell:

Since the business of Gainsborough, the hearts of our men have been so deaded that we have lost most of them by running away. So that we were forced to leave Lincoln upon a sudden; and if I had not done it then I should have been left alone in it. So that now I am at Boston; where we are very poor in strength; so that without some speedy supply, I fear we shall not hold this long neither.

My Lord General, I perceive, hath writ to you, to draw all the forces together. I should be glad to see it for that will not be, there can be no good to be expected. If you will endeavour to stop my Lord of Newcastle, you must presently draw them to him and fight him! For without we be masters of the field we shall be pulled out by the ears, one after another.

The foot, if they will come on, may march very securely to Boston; which to me will be very considerable to your Association. For if the enemy get that town, which is not very weak for defence for want of men I believe they will not be long out of Norfolk and Suffolk.

I can say no more; but desire you to hasten.[87]

The evacuation of Gainsborough came hot on the heels of Newcastle's victory at Adwalton Moor, near Bradford on 30 June, where he had defeated Fairfax's much weaker army. Almost half of the Northern Association are said to have been either killed or captured and opened the north to the Royalists with only Hull standing in their way of any advance into Lincolnshire and subsequently the counties of the Eastern Association. With Newcastle's army on their borders the counties of the Eastern Association looked to their defence who feared 'the whole association will be exposed to the fury and cruelty of the Popish army'.[88] On 6 August Cromwell wrote to the Committee of Cambridge, his panic is obvious:

Raise all your Bands, Send them to Huntington, get up what volunteers you can, hasten your horse. Send these letters to Norfolk, Suffolk and Essex without delay. I beseech you spare not but be expeditious and industrious. Almost all our foot

---

87   Ibid., p.146.
88   BL: Egerton, MSs 2647 f.93, Committee of the Eastern Association to Sir Thomas Barrington.

have quitted Stamford, there is nothing to interrupt an enemy but our horse that is considerable. You must act lively, do it with distraction, neglect no means.[89]

Despite the urgent need for infantry, four days previously Cromwell had written to the 'young men and maids' of Norwich to try and persuade them to convert the companies they were raising into a troop of horse for his regiment:

I approve of the business; only I desire to advise you that your foot company may be turned into a troop of horse which instead will, by God's blessing, far more advantage the Cause than two or three companies of foot … therefore my advice is, that you would employ 12 score pounds to buy pistols and saddles, and I will provide four score horses; for £400 more will not raise a troop of horse. As for the muskets that are bought I think the country will take them off you. Pray raise honest Godly men and I will have them of my regiment.[90]

The people of Norwich took Cromwell's advice and the 'Maiden Troop', as it was known, was put under the command of Captain Robert Swallow.[91]

On 8 August Cromwell again wrote to the Committee at Cambridge:

Finding our foot much lessened at Stamford and having a great train and many carriages, I held it not safe to continue there, but presently after my return from you I ordered the foot to quit that place and march into Holland to Spalding which they did on Monday last. I was the rather induced so to do because of the letter I received from my Lord Willoughby …

I am now at Peterborough whither I came this afternoon. I was no sooner come but Lieutenant Colonel Wood sent me word from Spalding that the enemy was marching with 12 flying colours of horse and foot within a mile of Swinstead; so that I hope it was a good providence of God that our foot were at Spalding.

It much concerns your Association and the Kingdom that so strong a place as Holland is be not possessed by them. If you have any foot ready to march, send them away to us with all speed. I fear lest the enemy should press in upon our foot; he being this far advanced towards you. I hold it very fit that you should hasten your horse at Huntingdon, and what you can speedily raise at Cambridge, unto me. I dare not go into Holland with my horse, less the enemy should advance with his whole body of horse this was into your Association; but remain ready here endeavouring my Lord Grey's and the Northamptonshire horse towards me, that so, if we be able we may fight the enemy, or retreat unto you with our whole strength. I beech you hasten your levies, what you can; especially those of foot! Quicken all our friends with new letters upon this occasion; which I believe you will find to be a true alarm. The particulars I hope to be able to inform

89   Printed in Charles Henry Cooper, *Annals of Cambridge* (Cambridge: Warwick and Co, 1845), vol. III p.355.
90   Carlyle, p.145.
91   Laurence Spring, *The Army of the Eastern Association* (Romford: The Pike and Shot Society, 2016), p.29.

you speedily of, more punctually having sent in all haste to Colonel Wood for that purpose.[92]

To meet this threat the Committee of the Eastern Association called upon all able-bodied men to rendezvous at Cambridge with any arms and money they could raise and that 'all gentlemen and others that are true lovers of their country, religion and liberty will now in this great exigency manifest their good affection by their personal coming into the field, which we expect and desire with all expedition to be performed'.[93]

As early as March 1643 there had been rumours that the governor of King's Lynn, Sir Hamon L'Estrange, had Royalist sympathises, but encouraged by Newcastle's advance on 13 August he declared for the King. At the beginning of the war new fortifications had been erected to strengthen its medieval defences and the surrounding trees were cut down so that any besieging army would not have shelter as it approached the town. A source also says the garrison had 40 pieces of artillery for their defence as well as 500 barrels of powder.[94] With the invasion of East Anglia, coupled with the defeat of Sir William Waller's Western Army at Roundway Down in July and Essex's army ravaged by sickness, things were looking very bleak for the Parliamentarian cause, and it was obvious that the situation had to be improved if the counties of the Eastern Association were not to be overrun altogether.

---

92   Carlyle, pp.148–152.
93   BL: Egerton, MS 2647 f.93, Committee of the Eastern Association to Sir Thomas Barrington.
94   BL: Egerton, MS 2643 f138.

2

Manchester Takes Command

As early as the 23 July 1643 the House of Commons ordered the Committees of Huntingdon and Cambridgeshire to gather 2,000 foot to Cambridge with a month's pay because 'considerable forces of the enemy are approaching towards the confines of the six associated counties'.[1] However, with the arrest of Lord Grey of Warke and his dismissal in August, a new commander had to be found. Despite his successes and more military experience, Cromwell was overlooked for this position in favour of Edward Montagu, 2nd Earl of Manchester. Nevertheless, both men seem to have 'worked effectively until the summer of 1644'.[2]

Between 22 July and 4 August the counties of the Eastern Association were ordered to raise 4,000 men, plus the 1,000 dragoons which were being raised in Essex for Waller's army, which were to be placed under Manchester's command. On 16 August, the associated counties were ordered to raise 20,000 men either by volunteers or impressment 'with so many gunners, trumpeters and surgeons … for the defence of King, Parliament and Kingdom'.[3] This is what Grey and Cromwell had been crying out for since the beginning of its formation and Manchester set about raising his own regiments of cavalry, foot and dragoons, while Cromwell's regiment was increased in strength to 10, and later 14, troops. Other regiments were also raised, such as Colonel Edward Montagu, who was commissioned to raise a regiment of foot on 23 August 1643.

For his train of artillery on 16 August, six brass drakes were ordered to be delivered to Manchester 'with a proportion of shot for them, as also a proportion of shot for the three brass sakers formerly ordained to be delivered for the Earl of Manchester'. However, the carriages for these sakers appear to have been unusable since on 25 August the office of the ordnance reported that there were no spare saker carriages in store and that to make 'three new

---

1   *Journal of the House of Commons*, vol. III p.179.
2   Ian J. Gentles, 'Montagu, Edward second Earl of Manchester' in *Oxford Dictionary of National Biography* (accessed online 31 March 2020).
3   F. J. Varley, *Cambridge During the Civil War* (Cambridge: W. Heffer and Sons Ltd, 1935), p.93. According to Varley, 500 came from Suffolk, 600 from Norfolk, 200 from Cambridge and 100 from Huntingdon; Firth and Rait, pp.248–249.

The Earl of Manchester.
(Public Domain)

field carriages with fore carriages with iron and shod wheels would cost £16 a piece'. Therefore Parliament agreed to purchase the saker carriages for £48. On 7 September a further 'two culverin of brass with two complete field carriages and 60 shot round and a demi cannon mortar piece, six petards, 40 grenades for the mortar and 60 hand grenades' were also to be delivered to him.[4]

To help raise the men, Parliament turned to propaganda with the publication of a letter said to have been written by a Captain John Williams in about September 1643, which warned that if the Cavaliers invaded the Eastern Association then the Cavaliers had:

grown so insolent that they grievously oppress all countries whereever they come and daily brings them [i.e. the population] to slavery, some of them being Irish Cavaliers, some Walloons, some Blackamores and others which name themselves to be of the Queen's Army, they do more harm then any of the rest.[5]

The Irish involvement in the Civil War is well known, but not that of the 'Blackamores' or Black soldiers, although there is evidence to suggest that both sides recruited these soldiers. Early in 1643 the Earl of Stamford freed 'divers Turks out of Launceston gaol' to recruit his army and when the western horse under Sir Edward Massey were discharged in 1646 some were going home to Egypt, Mesopotamia and Ethiopia. What percentage of Massey's soldiers came from these countries is not known, but Black soldiers were not just confined to the army: in June 1645 the East India Company ship *John*, which was bringing arms for the Royalist war effort, had a crew of 90 men, 17 of whom were reported to be Black.[6]

4   TNA: SP 28/264 ff.206; WO 55/460.
5   Williams' letter is printed in *London's Love to her Neighbours in general and in particular to the Six Associated Counties, namely Norfolk, Suffolk, Essex, Cambridge, Hertford and Bedford* (London: John Hammond, 1643), pp.7–9. Although the pamphlet is not dated exactly, it does refer to the fall of Bristol to the Royalists and the siege of Gloucester.
6   Joshua Sprigg, *Anglia Rediviva, England's Recovery being the history of the motions, actions and successes of the army in the immediate command of His Excellency Sir Thomas Fairfax* (1647),

Having set the scene about what he believed would happen in the event of a Royalist advance into the counties of the Eastern Association, Williams goes on with a rallying cry that Shakespeare would have been proud of:

> rouse up your spirits therefore you noble minded citizens and countrymen, by no longer under the burden of oppression, be valiant and courageous: show yourselves like men, and let it not be said that you suffered such a crew once to set foot in your countries, take sword in hand and fight valiantly against them that seek the utter ruin and destruction of you and all that belong to you, fight I say for King and Parliament, laws, liberties and rights … Consider I pray you, for your own sakes, would it not grieve your hearts to depart from your soft beds, and to be carried away to some loathsome prison where is nothing but hunger and cold chains, and irons, bloody stripes, and all manner of cruelties used: would it not pierce your tender hearts to see your wives abused, your daughters ravished, and your children turned out of doors? And children what torment will it be to you to see your loving parents thus barbarously dealt withal? It wounds my heart to think what will become of you., your homes will be the streets, the blocks your beds, water your drink and your food will be what you can beg of the merciless enemy.[7]

If Williams' letter was not enough, the pamphlet continues:

> Masters, servants and apprentices, all sorts of men: rich and poor, that are able to bear arms, I desire you to up for your Religion, and those that are not able to bear arms, let them show their bounty and liberality in sending money … Wives put on your husband's backs to love themselves, you and your children, and as they love you and would have you safe, so let them use a means to keep you safe to rise in a body and fight against these cursed men that intend nothing but destruction, up quickly and … for the cause and the love of heaven, the mover of all hearts, stir you up to the work and prosper in it, that we may see a happy end of this unhappy War.[8]

It is not known how successful this propaganda was, but even before the Ordinance was passed in July a Colonel Mazieres was commissioned to raise a regiment of horse. Little is known of Mazieres, but he was a Frenchman and his regiment made slow headway. On 9 September 1643 Edward Birkhead wrote to Sir Thomas Barrington:

> With much industry I have completed Colonel Mazaries troop, but I never saw such an indisposition in men to the service in my life, for … they have lain here a month, yet were not provided of trumpets, or colours for their troop. I think

p.310; John Lynch, *For King and Parliament, Bristol and the Civil War* (Stroud: Alan Sutton, Ltd, 1999), p.117.
7   Williams' letter, pp.7–9.
8   Ibid., pp.12–14.

we must have another troop to force these out, but I hope this day to send them packing.[9]

Only one other troop can be identified as belonging to this regiment, and in April 1644 the regiment was disbanded. As to his own regiment, Cromwell boasted: 'My troops increase. I have a lovely company; you would respect them ... they are honest sober Christians; they expect to be used as men'.[10] However he denied that any of his men were Anabaptists. In contrast to his own regiment, on 11 September 1643 Cromwell wrote to Oliver St John at Lincoln's Inn appealing for help since 'Many of my Lord of Manchester's troops are come to me: very bad and mutinous'. The trouble was that though Parliament and the various committees within the Eastern Association were demanding extra forces, they lacked the money to pay the soldiers. Cromwell continues:

> Of the £3,000 allotted me, I cannot get the Norfolk part, nor the Hertfordshire: it was given away before I had it. I have minded your service to forgetfulness of my own soldiers' necessities. I desire not to seek myself; but I have little money of my own to help my soldiers ... If you lay aside the thought of me and my letter, I expect no help. I believe £5,000 is due ... There is no care taken how to maintain that force of horse and foot raised and a raising for my Lord Manchester. [If] he hath no one able to put on that business. The force will fall if some help not. Weak councils and weak acting undo all! ... [and] all will be lost if God help not![11]

Pay was not the only problem for the soldiers, but also clothes and arms. On the 31 August the Committee of Cambridge wrote to the Deputy Lieutenants of Essex informing them that:

> Some companies of foot which are sent hither from you, but in so naked a posture that to employ them were to murder them. Their demands are arms, coats, clothes and shoes, wherein how far you are engaged to them by promise or how far by the common use and custom, we do not certainly know; but things of necessity, as weapons, arms, drums and colours, must be had, and that at the charge of your county. If not sent at once there will be a mutiny. The magazine at Cambridge affords them not. [We] ask that they may be sent at once, and to stay other companies till they can come completely furnished to serve. The future rendezvous of all Essex foot is to be at Chesterton (a small mile wide of Cambridge), with direction to send to the writers for further order to march.[12]

Nor was it just the infantry that suffered from lack of clothing. In an undated letter written sometime during the latter part of 1643 or early 1644, Colonel

---

9   HMC: 7 Report, p.562.
10   Carlyle, pp.155–157.
11   Ibid.
12   BL: Egerton, MS 2647 f.197.

Vermuyden wrote to the Committee at Norwich, that 'our troops go barefoot and naked this winter and their horses go unshod for want of your assistance'.[13]

In September 1643 a note concerning the army recalls that it had 9,990 men besides officers, divided into the following counties:[14]

County	Foot	Dragoons
Essex	2,112	360
Suffolk	[blank]	[blank]
Norfolk	2,112	360
Norwich	124	20
Hertfordshire	704	120
Huntingdonshire	342	50
Cambridgeshire	697	119
Isle of Ely	342	58
Total	8,545	1,445

These men were divided into the following regiments:

Essex	Two regiments, whereof one of 1,200 foot and 360 dragoons
Suffolk	Two regiments
Norfolk and Norwich	Two regiments
Cambridgeshire and Ely	One regiment
Herts and Hunts	One regiment

In the last case Hertfordshire was to choose the colonel and Huntingdonshire the lieutenant colonel, while both counties would choose the major. In theory a troop of horse or dragoons were to be attached to each regiment 'to make discoveries on all occasions and to fetch in provisions if need be'.[15] However, there were not enough horses to mount these men and those that were, were later formed into a regiment of dragoons. Moreover, not all served with Manchester's field army, which in 1644 had just six regiments of foot.

In September 1643 despite Russell's regiment of foot being raised in the county, Cromwell wrote to the Committee of Suffolk advising them on how to raise the regiments:

> You have no infantry at all considerable; hasten your horses; a few hours may undo you … I beseech you be careful what captains of horse you choose, what men be mounted; a few honest men are better than numbers … If you choose Godly honest men to be captains of horse, honest men will follow; and they will be careful to mount such … I had rather have a plain russet coated captain

13   Norfolk Record Office, (NCR): 13b/3.
14   BL: Egerton, MS 3651 f.164. The table does not add up, perhaps the difference is the missing figures omitted for Suffolk.
15   Ibid., ff.64, 174.

that knows what he fights for, and loves what he knows, than which you call 'a gentleman' and is nothing else. I honour a *gentleman* that is so indeed![16]

Cromwell added, do not, 'send such men as Essex hath sent, it will be to little purpose'. The 'russet coated' was Ralph Margery who became a captain in Cromwell's regiment of horse, who 'hath honest men [that] will follow him'.[17]

Captain Dobson would later claim that:

> Cromwell [in] raising of his regiment makes choice of his officers, not such as were soldiers or men of estate, but such as were common men, poor and of mean parentage, only he would give them the title of godly precious men; yet his common practice was to cashier honest gentlemen and soldiers that were stout in the cause … When any new Englishman or some new upstart Independent did appear there must be a way made for them by cashiering others, some honest commander or other, and those silly people put in their command … If you look upon his own regiment of horse see what a swarm there is of those that call themselves the godly; some of them profess they have seen visions and had revelations.[18]

It was not just Cromwell's regiment that this officer accused:

> Look on Colonel Fleetwood's Regiment with his Major Harrison, what a cluster of preaching officers and troopers there is. Look what a company of troopers are thrust into other regiments by the head and shoulders, most of them Independents, whom they call Godly precious men; nay, indeed, to say the truth, almost all our horse be made of that faction.
>
> If you look on Colonel Russell's Regiment, Colonel Montagu's, Colonel. Pickering's, Colonel Rainsborough's, all of them professed Independents entire, and besides in most of our regiments they have crammed in one company or other that they or their officers must be Independents.[19]

Despite the state of his army, Manchester began to look towards recapturing King's Lynn, and during the middle of August Captain Poe's troop of horse was sent to seize the bridges at Downham and Lynn, hoping to blockade the garrison until the main force arrived. On 19 August he informed the Committee and Deputy Lieutenant of Essex:

> this last night they [the garrison] likewise dallied out with a great body of horse, intending to have taken me and my troop, as also three or four hundred beefs from Setch market, but by God's providence I prevented all, and made them retreat, keeping them in alarm all night, which hath caused them to discharge above a 100 pieces of ordnance at least, the bullets whistling about our ears but

---

16   Carlyle, pp.153–154.
17   Ibid.
18   Printed in John Bruce and David Masson, *The Quarrel between the Earl of Manchester and Oliver Cromwell* (Camden Society, 1875), pp.72–73.
19   Ibid., pp.72–73.

without hurt, only my lieutenant and three of my soldiers are taken prisoner by them, and I have taken some of them.[20]

There is no way to verify whether the town did fire 100 shots at his troop, but Poe recommended that the besieging force should 'speedily get good store of ordnance and plant them on every side of the town, playing upon them night and day, till they either yield it up or we beat it down'.[21]

Manchester's force arrived at the town at the end of August, establishing his headquarters at Setchy Bridge. The town was said to be so well fortified that 'no ordinary power could take it'. According to *A Brief and True Relation of the Siege*, it was debated whether to besiege the town or to storm it. Finally it was decided that the town should be stormed, despite the town's formidable defences and Manchester only having about 3,000 horse and 1,500 foot then under his command, the latter consisting of Colonel Valentine Walton's regiment of foot and that of Colonel Francis Russell's. Although recruits were being raised to send to Manchester, they were of poor quality and on 7 September Manchester wrote:

> I have here divers men sent out of Essex, and as many of them, I believe, are run away as come; and those whom you have sent have no arms, nor clothes nor colours, nor drums, so as I confess to you I am more troubled to see these distractions than I Can express to you … I earnestly entreat you to send arms and other provisions with these men you send, or else I pray send no more.[22]

The Earl of Essex had wanted Cromwell's cavalry to reinforce his own army since he was preparing to relieve Gloucester, but in the end the taking of King's Lynn was considered too important, so Cromwell was ordered to prevent Newcastle's army relieving the town. On 29 August two brass demi-culverins and one of iron were delivered to Manchester for the reduction of King's Lynn along with two brass falconets and two which belong to Hobart's regiment. Although these were not siege pieces they could do a lot of damage to houses and other infrastructure. The Cambridgeshire accounts for the siege also record 'great guns' and mortar pieces, the latter being brought from Leicester.[23]

A detachment of the besieging force captured Old Lynn, a small town built on the west bank of the River Ouse. A battery was set up on the marshland by this town, which 'kept the town in continual alarm and did so terrify the people with their shot and grenadoes that they durst hardly abide in any of their houses that were toward that side, the shot flying daily into the houses in the Tuesday market place and other places'.[24] Another pamphlet, *Certaine Informations*, records that, 'Colonel Cromwell hath battered them sorely from Old Lynn, the shooting of whose ordnance hath slain divers

---

20   BL: Egerton, MS 2647 f.165.

21   Ibid.

22   Ibid., f.229.

23   TNA: SP 28/152, part 1 f12.

24   BL: TT E 67/28, *A Brief and True Relation of the Siege and the Surrendering of King's Lynn*.

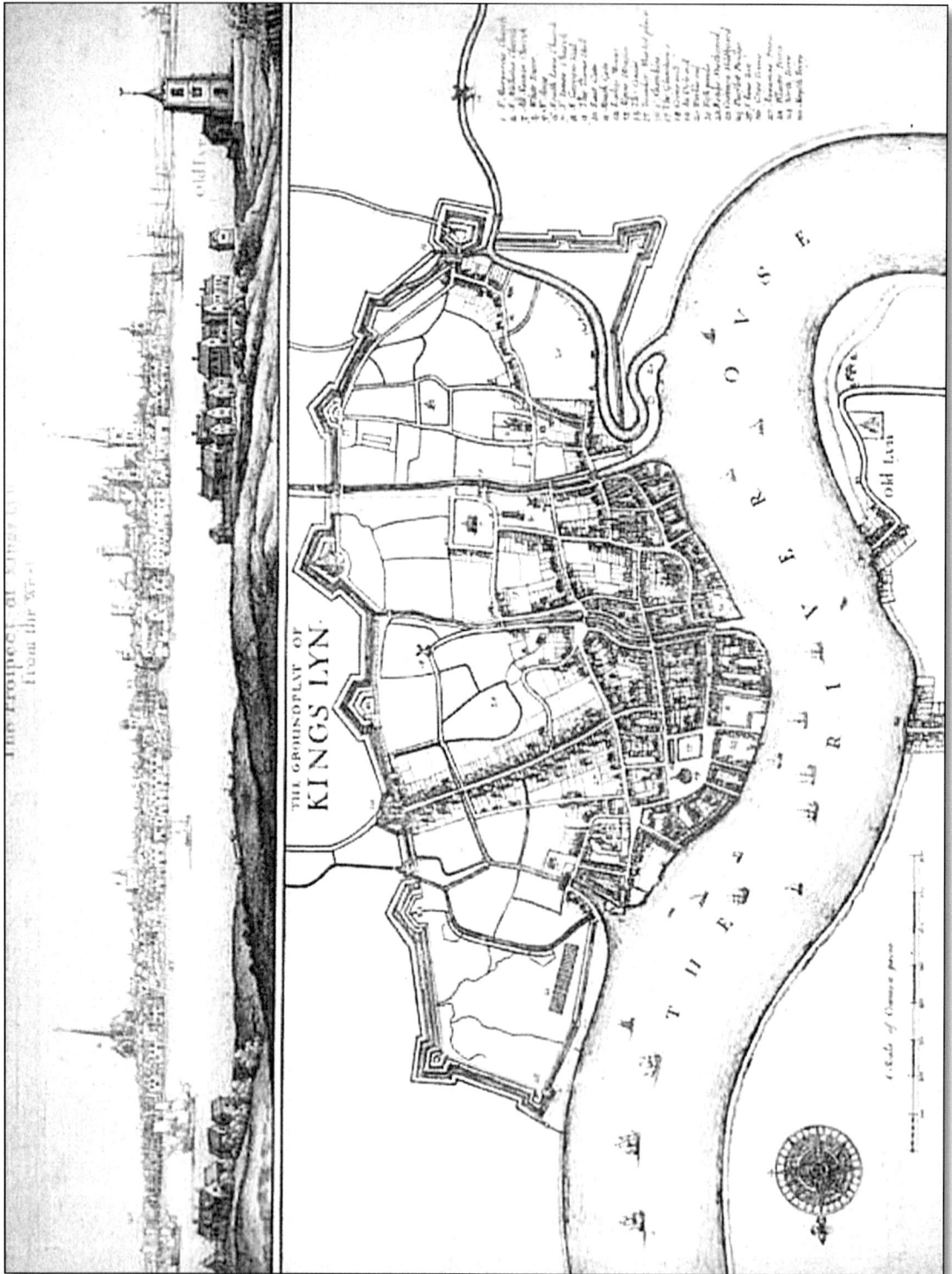

Plan of King's Lynn by Wenceslaus Hollar

N

0   150   300 yards

River Ouse

Kings Lyn

Old Lyn

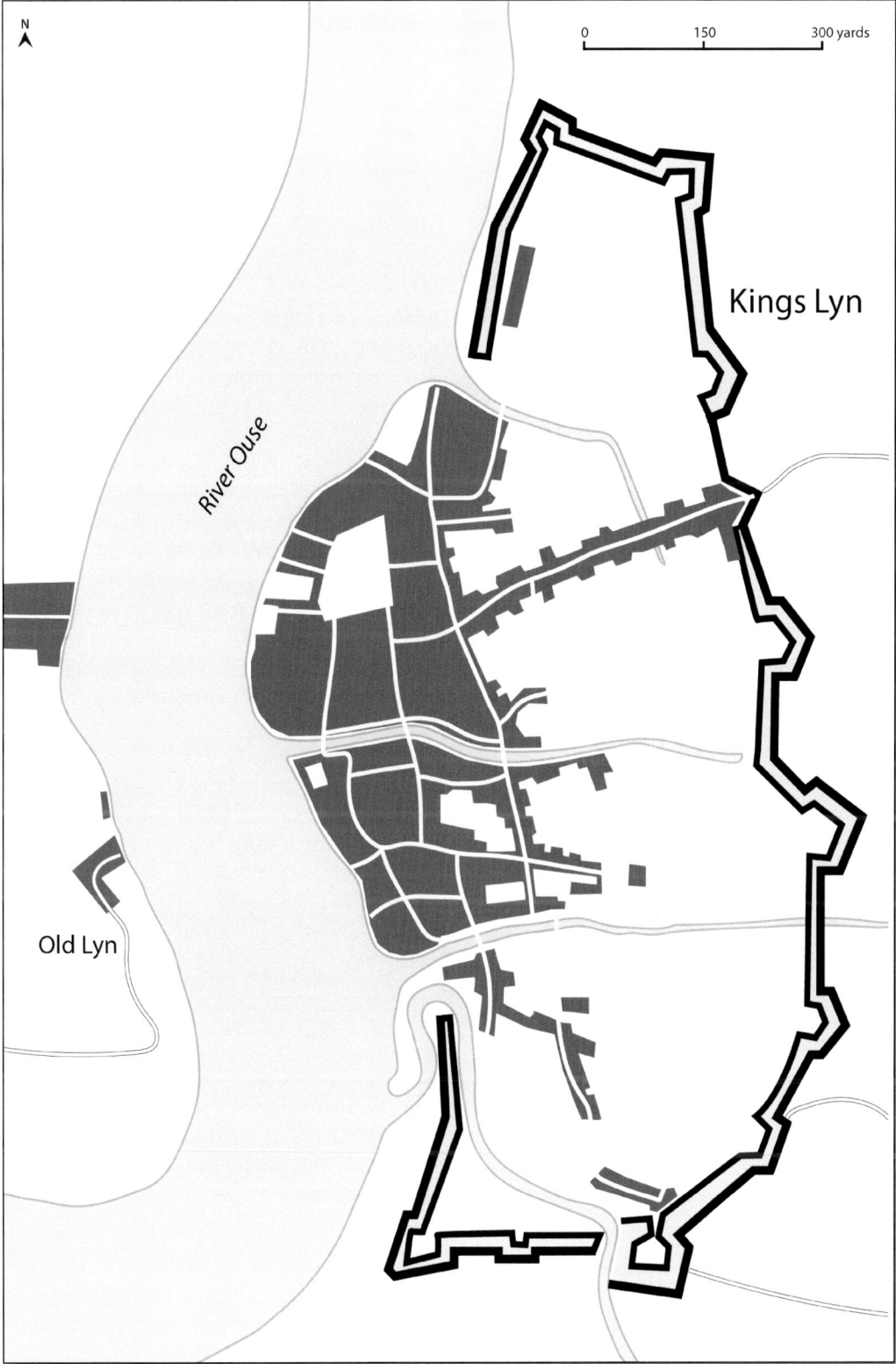

A modern interpretation of Hollar's map of King's Lynn

men, women and children and that the lamentable shrieks and cries of women and children are heard a great way out of the town'. It was during this bombardment that on 3 September a cannonball smashed the west window of St Margaret's church which caused the congregation to flee from the church. By 7 September Manchester's siege lines had come within 'musket shot of the town'.[25] Pioneers were sent for to dig approaches to the causeway and the east gate and soon they were within half musket shot of King's Lynn despite the garrison's attempts to prevent them by sallying out of the east gate. The garrison also attempted to burn the nearby town of Gaywood, but they only managed to set fire to two houses before the Parliamentarians extinguished the flames.

A second battery was also made on a hill close to the sea, which would bring most of the town within range of its guns. But as fast as the Parliamentarians breached the walls, the garrison repaired them. In preparation for the storming of the town, scaling ladders were brought up and boats assembled so that the town could be attacked from the river side. During this time the besiegers are said to have lost four men, including two who were mortally wounded, one a cannoneer who was hit by a shot from a drake and the other a lieutenant who had his arm shot off. However, the pamphlet continues, 'in this violent playing with cannon and small shot we believe above 80 lost their lives on both sides'.[26] Saturday 16 September was the day set to storm the town and Manchester sent word into the town that he would allow the women and children safe passage out of King's Lynn in order to avoid the shedding of innocent blood. This seems to have unnerved the officers in the garrison who on the Friday sent a message that they were willing to negotiate for the town's surrender.

The delegates met at Gaywood to discuss terms and after 24 hours negotiation the articles for surrender were agreed; which included the delivering up of the town with all its ordnance, arms and ammunition; that the gentlemen 'strangers' within the town were free to leave and each male inhabitant was to make a payment so that the Parliamentarian soldiers could receive 10 shillings per man, and the officers a fortnight's pay to prevent the town being plundered. The inhabitants of the town would also receive an amnesty for their actions.

However, despite these terms the garrison still opened fire on the Parliamentarians and tried to flood their works by cutting ditches for when the spring tide came in. When the Royalists were threatened with being made prisoners of war they used delaying tactics, including claiming that they could not open the large gate, so the men of Colonel Russell's and Colonel Walton's regiments of foot would have to enter the east gate one at a time. When finally this was agreed to, these two regiments were informed that they could not enter due to a 'rude multitude' who sought to prevent their entry. Finally after 24 hours the Parliamentarians were allowed to enter the town, and with Manchester at the head of his lifeguard, a thanksgiving service was held for its delivery. Colonel Valentine Walton became the town's governor.

---

25   BL: Egerton, MS 2647 f.229.
26   BL: TT E 67/28.

Amongst the besiegers was Thomas Butcher of Langham in Essex, whose petition stated that he 'being pressed in the service of parliament against Lynn ... he returned from the said service sore and dangerously wounded; so that he has been disabled ever since from following his calling.' In 1657 he was granted a pension of £4 per year.[27]

According to Captain William Dobson after the surrender of King's Lynn, on Sunday:

> the soldiers have gone up into the pulpits both in the forenoon and the afternoon and preached to the whole parish, and our ministers have sat in their seat in the church, and durst not attempt to preach, it being a common thing to preach in private houses night and day ... because they profess themselves Independents ... [and] frequently re-baptise the people of that Isle [of Ely].[28]

On 26 August 1643 Parliament passed the ordinance, *For the utter demolishing, removing and taking away of all monuments of superstition or idolatry.* This called for the removal of all 'Altars, tables of stone, Communion tables, tapers, candlesticks and basons, Crucifixes and Crosses, images and pictures ... of any one or more Persons of the Trinity, or of the Virgin Mary and all other images and pictures of Saints, or superstitious inscriptions'. The altar rails were also to be removed, although tombs, coats of arms, pictures and other non religious images were to remain. On 9 May 1644 Parliament went further and ordered that the ground 'raised for any Altar, or Communion table to stand upon, shall be laid down and levelled; And that no Copes, Surplices, superstitious vestments, Roods, or roodlons, or Holy Water Fonts shall be, or be any more used in any Church or Chappel within this Realm'. Also 'no Cross, Crucifix, picture, or representation of any of the persons of the Trinity, or any Angel or Saint shall be [used] ... And that all organs and the frames or cases ... shall be taken away and utterly defaced wherein they stand'.[29]

Despite these iconoclasm ordinances stating that this work should be completed in all places of worship in England and Wales by 1 November 1643, it was not until 19 December that Manchester appointed William Dowsing to destroy all such religious images 'within the Associated Counties'. He was to be aided by 'all mayors, sheriffs, bailiffs, constables head [of] boroughs, and all other [of] His majesty's officers and loving subjects'.[30] Dowsing, with assistance of seven others, like Thomas Westhorp of Hundon, who was described as a 'Godly man', quickly began their task by visiting the churches and the chapels of the universities in Cambridge. On 6 January 1644 he turned to the churches, visiting the parishes of Haverhill, Huden, Wixoe and Withersfield in Suffolk and destroyed their 'Popish' pictures and

---

27   ERO: Q/SBa2/100.
28   Bruce and Masson, pp.73–74.
29   Firth and Rait vol. 1, pp.265–266, 425–426.
30   William Dowsing, *The Journal of William Dowsing of Stratford, Parliamentary visitor appointed by the Earl of Manchester for demolishing the superstitious pictures and ornaments of church etc., within the county of Suffolk in the year 1643-1644,* ed. Rev. C. H. Evelyn White (Ipswich: Pawsey and Hayes, 1885), pp.6–7.

statues, including one of 'seven friars hugging a nun'. That day he also visited the parish of Clare, where he recorded in his journal:

> we brake down 1,000 pictures superstitious; I brake down 200; three of God the Father, and three of Christ and the Holy Lamb and three of the Holy Ghost like a Dove with wings; and the 12 Apostles were carved in Wood, on the top of the roof which we gave order to take down and 20 Cherubines to be taken down; and the Sun and Moon in the East Window, by the King's Arms, to be taken down.[31]

His journal covers the period 6 January until 1 October 1644 and records that he visited 149 churches mainly in Suffolk, although there is a gap in the journal between 16 April until 15 July. Sometimes he would arrive at a church to find that the icons had already been smashed, while others had

Horse and Foot in London 1643. Detail from an engraving of the destruction of The Eleanor Cross at Cheapside in May 1643. (Cross to the right of the picture) This is not, for once, a reused illustration and shows the general appearance of the rank and file. Note the fashionably short coats (which of course used less cloth and therefore cost less) and the unusual cornet carried by the horse. (Stephen Ede-Borrett collection)

31   Ibid., pp.15–16.

probably been taken away by the church officials for safe keeping. On other occasions he would leave the destruction of a church's ornaments to others, although they did not always obey his instructions since when he returned to a church he sometimes found them still intact.

No doubt he saw justification in his work when, on 8 April, he was told by a Mr Ellis, a high constable of the parish of Frostenden, that he had seen an 'Irishman' (that is, a Catholic), 'bow to the cross on the steeple, and put his hat to it' as a mark of respect. However not all felt the same as Dowsing and his deputies: on 31 August Dowsing visited Ufford, which he had visited before on 26 January, but this time the parish officials refused to let him in and Dowsing had to wait two hours before the keys to the church were found. His journal only records his own acts of iconoclasm, because incidents at the churches in the Hundreds of Mutford and Lothingland, which were visited by his deputy Francis Jessop, are not recorded.[32]

Neither was it just the Suffolk's churches that suffered, a Captain Gilly appears to have been active in Norfolk, while on the 24 January 1644 the Committee at Norwich ordered that the sheriff and several alderman were to 'take notice of such scandalous pictures, crucifixes and images as are yet remaining in the … churches and demolish or cause the same to be demolished.' Nor was it just the churches that the Parliamentarians looked to, but also the clergy themselves. Originally 'scandalous ministers' were dealt with by Parliament itself, but in the summer of 1643 the responsibility passed to the various county committees. In March 1644, Manchester issued a set of instructions for the committee members to follow. Clive Holmes has identified three categories under which a clergyman, or schoolmaster, was charged: when their religious views differed from their congregation; when they were against the Parliamentarian cause; when their morals were impugned.[33] However, a fourth category could be dereliction of their duties, due to being 'idle and lazy', or from absenteeism. Of the 14 articles brought against the rector of Copdock, William Aldus, the majority were for drunkenness, including that he was often so drunk that he could not perform his duties such as burying his own sister, and that on another occasion he failed to turn up to bury a child of Jeffrey Blanchflower.[34] Being a 'common drunkard and haunter of taverns' was a common accusation against the clergy. The vicar of Chassiham, Jeremiah Ravens, who was also the rector of Great Blakenham was not only accused of adultery but also that he had, 'hung up his wife by the heels and hath tied his wife to the bedpost and whipped her'.[35] On the other hand Robert Sugden, the vicar of Benhall was accused of sleeping with members of his congregation and getting at least one, 'Anne Shepherd, a singlewoman', pregnant.[36] Since the parishioners had to travel to where the committee was sitting, only a handful of the congregation usually

32   Ibid., pp.27, 29, 56.
33   Clive Holmes, *The Suffolk Committees for Scandalous Ministers* (The Suffolk Records Society, 1979), p.18.
34   Ibid., pp.66–67.
35   Ibid., pp.39–41.
36   Ibid., pp.68–69.

accused their minister of these charges. The accused clergyman could offer a defence, so not all the charges were proven and the case against them was dismissed; but what is clear from the examples given (and others which appeared before the Committee of Scandalous Minister for each county is that this was sometimes not a bad thing.

While Manchester was besieging King's Lynn for much of September, Cromwell remained at Boston waiting for Newcastle's advance which never came. Instead Newcastle decided to lay siege to Hull, and arrived at the city on 2 September, although he failed to occupy the southern bank of the Humber, so the town could be easily supplied with provisions. Lord Fairfax, who had retreated to Hull after his defeat at Adwalton Moor, had sent off a despatch to Manchester for assistance. Unfortunately Manchester was besieging Kings Lynn at this point and could do little. But with the surrender of the town on 16 September, he despatched Cromwell with 14 troops of horse and three companies of dragoons to assist Hull, while Lord Willoughby brought a further six troops of horse.

Portrait of the Marquis of Newcastle (Public Domain)

On 22 September Cromwell and Willoughby arrived, but their cavalry could do little since there was no way of coming to grips with the Royalists. Therefore, according to Sir Thomas Fairfax, the cavalry within the town were 'now useless, and many [horses] died every day, having nothing but salt water about the town. I was therefore sent over [the Humber] with the horse into Lincolnshire'.[37] As the cavalry of the northern horse were ferried over the river in small boats, Cromwell's forces guarded the opposite bank. Both Cromwell and Fairfax do not appear to have known that about 40 troops of Royalist horse under Sir John Henderson had set out from Newark to intercept them and were shadowing their movements, while Fairfax 'trusted to the care of our new friends, being strangers in those parts'. Finally near to Horncastle, Henderson pounced and beat up some of the outposts, which caused some 'newly raised' soldiers to flee to Lincoln, while others were in disorder and it was sometime before the Parliamentarians could reform. Fortunately 'my Lord Willoughby

---

37   Thomas Fairfax, *Short Memorials of Thomas, Lord Fairfax Written by Himself*, p.65.

with his horse, and my dragoons, commanded by Colonel Morgan, brought up the rear and after some skirmishes we lodged that night in the field'.[38] However, Cromwell blamed Willoughby for their quarters being surprised: in a letter to two members of the Suffolk committee he said, 'if God had not been merciful [the royalists] had ruined us before we had known it, the five troops [of Willoughby's] we set out to keep watch failing much in their duty'. In a letter to William Harlakenden he went further, 'divers troops of Lord Willoughby of Parham had an alarm from the enemy … and all those troops did run away and give no alarm to any of the rest … and it was God's infinite mercy their throats were not cut in their beds'.[39]

The siege of Hull continued from where on 27 September Robert Burton wrote to Sir Thomas Barrington:

> By reason of the Earl of Newcastle's forces coming together all men's estates … are so weakened and decayed that I fear few men will be able to pay any rents; for all our horses, beasts and sheep are driven away, the most of our houses plundered, our corn lost in the fields, our hay devoured, spoiled and wasted'.[40]

The besiegers dug earthworks between Hessel and Hull and at Gallows Clowe and made fortifications 'slating nearer and nearer towards the town'.[41] Sir Philip Warwick inspected the Royalists' siege lines and found that:

> (the season having been very wet) his men standing ankle deep in dirt a great distance from the town; so as I conceived those without were likelier to rot than those within to starve; and by assault there was not the least probability to carry it. Upon my return to him [Newcastle], relating but faintly and modestly my thoughts (for he knew I had not the least part of a soldier to warrant a discourse upon that subject) he merrily put it off, saying, 'You often hear us called the Popish Army: but you see we trust not in our good works.[42]

Burton continues that the Royalists:

> were come so near that I have been an ear witness of musket bullets coming over the walls. Before all this at their first coming they cut out from us our fresh water, so that in the end both water and grass grew very scarce, by reason of the multitude of horses and other cattle about the town.[43]

Lord Fairfax had to slaughter a great number of oxen and sheep within the city so their meat could be preserved. Burton continues:

---

38 Ibid.
39 Carlyle p.159; BL: Egerton 2647 f.286.
40 Ibid., p.567.
41 Ibid., p.568.
42 Warwick, *Memoirs*, pp.294–295.
43 HMC: Appendix to 7th Report, p.568.

> Nevertheless, we were so strait holden up both on the west side and north side of the town that our cattle were sore pinched, and many of them were shipping away, the enemy watching for them as a ravenous kite from a silly bird; They could no sooner straggle twice 12 score from the town but they were snatched from us.[44]

Among Newcastle's artillery were:

> two very great guns, which were called the Queen's pocket pistols. One of them lay between Scylscotte and Hull, and the other towards Hessel out of which they shot many fiery hot bullets into the town above 80 at the least and yet [they] did very little execution … These bullets weighed 35 pounds a piece and more. They shot one Sunday morning in prayer time three bullets at the high church, thinking to spoil us there, but God prevented them.[45]

Sir Henry Slingsby, who was with Newcastle's army, confirms Burton's evidence: 'His excellence thinking to fire the town sent red hot bullets into it, but they did no hurt at all'.[46] This so incensed the garrison, and the population of Hull, that on 4 October they sallied out of the city which made the besiegers 'run like cowardly hares, and [we] took three of their works [and] demolished them'.[47] Once the sally was over, the Royalists reoccupied two of the works; 'the nearest work we never suffered them to repair'.[48]

On 5 October Sir John Meldrum broke through the besiegers' lines with reinforcements, which various sources put at between 400 and 1,000 men. With this reinforcement, plus the some of the townsfolk, on 11 October Lord Fairfax ordered an attack on the siege lines. After an initial success Royalist reinforcements arrived who beat back the soldiers and civilians and regained their works, which they had lost in the initial assault, while the four troops of Parliamentarian horse faced a much larger body of Royalist cavalry. The Parliamentarian retreat was covered by the town's artillery. Meldrum and Lord Fairfax rallied their men and launched another attack. The Royalists were again driven from their defences and the Parliamentarians turned their own guns on the fleeing besiegers, including a demi-cannon, and 'two commonly called the Queen's Pocket Pistols and Gog and Magog, a demi culverin and four small drakes in one carriage'. The remaining cavalry pursued the fleeing Royalists, but Meldrum was wounded in this attack. The besiegers rallied and retook their works, but Newcastle was forced to abandon the siege the following day.

After spending the night in the fields the following day Cromwell and Fairfax's force met up with Manchester, who having taken King's Lynn, now set his sights on capturing Bolingbroke Castle which had been besieged by local Parliamentarians since September. However, upon hearing that

---

44   Ibid.
45   Ibid.
46   Sir Henry Slingsby, *The Diary of Sir Henry Slingsby* (London: 1836), ed. Rev. Daniel Parsons, p.100.
47   HMC: Appendix to 7th Report p.568.
48   Ibid.

Sir William Widdrington was marching to relieve Bolingbroke Castle, Manchester had held a council of war of what to do. Unfortunately Fairfax's advice is not known, but according to one pamphlet, 'Colonel Cromwell who was no way satisfied that we should fight, our horse being extremely wearied with hard duty [for] two or three days together'.[49] Nevertheless, Manchester decided to fight and so when Widdrington arrived near to the castle on 11 October he found Manchester's Army, along with Fairfax's cavalry drawn up on Bolingbroke Hill near Horncastle.

According to one Parliamentarian pamphlet, 'the enemy drew that morning their whole body of horse and dragoons into the field, being 74 Colours of horse, and 21 Colours of dragoons, in all 95 Colours. We had not many more than half so many Colours of horse and dragoons, but I believe we had as many men.'[50] Manchester recalls that 'I drew up the whole body of horse and foot before the castle of Bolingbroke … word was brought [to] me, that the enemy was advancing towards me, with 80 colours of horse'.[51] About midday Manchester decided to advance to meet this force, and the cavalry moved off leaving their foot and artillery to catch up.

The Parliamentarians advanced between half a mile to a mile and when they came to the village of Winceby they could see the Royalists; 'little and little coming towards us', recalls a pamphlet, 'until this time we did not know we should fight, but so soon as our men had knowledge of the enemy's coming they were full of joy and resolution, thinking it a great mercy that they should fight with him. Our men went on in several bodies singing Psalms'.[52] On a piece of 'convenient ground', the Parliamentarians deployed their cavalry; Cromwell's and Manchester's regiments of horse forming the front line, while Fairfax's cavalry formed the reserve. The five troops of Colonel Bartholomew Vermuyden's regiment, which was supported by some dragoons, formed a forlorn hope. On the slope on the opposite hill the Royalists drew up: according to Widdrington, the ground where he drew up his cavalry was not wide enough to deploy all his cavalry, 'we had but three divisions charged, two divisions being Sir William Savile's, the second of my Lord Eythin's and Sir John Henderson's joined, but being eight troops. The third division, being of the left wing'. The remainder of his cavalry were probably formed further to the rear.[53] To distinguish the two sides the Parliamentarian's field word was 'Religion', while the Royalists chose 'Cavendish'.

How long both sides faced each other is uncertain, one pamphlet says an hour, while Sir Thomas Fairfax says 'a little while'.[54] The forlorn hopes were the first to come into contact, then the Parliamentarian cavalry charged:

49 BL: TT E 71/5 *A True Relation of the Late Fight between the Right Honourable the Earl of Manchester and the Marquess of Newcastle's Forces.*
50 Ibid.
51 *Journal of the House of Lords*, vol. p.255.
52 BL: TT E 71/5.
53 John Rushworth, *Historical Collections* (London: 1721), p.282.
54 Sir Thomas Fairfax, 'A Short Memorial of Northern Actions during the war there, from the year 1642 till 1644' in *Journal of the Society for Army Historical Research*, vol. V (1926), p.167.

> Colonel Cromwell fell with resolution upon the enemy, immediately after their dragoons had given him the first volley, yet they were so nimble, as within half pistol shot they gave him another; his horse was killed under him at the first charge, and fell down upon him and fell down upon him, as he rose he was knocked down again by the gentlemen that charged him, who we conceive was Sir Ingram Hopton; but afterword he recovered a poor horse in a soldiers hand, and mounted himself again. Truly this charge was so home given that the enemy stood not another but were driven back upon their own body that was to second them, and put into disorder, our men charged all in with him, and then they ran for it, leaving all their dragoons which were now on foot behind them.[55]

As the cavalry of the Eastern Association fought with those of Newcastle's army, according to Widdrington his left wing 'put the enemy to disorder'. With Fairfax looking on he decided to charge the Royalists in the left flank, with the words 'come let us fall on', and as he led his cavalry forward, Fairfax is quoted as saying 'I never prospered better than when I fought against the enemy three or four to one.'[56]

However, despite Widdrington's claim that his cavalry had disordered some of the Parliamentarian cavalry, the Royalists had had enough and with Manchester's infantry beginning to appear and Fairfax's cavalry bearing down on them, Savile's regiment, who was on the opposite flank, broke and according to Widdrington 'totally disordered and so put to rout our whole army'. Fairfax recalls 'the fight was hot for half an hour, but then we forced them to a rout.'[57] Manchester also wrote about Fairfax's charge; 'the second charge, our men had little else to do but to pursue a flying enemy, which they did for many miles.'[58]

With Cromwell out of action, having been knocked down by Hopton, Fairfax led the pursuit, 'our men fell upon them and pursued them four miles, killing many and taking prisoners all the way', records one pamphlet.[59] While another recalls:

> Colonel Carnaby, Colonel Hopton, and divers persons of great quality were slain, whereof many fell in the place of encounter. 1200 were slain, wounded, and taken prisoners, and as the countrymen report, betwixt 100 and 200 drowned in Horncastle river. The Earl [sic] pursued the enemy to Horncastle and there quartered for the night. Very many of our men are wounded, but we do not hear of above twenty killed. Let God have all the praise of this victory! Twenty-six colours, which were taken, are brought already to my lord.[60]

Manchester records that 'divers men of quality lay dead upon the place, and divers that rode away fell dead from off their horses in the towns some miles

---

55   BL: TT E 71/5.
56   *Scottish Dove*, 20 October 1643.
57   Fairfax, 'A Short Memorial', p.167.
58   *Journal of the House of Lords*, vol. p.255.
59   BL: TT E 71/22 *A True and Exact Relation of the Great Victory by the Earl of Manchester and the Lord Fairfax*, 19 October 1643.
60   BL: TT E 71/5.

off from the place where we fought. I have sent 800 prisoners to Boston. There were killed upon the place about 300 as we can guess.'[61]

According to tradition, Slash Lane near Winceby is named after this pursuit, as well as there being a gate which because of the crush of fugitives from the battle, the Royalists could not open since it opened inwards, thus adding to their casualties.

With this battle and the raising of the siege of Hull, Sir Thomas Fairfax records; 'These two defeats together (the one falling heavy on the horse, the other upon the foot), kept the enemy all winter from attempting anything'.[62]

On 24 October Captain Nathaniel Rich, while at Plyford, wrote to Sir Thomas Barrington:

We are now advancing towards Newark, conceiving it the most considerable garrison the enemy of the two, viz., it and Gainsborough. The winter is already come, and our lying in the field hath lost us more men than have been taken away either by sword or bullet; notwithstanding which (and many of our men lying scattered up and down the [county]).

Sir Thomas Fairfax (Public Domain)

The soldiers had not been paid for nine weeks, even so Rich adds:

We are ready to persist and unwilling to wait any opportunity of doing God honour and our county service; yet if God pleases to bring us safe to our winter quarters you must think of speedy recruiting our troops which are not a little battered and lessened with what service we have done.[63]

The army seems to have faced Newark for a few days before settling down into winter quarters in the counties of the Eastern Association.

The year 1643 had been the low point for the Parliamentarian cause, but on 25 September Parliament agreed a treaty with the Scottish Covenanters to enter

---

61 *Journal of the House of Lords,* vol. p.255; BL: Egerton, MS 2647 f.319.
62 Fairfax, 'A Short Memorial', p.167.
63 HMC: 7th Report, Appendix p.567. The author has replaced the word country with county since this is more appropriate.

the war on their side. On 19 January 1644 the Scottish Covenanter army, consisting of about 20,000, men crossed the Tweed to assist their new allies. Parliament agreed to pay for this army every day it was on English soil, and more controversially everyone in England and Wales had to swear to the Solemn League and Covenant. This treaty meant that if Parliament won the war then the Church of England would be based on Presbyterianism, which had been founded on the Calvinist form of Protestantism; whereas if the King won then Laudianism – which had been introduced by Charles' Archbishop of Canterbury, William Laud, and was seen as Catholicism in all but name – would be re-established as the basis of the Church of England. These two religions were unacceptable to Independents like Cromwell, who rejected state religion in favour of independent congregations. The hatred of these religions and for the Scots would drive Cromwell's actions in the forthcoming campaigns.

3

Newark

During the winter of 1643 to 1644, Manchester continued to reorganise his army, and on 1 February he appointed Lawrence Crawford to be Sergeant Major General of all the forces both of horse and foot in the Eastern Association. Crawford also received a commission to raise a regiment of foot and a troop of 100 horse, which was to be raised in Suffolk. Born in 1611, Crawford was a Scottish Presbyterian who had served in Danish and Swedish service during the Thirty Years' War and had been a lieutenant colonel in the army of Prince Charles Louis, Rupert's older brother. More recently he had commanded a regiment in Ireland, but when the Earl of Ormond demanded that all officers and men swear allegiance to the King on pain of imprisonment and the officers cashiered, he returned to England to fight for Parliament.[1]

Unfortunately, the appointment of Crawford would divide the Eastern Association as his fellow Scotsman, Robert Baillie, later wrote:

> Our Countryman Crawford was made General Major of that [Manchester's] army. This man proving very stout and successful, got a great hand with Manchester and with all their army that were not for sects. The other party finding all their designs marred by him, set themselves by all means to have him out of the way, that he being removed, they might frame the whole army to their devotion, and draw Manchester himself to them by persuasion, or else to weary him out of his charge that Cromwell might be general. This has been the Independents' great plot by his army to counterbalance us, to overawe the Assembly and Parliament both to their ends … [but] they require a council of war to remove him.[2]

No doubt the relationship of the two men must have soured even further when Crawford cashiered the lieutenant colonel of his regiment when he refused to obey orders. Lieutenant Colonel Packer, who is described as a

---

1   Laurence Crawford, *Colonel Crawford his Remonstrance, declaring why he deserted his employment in Ireland* (London: H. Elsing, 3 February, 1644).

2   Robert Baillie, *Letters and Journals of Robert Baillie*, ed. D. Laing (Edinburgh: Bannatyne Club, 1841), vol. II, p.229–230.

'notorious Anabaptist', complained to Cromwell, who on 10 March 1644 wrote to Crawford defending Packer:

> Sir, the State, in choosing men to serve them, takes no notice of their opinions, if they be willing faithfully to serve them, that satisfies. I advised you formerly to bear with men of different minds from yourself: if you had done it when I advised you to it, I think you would not have had so many stumbling blocks in your way. It may be you judge otherwise, but I tell you my mind. I desire you would receive this man into your favour and good opinion. I believe, if he follow my counsel, he will deserve no other but respect from you. Take heed of being sharp, or too easily sharpened by others, against those to whom you can object little but that they square not with you in every opinion concerning matters of religion. If there be any other offence to be charged upon him, that must in a judicial 'way' receive a determination; I know you will not think it fit my Lord should discharge an officer of the Field but in a regulate way. I question whether either you or 1 have any precedent for that. I have not further to trouble you, but rest.[3]

However, Crawford could not be persuaded and instead appointed Richard Warner as lieutenant colonel in Packer's place.[4]

Newark had been a thorn in the Eastern Association's side since the beginning of the war, and so began the famous siege. On 12 February seeing the Parliamentarian forces beginning to gather outside its defences, the town's governor Sir Richard Byron wrote to Lord Loughborough for assistance since:

> The forces from Lincoln, Gainsborough, and their other garrisons in Lincolnshire are already drawn out, and many of them lie within four or five miles of us, whereby they hinder and cut off all provisions and maintenance which should support us on [the] Lincolnshire side, and stay there in expectation of a confluence of the Earl of Manchester's and other forces, which (as we are informed) are now at Peterborough, within 30 miles of this place, to the number of 5,000 and are making all preparations to fall upon us speedily.[5]

However it was not until 29 February that Sir John Meldrum and Lord Willoughby decided to besiege the town and it would not be until 6 March that they finally arrived with a force of 2,000 horse and dragoons, plus between 4,000 and 5,000 foot.

Byron sent a despatch to a Mr Thorold, who was to notify Rupert of the town's predicament:

> On the south side of the town are all my Lord Willoughby's forces, and their new made colonel King, and Meldrum with all that they can draw out of all their garrisons of Boston, Lincoln and Gainsborough. My Lord Grey [of Groby's]

---

3   Carlyle, pp.170–171.
4   Warner was lieutenant colonel of Crawford's regiment until his death on 30 October 1644. Spring, *The Army of the Eastern Association*, p.50.
5   HMC: Hastings, vol. 2.

forces with all [the] Leicester, Melton, Nottingham and Derby can afford are gone on the north side of the Trent.

Another Royalist account states that there were five regiments of foot and a further four companies or 'colours'. This force included Sir Miles Hobart's, Sir John Palgrave's, Colonels Francis Russell's, Thomas Waite's and Edward King's regiments of foot, plus Willoughby's regiments of horse and foot. A list of prisoners within Newark on 9 April also records men from Sir John Gell's, Colonel Askew's and six troopers from Colonel Cromwell's regiment.[6]

Upon the besieging force's arrival, Colonel King looked to the capture of the Countess of Exeter's house, which 'after a sharp conflict', they captured. A Royalist counterattack failed to dislodge King's regiment and with Exeter House secured, Major John Lilburne tried to persuade Sir John Meldrum to occupy an island on the River Trent opposite the town of Newark. Meldrum was at first reluctant but 'the major and the resolution of the soldiers prevailed'. Lilburne's dragoons stormed Muskham Bridge and occupied the island. The garrison of Newark responded by sallying out to repel this force, but with the intervention of Colonel King's regiment of foot and two troops of horse, the Royalists fell back to the safety of the town. The Parliamentarians pursued the cavalry over a bridge and captured a fort overlooking it.[7]

The besiegers erected an earthwork near Exeter House which was known as the spittle, which was described as 'their chief work … little more than a musket shot from the town'. In the besiegers' lines was a detachment of Sir Miles Hobart's regiment of foot who being relieved from guard duty extinguished their match, which they used to fire their muskets, but about 100 horse from the garrison observed this and fell upon them and those who were not killed were taken prisoner. Two troops of Willoughby's regiment of horse who were escorting them to their quarters are said to have just looked on and did not intervene.[8]

Encouraged by this, some additional cavalry from Newark sallied out onto the island, where two companies of Colonel Edward King's regiment under Lieutenant Colonel John Bury attacked the Royalists and ordered 20 musketeers to line some hedges to prevent the Royalists' retreat. Bury also called upon some musketeers of Willoughby's regiment of foot, who had been ordered to support him, to do the same but 'could not obtain one man'. Unfortunately Bury's account then goes onto another episode of the siege so does not say what happened next, but presumably the Royalist cavalry managed to return to Newark with little loss.

By the middle of March Meldrum was confident that Newark would soon surrender, nevertheless he asked for reinforcements, but on 19 March he received the following reply from the Committee of Both Kingdoms:

---

6   HMC: Hastings, pp.124, 125.

7   Lieutenant Colonel Bury, *A Brief Relation of the Siege of Newark as it was delivered to the Council of State at Derby House by Lieutenant Colonel Bury* (London: Peter Cole, 26 March 1644).

8   BL: TT E 39/8.

You write for 500 horse more and 2,000 foot, with which we find you cannot suddenly be furnished. The pressing necessity of sending forces into Yorkshire and elsewhere is so great as we are of opinion that the making any attempt upon Newark which shall break those forces, or their long stay there, will be more inconvenient than the not taking that place.[9]

Prince Rupert (Public Domain)

Therefore Meldrum settled down to starve Newark into submission, but little did he know that Prince Rupert had been gathering a force to relieve the town. Early in the morning of 21 March he drew up his forces on Beacon Hill to the east of the town from where he attacked the Parliamentarian forces. Colonels Rossiter and Thornhaugh with their regiments of horse tried to prevent the Royalists' advance, as one Royalist newspaper recalls:

Our field word was 'King and Queen' and theirs 'Religion'. The fight began about nine of the clock, and after a while grew sturdy, especially on our right wing; the Rebels doubling march off suddenly, advanced their files from three to six deep, and charged our two utmost troops upon the flanks so hard, that Captain Martine [of Rupert's regiment] came timely in to help beat off the Rebels. The Prince himself having pierced deep into the enemies, and being observed for his valour, was dangerously at once assaulted by three sturdy Rebels, whereof one fell by his Highness' own sword, a second being pistolled by M Mortaine one of his own gentlemen: the third now ready to lay hand on the Prince's collar, had it almost chopped off by Sir William Neale: His Highness thus disengaged with a shot only in his gauntlet, with Sir Richard Crane and his own troop charged quite through that body of Rebels; pursuing them in rout home to their very works at the Spittle.

Presently after this, his Highness' Regiment with their seconds, likewise routed the three other bodies; four of the troops charging even into the work, and bringing away a captain prisoner.[10]

Lucy Hutchinson recalls that on hearing of Rupert's approach that Meldum:

had drawn all his ordnance within the walls of a ruined house, called the Spittle, and the horse were the first to charge the enemy. Colonel Thornhaugh and Major Rossiter gave them a very brave charge, routed those whom they first encountered, and took prisoners Major General Gerard and others, and had they

---

9   CSPD 1644, p.61.
10   Anon., *His Highness Prince Rupert raising of the Siege of Newark upon Trent, 21 March 1643 written by an eyewitness to a person of honour.*

been seconded by the rest of the horse, had utterly defeated the prince's Army; but the Lincolnshire troops fled away before ever they charged, and left Colonel Thornhaugh engaged, with only his own horse, with the Prince's whole body, were, they say, he charged very gallantly through the whole army, with a great deal of honour and two desperate wounded, one in the arm, the other in the belly. After the Lincolnshire horse were run away, Sir John Meldrum sent the Derby horse and the Nottingham foot, with two companies of Colonel King's to keep Muskham bridge, and Molanus, the Derbyshire major, to be their commander … Sir John himself with the few horse and dragoons that were left from Nottingham and Derby, being about 500, went into the spittle to his foot.[11]

According to Lieutenant Colonel Bury, Meldrum commanded 'the Derby horse to guard the 200 pioneers and 400 musketeers which Sir John then sent into the island to make a Fort Royal'.[12] He continues:

the enemy drew down half their horse and the greatest part of their foot to force the bridge, which was gallantly maintained by Colonel King's company and two to three of Yorkshire Companies, although hotly assaulted by the Welsh Regiment, they were forces to retreat with much loss; all this time our cannon played upon their horse, the Master Gunner with the great piece did excellent execution the enemy's expectation of the bridge being frustrated, they drew out the Newark foot with a considerable strength of horse, not giving Sir John time to raise his fort Royal, possessed themselves of the island and entrenched themselves there to cut off our provision. The three companies of Colonel King's and the three Nottingham companies in the night, (Sir John not knowing thereof) quitted the Fort and passed over Muscom Bridge, brake up the bridge, and so secured themselves and our horse on that side.[13]

However, the Royalist cavalry did not have it all their own way:

My Lord Loughborough also deported himself honourably, and when some of his shrunk, at the second charged himself rode back to rally and bring them up again: Major General Porter charged with bravery enough … though some of his [men retired up the hill in some has and disorder. Colonel Charles Gerard (who never carried himself but gallantly) did here like himself: but by the fall of his horse, was bruised, shot in the arm and taken prisoner.

After a while both sides began to rally and make ready for a second charge; ours to make the impression and their to receive it: and though for a good while they disputed it toughly, yet by fine force were they and all the rest driven quite out of the field; not half of our horse charging, for our rear was not yet come up. Now fled the enemy quite beyond their own work … at the Spittle.[14]

---

11   Hutchinson, *Memoirs*, pp.220–221.
12   Bury, *A Brief Relation.*
13   Bury, *A Brief Relation.*
14   Anon., *His Highness Prince Rupert.*

The Parliamentarian cavalry were forced to withdraw over a bridge of boats which had been especially constructed by the besiegers for better access to the island. In this cavalry melee the Royalists are said to have taken five cornets. With the Parliamentarians trapped on the island there was a lull in the fighting for three hours, 'of silence excepting that the enemy's cannonades (though with very little effect) disturbed it'. Rupert was waiting for his infantry to come up as well as the remainder of his cavalry units.

When the Royalists infantry finally arrived they could not be thrown into the battle immediately because they were too tired after their long march, so they rested for a while on Beacon Hill. The infantry included 1,000 musketeers drawn from the regiments from Colonel Tillier's and Broughton's, which were had recently arrived from Ireland, as well as 120 musketeers from Sir Fulk Huncks regiment. Once they had rested enough, Tillier with the regiments from Ireland:

> marched down bravely in the face of the enemy, hooting at their cannon. These flanked with some horse, were wheeled to the right, by and by, into a meadow. At their coming the Rebels drew all their horse and foot within their Spittle work … our men came against both sides saluted one another at too far a distance, with a short volley. But Colonel Tillier was not to stay here; as being, by his orders to march up to the very river side, to recover the boat bridge from the enemy. But this being too well guarded, ours drew off.[15]

Tillier's men withdrew out of the range of the Parliamentarian cannon. Meanwhile other bodies of Royalist infantry had advanced down the hill who also charged the Parliamentarian works and 'killed many'. Seeing this Sir Richard Byron, also sent forces to draw up on the south east side of the town. Meldrum now found himself hemmed in on three sides and trapped on the island, although the soldiers from Nottingham appear to have been cut off from the island and so leaving their lighted match behind them withdrew under cover of darkness. Lucy Hutchinson praised this manoeuvre, which she calls 'a very seasonable mercy, for had they stayed the choicest arms in the garrison had been lost, and the best and most confiding soldiers disarmed'.[16] Rossiter covered the Parliamentarians' retreat and about 500 troopers appear to have broken out leaving the rest of the army to their fate.

With only two bridges leading to the island the Parliamentarian infantry could not break out, nor could the Royalists attempted to storm it without suffering heavy losses, so now the besiegers became the besieged. Due to its close vicinity to Newark itself no provisions or ammunition appears to have been stored on the island, so a Major Molanus declared that he would break out and ride to the next village to get some bread. According to Lucy Hutchinson he was never seen again. Could he be the unnamed prisoner captured by the Royalists who told Rupert that 'the Rebels were so distressed for want victuals, that they were not able to live there two days', which encouraged him to offer terms of surrender? However, according to

---

15   Anon., *His Highness Prince Rupert.*
16   Hutchinson, *Memoirs*, pp.221–222.

Lieutenant Colonel Bury it was the Royalists forcing Muskham Bridge and the mutiny of Palgrave's regiment which he refers to as the 'Norfolk redcoats' that prompted Meldrum to call for a parley.[17]

On 22 March Hobart and Palgrave on behalf of Sir John Meldum signed the articles of surrender. The Parliamentarians had to give up their arms, except their swords, but were allowed to keep their drums and colours, although the officers were allowed to keep their arms, baggage, servants and horses. The Royalists were also to escort the Parliamentarians until within two miles of Lincoln, but when they marched out the following day with some of their arms the Royalists declared they had broken the terms of surrender and fell upon them and it was said plundered them of their clothes. Prince Rupert himself is said to have set about his men in an effort to restore order.

It was rumoured that Rupert's dog, 'Boy', had been killed in the fight. The Parliamentarians claimed that Rupert was a witch and his dog was his 'familiar' through whom he communicated with the Devil. Upon hearing the news in London, bonfires are said to have been lit to celebrate, but these rumours soon proved to be unfounded.[18]

Newark is seen as Rupert's finest hour, but he lacked the resources to follow up his success in invading the territory of the Eastern Association and so retired to Shrewsbury. However the disaster at Newark had far reaching results, and a large part of Lincolnshire was abandoned to the Royalists including Lincoln itself. Newark would also be the last action that Lord Willoughby of Parham took part in; with pressure on him in Parliament from Manchester and Cromwell over his abandoning Gainsborough and pressure from Colonel Edward King and his officers, Willoughby finally resigned his commission.

On hearing of these events Robert Baillie wrote:

> The disaster at Newark was ascribed by some to my Lord Willoughby's treachery for his envy to Manchester, and desire to see his forces there broken; others to the malcontent of the Independent soldiers, who did mutiny; others to the slackness of Colonel Cromwell, the great Independent, so send Meldrum timeous relief. But when all is well considered and Sir John Meldrum's own letters looked upon it seems his own unprovidence alone has procured that mischief … He assured in every letter after he lay down [before the town] to carry it in four or five days. When it was told of him of [the] Prince Rupert's coming, he wrote of it hither, but as not believing it; when he was assured of his coming he would not rise but would fight him in the fields. When he was assured of his being within eight miles, with seven or eight thousand effective [men], he drew the council of war to a foolish conclusion to make good the Isle of Trent for one day to keep the place where he lay, and a bridge on the other side of the Isle, whether they would retire at night and cut the bridge and so retire in safety. But the first thing the enemy was to enter Newark and by it the Isle and to lay themselves down betwixt Sir John and his bridge; which presently made a parley to be sounded, and a shameful capitulation to be closed to render cannon munitions, muskets pistols and all fire

---

17   Hutchinson, *Memoirs*, p.221–222; Anon., *His Highness Prince Rupert*; Bury, *A Brief Relation*.

18   BL: Egerton, MS 785 unfoliated.

weapons; but attour all arms and colours and money, and clothes almost all pulled off them: and so one of the most considerable parts of our forces clean dissipated. Sir John with two thousand naked foot came to Hull; whence he wrote the story not in so humble terms as his condition requires.[19]

The situation was serious and so the Parliamentarian propaganda machine when into action; on 6 April to raise moral a payment was made to Roger Daniel for printing 2,000 copies of *A Catalogue of Remarkable Mercies* for the county of Huntingdon.[20] In 11 points this catalogued the victories the forces of the Eastern Association had obtained since Cromwell's capture of Lowestoft in March 1643 and referred to Sir William Waller's recent victory at the battle of Cheriton on 29 March 1644. Another publication printed in 1644 was *The Soldiers' Catechism,* which argued that they were fighting for 'King and Parliament', in order to rescue him from 'the hands of a Popish Malignant company' and that they were fighting 'against the enemies of Jesus Christ, who in His Majesty's name make war against the Church and People of God'. Whereas as Parliament 'under God, consists the glory and welfare of this Kingdom'.[21] However, it did not just criticise the Royalists, but also the commanders of the Parliamentary armies. Under the question 'what is the reason then that there be so many lewd and wicked men in the Parliament's Army', it gives the following answers:

> 1. Because commanders in chief are not more careful in choosing Godly officers.
> 2. Because honest religious men are not more forward to put forth themselves in this service of God and his church.
> 3. Because order and discipline is not more strictly executed by superiors.
> 4. Because officers in towns and counties aim to press the scum and refuse of men, and so by easing themselves, posture our armies with base conditioned people.[22]

How widely these views were accepted is not known.

By now the Scottish army under Alexander Leslie, the Earl of Leven, who had fought for many years in the Swedish army, had altered the balance of power in the north. With this new threat Newcastle's army headed north leaving Fairfax's Northern Association to capture Royalist garrisons in Cheshire, Lancashire and West Riding, including Halifax, Bradford and Howley Hall, and then on 11 April Selby, where the garrison had been reinforced by a large part of the garrison of York commanded by the city's governor, John Bellasis (or Belasyse). The Parliamentarians stormed the town 'in three several places at once, and after two hours took it'. Among the 79 officers and 2,100 soldiers prisoners was Bellasis himself. Seventeen ensigns

19 Baillie, *Letters and Journals*, vol. II, p.153.
20 TNA: SP 28/223 part 5, unfoliated.
21 Anon., *The Soldiers Catechism: composed for the Parliaments' Army: consisting of two parts wherein are chiefly taught 2 the qualification of our soldiers. Written for the encouragement and instructions of all that have taken up arms in this cause of God and his people; especially the common soldiers.* (James Cranford, 1644), pp.3–9.
22 Ibid., pp.19–20.

were also captured.[23] The Earl of Newcastle, who was then at Durham, heard about this disaster the following day and knew that the remaining soldiers in York were nowhere near strong enough to hold the city. Therefore he abandoned any inclination of confronting the Scots and set off south for York, followed by the Scots under the Earl of Leven. Exactly when Newcastle arrived at York is open to debate, secondary sources suggest the 14 or 16 April, but according to Rushworth on 13 April 'the Marquis [of Newcastle] having sent for what forces could be spared out of Newcastle and Lumley Castle, to strengthen his foot, began to remove his whole force from Durham and that in a great deal of haste … left cumbersome provisions behind him … hastened his march for York, where he arrived April the 19th.'[24]

Meanwhile Manchester continued to increase the size of his army. On 18 March Colonel John Pickering was commissioned to raise a regiment of foot and on 31 March, the regiment's major, John Jubbs, received £50 for conducting 500 men out of Norfolk, who judging by its later actions were presumably 'honest religious men', rather than 'scum' as described in *The Soldiers' Catechism*.[25]

On 6 April with the King mustering his forces again for the forthcoming campaigning season, the Committee of Both Kingdoms wrote to Manchester to muster his forces and march to Aylesbury by 19 April. On the same day as the muster a further 'two saker drakes of brass' were ordered to be delivered to Manchester.[26]

The strategy for the campaign was the destruction of the King's main Oxford army by the armies of Manchester, Essex and Waller. However, on 13 April the Committee again wrote to Manchester having received intelligence that the Royalists intended to capture Boston and that he should look to the relief of 'Boston, and the security of the Association, whereby you will keep those parts from danger and not be hindered from coming to the rendezvous, which diversion perhaps was their main design'.[27] On 15 April the Committee again wrote to Manchester:

> the enemy with about 2,600 horse and dragoons is come before Boston and has driven the horses and cattle out of Holland. We exceedingly apprehend the loss of that town (which we hear has not above 500 men in it), and that Marshland must then in all probability be lost, and the enemy will break into Norfolk, where, and in other parts a great army may be speedily raised against the Parliament and this place much straitened for provisions, and your whole Association be much shaken. We desire you therefore to send forthwith such supplies as may relieve [it] and secure the Association and [so] prevent these inconveniences, and with the rest to proceed in your intentions for the rendezvous.[28]

---

23 Hamilton, *Calendar of State Papers Domestic* (1644), p.125.
24 Rushworth, *Historical Collections of Private Passages of State*, vol. V 1642–1642 (London: D. Browne, 1721).
25 TNA: SP 28/128 part 8, f.8.
26 TNA: WO 47/1 f. 23.
27 CSPD 1644, pp.101, 116.
28 CSPD 1644, p.120.

In April 1644 Manchester's army consisted of the following infantry regiments:[29]

Regiment	Strength in May 1644
Manchester's	1,628
Crawford's	850
Pickering's	738
Hobart's	883
Montagu's	759
Russell's	932
Palgrave's (later Hoogan's)	804
	6,594

This figure falls far short of the 10,000 foot which had been proposed for the army, and the strength of the cavalry at this point is not known since many of the pay accounts have not survived. Although the muster payments of the ones that do survive show that the troops mustered between 42 and 100 troopers, which gives about 2,956 troopers, which is almost the paper strength of the Eastern Association's cavalry being 3,000 men.[30]

The Capture of Lincoln

After the disaster of Newark, Manchester set about recapturing the territory that had been lost. On 3 May he arrived at Lincoln, and sent a trumpeter with a message for the Royalists to surrender. However, when the trumpeter returned, it was with 'a very uncivil answer'. Since it would take too long to starve the garrison into surrender, there was no option but to the storm the town. Montagu's and Russell's regiments were chosen for this task, who were led by their colonels 'with good alacrity and resolution, being led on by those two valiant and religious Colonels, who, through the might of God, so undauntedly approached the enemy that after a very short dispute, terror seized upon their spirits, and our men seized upon their works'. After a brief fight the Royalists fell back to the castle and the minster, setting light to some houses to cover their retreat. Manchester planned to storm the castle the following day, however according to Rushworth 'there fell so much rain as hindered any great action'. Manchester postponed the attack due to the 'weather continuing so violent', since the ground leading to the castle was so steep and very slippery from the rain. As one account put it 'the Mount whereon the Castle stood being near as steep as the eaves of a house'.[31]

---

29   Holmes, *The Eastern Association*, Appendix 8.
30   Clive Holmes, *The Eastern Association*, Appendix 9. The overall figure is based on the average number of known troops strengths multiplied by 36 or the number of troops which made up Manchester's regiments.
31   BL: TT E 47/2 *A True Relation of the taking of the city, Minster and Castle of Lincoln …* (London, 1644).

Despite the inclement weather, when news arrived later that morning that General George Goring was marching with 5,000–6,000 cavalry to relieve Lincoln, Manchester had no choice but to act fast and ordered scaling ladders to be brought up and issued to his infantry. He intended to storm the castle that afternoon, but a subsequent despatch arrived informing him that Goring was still some distance away and that he would not be able to relieve the city any time soon, therefore the assault was delayed. However, Manchester did send Cromwell with 2,000 cavalry to shadow Goring and intercept him if necessary.

Keep of Lincoln Castle
(from J Brittons's
Antiquities of Cities, 1828)

Seeing the Parliamentarian infantry stand down, the Royalists 'perceiving, it caused them to insult, hooping and hollowing against us, thinking we were afraid to set upon them; but the next morning, they sang another note in another tune'.[32] That night the infantry slept in the positions they had taken up that day and at 2:00 or 3:00 a.m. on 6 May, six great pieces of ordnance opened fire, the signal for the assault. As the Parliamentarian infantry pressed forward, the Royalists 'met them with all their shot', records one account, 'which they poured out like hail'.[33] The musket shot soon gave way to heavy stones thrown from the parapet, 'by which we received more hurt than by all their shot'.[34] Rushworth also mentions this incident, the Parliamentarians:

> got up to their works, though the King's forces made a gallant resistance; and
> being under their works, set up their scaling ladders, whereupon those with

---

32   Ibid.
33   Ibid.
34   Ibid.

left firing, and threw down mighty stones from over their works, which did the assailants more prejudice than their shot, yet at last up they got, and slew about 50 in their works, and the rest cried for quarter, which was given them.[35]

The Parliamentarians were soon over the walls of Lincoln Castle and the Royalists threw down their arms and surrendered. According to Rushworth the assault had taken just a quarter of an hour, although another account puts it at an hour, which is probably more likely. Four colonels, two lieutenant colonels, two majors, 20 captains and 800 soldiers, including 100 troopers were captured. As a reward the Parliamentarian soldiers were free to pillage the upper part of Lincoln, a city that was part of the Eastern Association. Rushworth claims that there were eight killed and 40 wounded on Parliament's side, which included Henry King of Helions Bumpstead, who belonged to Captain William Walden's company of Manchester's regiment of foot who, 'by the blowing up of a barrel of gunpowder at the receipt of ammunition … [his] eyes were exceedingly blasted, whereby he is rendered incapable to follow his labour towards the maintenance of his wife and three small children, which are in necessity'. Despite his injury it was not until October 1656 that he was awarded a pension of 20s a year.[36]

The *Parliament Scout* praised 'Colonel Russell and Colonel Montagu, of whose affection to the Cause, freeness from self ends, hatred of covetousness, we have had sufficient testimony, and now lastly of their valour, who led up their men, and fought bravely in their own persons, one of which gave a Colonel of the other side several wounds'. Meanwhile the *Particular Relation* states that 'The Colonels and other superior officers were in the face of all the dangers, performing equal service with the meanest soldier (who undoubtedly received much life and courage from the undaunted resolution and forwardness of their commanders)'.[37] A thanksgiving service was held in the cathedral on 8 May after which Manchester planned to set out for York. However, on 22 May Manchester was still at Lincoln, when he wrote to the speaker of the House of Lords:

> I am still at Lincoln with four regiments of foot, I have quartered four more at Gainsborough, Torksey Bridge, and Saxilby, being in readiness to march towards the Scotch Army upon certain notice of Prince Rupert's marching that way. Most of my horse are joined with the Scotch horse already, and lie quartered on the either side of [the] Trent. The Derby and Nottingham horse intend to join with me. Those on the other side [of the] Trent will make near 6,000 horse and dragoons.[38]

The Derby and Nottingham horse do not appear to have joined him and so on 1 June he again wrote to the Committee of Both Kingdoms, 'upon

35   Rushworth, *Historical Collections*, vol. III, part 2, p.620.
36   D.H. Allen, *Essex Quarter Sessions Order Book, 1652–1661* (Chelmsford: Essex Record Office Publications, 1974), p.93.
37   BL: TT E 47/26 *Parliament Scout*; TT E 47/- *Particular Relation*.
38   Lincolnshire Archives (LA): reference no. HILL/39/2.

Monday I shall march to the leaguer [before York], and take up my quarter there'.[39] Despite being in desperate need of money to pay the soldiers' wages, Manchester finally set out to join the Scottish army under Leven and Fairfax's Northern Association who were besieging York.

39   CSPD 1644, p.191.

4

Siege of York

York is an ancient city surrounded by a medieval wall, which during the Civil War had been reinforced by various fortifications to strengthen its defences. Unfortunately, there is no map depicting these fortifications but various accounts speak of sconces or forts. John Speed's map of 1611 shows the city to have about 30 churches and a cathedral, and the southern part of the city was isolated by the River Ouse with only a bridge connecting both parts of the city. To the east of the city is the River Foss, which also connected two parts of the city with a bridge. Also on the eastern side was Wawgate (also referred to as Walmgate and Wangate) and to the south east, Fisher Gate. On the western side of York was Mary Gate and Gilly Gate and on the south side of the city is Micklegate and across the Ouse is the York castle. Many of the roads today have similar names as in the seventeenth century, for example to the north east of the city was located the suburb of Boudam and the road is now known as Clifton Bootham.[1] Outside of the walls Speed's map shows many windmills scattered on four sides of York, however by the time that Benedict Horsley's map of the city was published in 1694 only a few windmills remained and the suburb opposite Walmgate had disappeared, almost certainly due to the siege.[2]

In 1642 the accounts for the city show that payments were made for repairing the walls and gates, including 12s 11d for making a door at Monk's Bridge. The Horsley map also shows that the breastworks around the city walls were still there apart from the eastern part of York where the River Foss formed a natural defensive line. These earthworks were still visible in the 1720s when Daniel Defoe visited York and recalls 'The old walls are standing, and the gates and posterns; but the old additional works which were cast up in the later rebellion, are slighted; so that York is not now defensible as it was then'. Descriptions of the siege mention three sconces to the west of the city; one of which is referred to as being nearest to the city and protected by a double ditch, and was possibly on the site of Nunmill Hill or which is sometimes referred to as Clementhorpe Hill.

---

1   There is also now a Fairfax Street and a Cromwell Road, but no Manchester or Leven Road.
2   Two undated and anonymous maps of York, c. 1600; *The Ichnography or ground plot of the City of York*, surveyed by Benedict Horsley, 1694.

N

to the North

River Foss

to Scarborough

Clifton

M A N C H E S T E R

Bridge of Boats

The Manor

Monk Gate

Leyrethorp Gate

S C O T T I S H

To Boroughbridge & Knaresborough

to Marston Moor & Wetherby

Mickle-gate

Skelders Gate

Castle

Walm Gate

St. Lawrence's Ch.

Fisher Gate

F A I R F A X

to Hull

River Ouse

Heslington

to Tadcaster

Fulford

Bridge of Boats

Middlethorpe

0   ½ mile

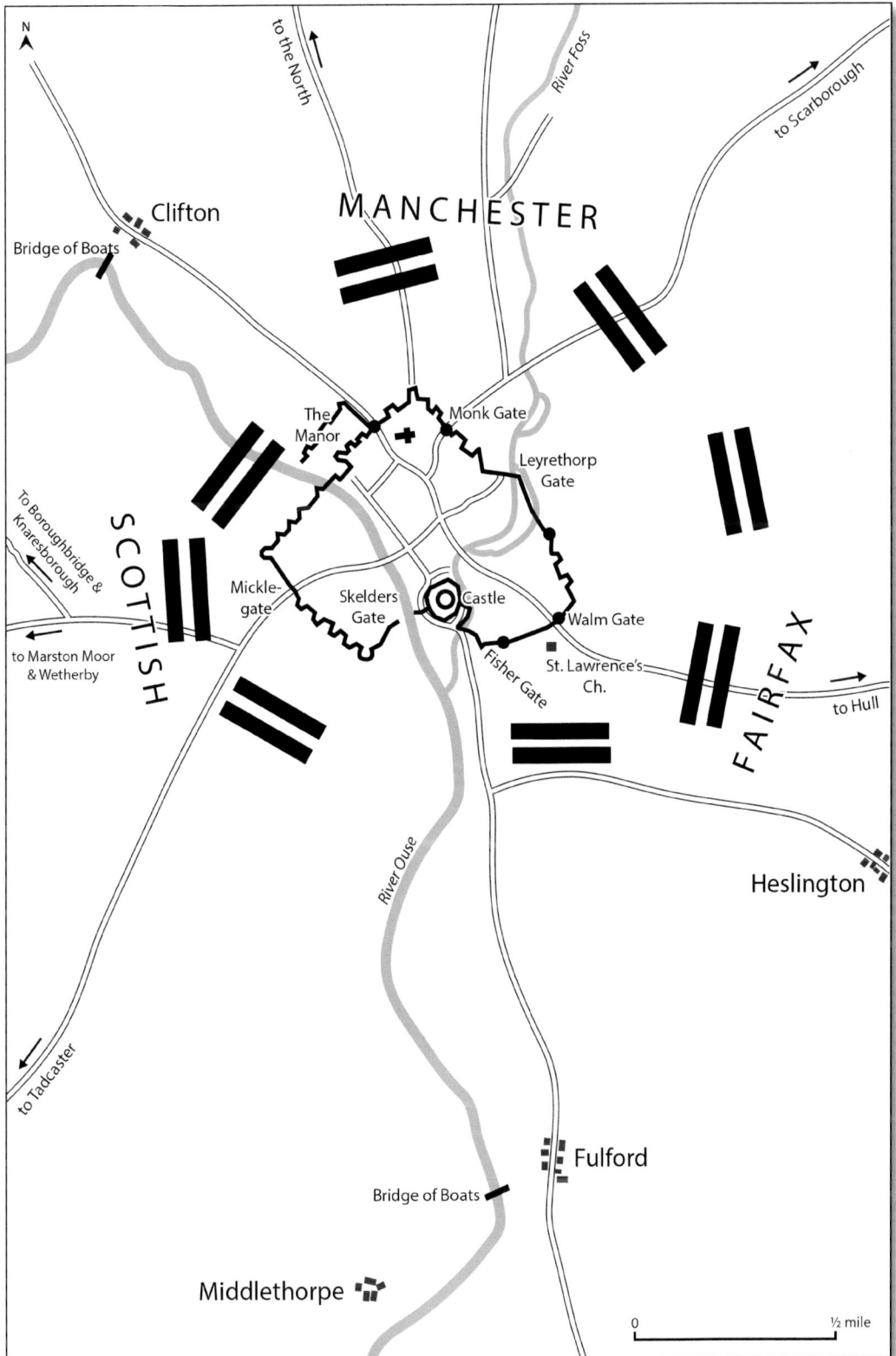

The Siege of York.

Another sconce was on the Mount, which Simeon Ashe, a chaplain to the Earl of Manchester, records as 'the Royal Fort, which is a curious and strong work'. When William Stukeley saw it in 1725 he described it as 'a great sconce a little way off [from] York called the Mount, consisting of four bastion raised in the Civil War'.[3] This appears to be an old burial ground since during the widening of the road in 1742 the workmen discovered some skulls and it was estimated that it contained between 1,200 to 1,300 skeletons. A coin was also found dating back to the Roman Emperor Nerva in 96 A.D. The excavation also found two cannonballs, a cross bar shot and some musket balls buried in the ramparts which had been fired at the Parliamentarians by the Royalists at Micklegate Barr.[4]

Micklegate Bar, York (J Britton, Antiquities of Cities, 1828)

The third earthwork was on Holgate Hill which is now known as Wilton Rise, and appears to be much smaller than the one on Clementhorpe Hill having about 50 men rather than 120 soldiers to defend it. This earthwork appears to have been still visible in 1930 when it was described as 'a rectangular earthwork, with rounded corners measuring 148 feet [by] 160 feet'. There was also a work which is described as 'the work at the brick kilns in or near Holegate Fields'. This protected a bridge of boats near Clifton or Poppleton, which was ordered to be demolished in May 1645.

To the south east of the city was an earthwork on Lamel Hill, which is just off the Heslington to York Road. Rushworth calls it 'a hill near Walmgate Barr', and Hildyard as 'the mill hill above St Laurence Leyes, without Walmgate Barr'. This is probably the earthwork referred to in a letter by one of the besiegers dated 7 June which records that:

3   Quoted in Peter Wenham, *The Great and Close Siege of York* (York: Session Book Trust, 1994), p.202.
4   *The Newcastle Courant*, 3 July 1742.

upon Wednesday night last, was a battery made at the windmill betwixt York and Heslington about eight score [yards] distance from the walls, and five pieces of great ordnance yesterday placed in it, and divers shots made into the city … another battery was yesterday got at St Laurence's church, made within the churchyard next [to] Wombgate about fifty yards from the gate, and here and in the church and houses there are about 3,000 of our men.[5]

During the 1840s, skeletons were found just below the surface of this earthwork which were at first believed to date from the Civil War period since among the other finds was a Charles I silver penny and two or three Scottish farthings, plus part of an iron camp kettle. However, upon further excavations more skeletons were found with artefacts dating from Anglo Saxon times: so it is believed that the skeletons found in the upper layer were probably disturbed when the besiegers were adapting the mound into an earthwork.[6]

Ashe also refers to a fort on the eastern side of the city probably on Baile Hill and to the north of the city was another earthwork near St Peter's School at Clifton, although according to Sir Henry Slingsby this was dug by Manchester's army rather than the garrison. Writing about the history of York in 1664 Christopher Hildyard states that it was in 1640 during the Bishops' Wars rather than during the Civil War that many of these 'bulwarks [were] raised and a bridge of boats was made over the River Ouse'. He also refers to '30 great brass pieces of ordinance from Hull' being delivered to the city for its defence in case the Scots should attack it.[7]

Newcastle's army had arrived at the city just before those of Fairfax and Leven. On 2 May Christopher Hildyard records that 'the seven windmills on Heworth Moor were burnt by the enemy and the next day the watermills, called Abbey Mills, and the windmill adjoining the pepper mill, were also burnt'.[8] Another person who had been at the siege since the 20 May recalls that:[9]

during which time there were divers small skirmishes at a windmill within musket shot of the town on the south east side, which was divers times won and lost with small loss on either side … Our men keep guard in a church which stands by the said mill, out of which they are continually playing their muskets against York, and York likewise at them.

On one occasion he records that 'a woman that came to sell provisions to the leaguer, having passed the guard next to the town being well horsed rode full gallop into the city: the guards shot at her but missed'.[10]

5   BL: TT E 50/30, *An Exact Relation of the Siege of York*.
6   John Thurham, 'Description of an Ancient Tumular cemetery, probably of the Anglo Saxon Period at Lamel Hill, near York', in *Archaeological Journal* vol. 6 (1849), p.31.
7   Wenham, pp.96–97, 143–152.
8   James Torr, *The Antiquities of York City and the civil government thereof … collected from the papers of Christopher Hildyard* (London: G. White, 1719), pp.105–106.
9   H.G. Tibbutt, *The Letterbooks of Sir Samuel Luke*, letter 157.
10   Ibid.

On Sunday 2 June Manchester's army rested before continuing its marched towards York. Early on the following day, through:

> long and strong showers, and although the ways were tedious and tiring … the commands of much honoured commander, carried the poor soldiers forward … with much cheerfulness … because the Earl himself, for their encouragement marched along with them the greatest part of the way. This day's march (considering divers diversions by waters and deep ways) was little less than 12 Northern miles, which was more longsome than 20 miles at another time, and elsewhere would have been accounted.[11]

On 3 June Robert Douglas, who was a chaplain in the Scottish army, recorded in his diary, 'Manchester cometh up to us with 6 regiments of foot and 6 troops of horse'.[12] The soldiers were tired after their long march, and Simeon Ashe and William Good, both chaplains to Manchester wrote:

> The tired soldiers took some rest though some of them upon their own accord went up to the walls of York and fetched out the pastures there oxen, kine and some horses. That day the three worthy commanders, with some of their field

Soldiers of Manchester's Army 1644. Engraving from a London newsbook of 1644, the legend reads: "The souldiers in their passage to York turn unto reformers pull down Popish pictures, break down rayles, turn alters into tables", confirming that the illustration depicts Parliamentarian troops, presumably horse from the fact that they are all wearing boots. (Stephen Ede-Borrett collection)

The Souldiers in their passage to York turn unto reformers pull down Popish pictures, break down rayles, turn altars into Tables,

11   TT E 51/3 *A Particular Relation of the most remarkable occurrences, 1 to 10 June* (London, 1644).
12   Robert Douglas, 'Diary of Mr Robert Douglas when with the Scottish Army in England', in *Historical Fragments relative to Scottish Affairs from 1635 to 1664* (Edinburgh: Thomas Stevenage, 1833), p.59.

officers, met as a council of war, to consult in what manner to carry on their intended assault against the city. All this day and the next there were some sleight encounters between our soldiers and theirs, the greatest loss by far falling on their side and all this while the cannon from Clifford's Tower and another fort eastwards in the city played frequently upon our men, as they espied any advantage, yet through God's good providence there were not any one of ours slain.[13]

However, Manchester's men did not have a rest for long because on the following day, Ashe and Good record:

Upon Wednesday most of the Scots regiments and all the Earl of Manchester's were drawn forth in nearer approaches towards the town to amuse the town whilst the Lord Fairfax with his forces raised a battery within less than musket shot of the town upon a hill westward, where a windmill stood heretofore: They quartered all night in the field, the enemy from the town spent upon them with their cannon in the night and the next morning (as tis thought) about two hundred shot and yet not above five or six slain and about so many hurt.[14]

This battery, according to the *Exact Relation* was:

raised upon a hill near Walmgate, where there are four pieces of battery already planted, that have played all this afternoon upon the castle, tower and town; and they from the town have sent us at least a hundred bullets from several platforms in the town, but they have done us very little hurt, not above one man killed and what execution our ordnance do in the city we cannot yet tell; but we are getting more pieces up to our new work, which we know hath already put them into very great fear.

Slingsby calls this hill Windmill Hill, where he reckoned there were five pieces of ordnance, 'which plays continually into the town, they come near to us and takes the suburbs without Walmgate Barr, [and] plants two pieces in the street against the Barr'. Fairfax's forces also began to dig a mine.

On 5 June Douglas mentions that Major General Crawford with Manchester's foot lodged 'in Clifton before Bouden barr.'[15] A few days after the arrival of Manchester's army, a H. Sidney wrote to Manchester's wife to inform her of the situation:

The Scots as I am told have not above 10,000 men, I hear [the] foot seem to be good, [but] I hear the horse are very marmed and worse mounted they seem lye on the west and south side of the town. My Lord Fairfax with four regiments of Scots is on the south east. My Lord of Manchester's foot is quartered on the north side, they have already entrenched themselves and gotten close under the walls of the town … Most of the … [inhabitants] as we are told are weary of my Lord of Newcastle tyranny, but dare attempt nothing in favour of us. There is certainly

---

13   TT E 51/3 *A Particular Relation of the most remarkable occurrences, 1 to 10 June* (London, 1644).
14   Ibid.
15   Douglas, 'Diary of Mr Robert Douglas', p.59.

Walmgate Bar, York (J Britton, Antiquities of Cities, 1828)

no great want of victuals or ammunition within the towns force must make us masters of it, and I think it cannot hold out long for the place is weak and hath not at the most above 4,000 men within it. It may be that within a few days I hear continual watching will bring them into a condition to be fit to be stormed, nevertheless they still expect Prince Rupert coming and in him is their only hope. But I am confident though he be a bold man he will not dare to attempt relieving York and our only fear here is that we shall be fain to seek him out near Oxford.[16]

On 6 June Ashe and Good record:

The Earl of Manchester's forces on Thursday morning entered the suburbs on the north side and maintained what they got, with the loss of 5 or 6 men at the most and so many wounded. About 27 of the Earl of Manchester's Regiment being voluntarily led on by a corporal of horse into the east suburbs, killed 5, took some goods and retreated without any loss.[17]

Was one of these men lost Daniel Emming of Coggeshall in Essex, whose widow Martha Emming petitioned the Essex Quarter Sessions?

---

16   Parliamentary Archives (PA): Wil/2/43. The letter is dated 7 May, but this must be an error for June.

17   TT E 51/3.

That your petitioners husband and two of her sons did some eight years since take up arms for the service of the Parliament and under the command of Captain Boyce in which employment at the siege of York in a town called Hasselton within a mile ... [of] the city it pleased God to take away the life of my said husband and soon after him one of my sons in Ireland to the great grief and also the hindrance of your poor petitioner. She being very aged and past her labour and had long before this time come to the charge of the parish had not her son helped to provide for her.[18]

The petition was written for her since she made her mark at the bottom of the page, and she was awarded 40 shillings gratuity.[19] Another soldier of Manchester's regiment of foot at the siege was Richard Ellsing, a weaver of Helions Bumpstead who in 1646 petitioned the Essex Quarter Sessions:

About three years since impressed in the said parish for the service of the State under the command of Captain Walden. And at the siege of York in the said service had one of his legs shot off with a cannon, whereby he is altogether disabled to follow his trade and hath been ever since very chargeable to the said parish (his allowance being 2 shillings 6 pence by the week).[20]

He was granted a pension of £3 per year.[21]

Up to the 10 June there were also some lucky escapes, such as a cannonball which passed through the tent where the Earl of Leven was having a council of war with the rest of his officers, but no one was hurt. If Simeon Ashe and William Good are to be believed, another cannonball took the crown of a soldier's hat off without hurting him, and a soldier lying on the ground had the heel of his shoe struck off by a cannonball, 'which scratched his foot, and did no more harm'. However a lieutenant was swept off his feet by a passing cannon shot.[22]

The following day they continue:

About midnight, a commanded company of the courageous Scots assaulted fiercely and bravely the three forts on the west side of the city, and after a very hot service, for the space of two hours (whereof many of us, with deep affections were eyewitnesses at a distance) they became possessors of two of them. The one of the forts (which was nearest to the town) was strengthened with a double ditch, wherein there were 120 soldiers, above 60 were slain, and all the rest taken prisoners. The other fort taken, had only 50 men to maintain it, who were all either killed, or taken prisoner desiring quarter. And the third fort had been

---

18   ERO: Reference no. Q/SBa2/82, Petition of Martha Emming, widow of Coggeshall, Essex.
19   Although the petition does not record her husband's name, the Coggeshall register records two possibilities, Martha Squire who married a Daniel Emming on 27 November 1614, or Martha Sutton who also married a Daniel Emming on 3 July 1621.
20   ERO: Reference no. Q/SBa2/61, petition of Richard Ellsing, a weaver of Helions Bumpstead, 1646.
21   There is also a baptism entry for a Richard son of Richard and Elizabeth Ellsing on 22 May 1621, which would make him about 23 years old during the siege.
22   TT E 51/3.

possessed by the Scots also, if a strong party of both horse and foot, had not come out of the town for the relief thereof. In this brave and bold service the Scots lost three captains and some others (whether 6, 7 or some few more as yet is not manifested) were killed, one lieutenant colonel and two captains deadly wounded, with many others wounded, but (as its hoped) not in danger of death. The Earl of Manchester's Army is possessed of the suburbs on the north side of the city, where the soldiers have fortified themselves, and are come up to the gates of the city.

Yesterday morning the enemy began to fire the suburbs, and in the beginning of the night, there was a lamentable fire in those places, most doleful and dreadful to many of us, who with sad hearts saw that fearful fruiting of wasting war.[23]

H. Sidney's letter also mentions that the Scots attacked three fortifications:

The Scots have this night taken two of the enemy's outworks, slain about 100 of them and took four score prisoners with very small loss on our side … They attempted another but were beaten off by a sally of horse and foot out of the town. My Lord Fairfax hath planted a battery that we hope will much … damage and terrify the enemy.[24]

The *Exact Relation* gives some additional information about the destruction of the suburbs:

This day they [the Royalists] have fired most part of the suburbs and drawn their people into the town; our men fall into the suburbs and beat them in when they sally out either to fire houses or fetch in goods; but whilst they skirmish the fire consumes the houses, they will not suffer our men to quench it, for if the houses could have been saved, they would have been a great shelter for our men in their approaches.

And the suburb without Bootham, where there were many fair houses, being fired, the Earl of Manchester's men nevertheless entered and beat in the enemy this morning and saved much of the houses from the fire, and so gallery through them close to the wall.

According to Douglas the Scots only assaulted two forts that day:

[The] sconce on the right hand taken by storm, 50 of them killed, 85 taken. Lieutenant Colonel Carmichael deadly shot, whereof he dieth the next day. Captain Campbell killed and 10 soldiers. [The] sconce on the left assaulted, but not taken; 18 of theirs killed, 33 taken; we lose Captain Panther and 10 soldiers: at Wingate Barr we take two houses and fill them with earth and plant them with cannon.[25]

Ashe and Good continue:

23 Ibid.
24 PA: Wil/2/43. The letter is dated 7 May, but this must be an error for June.
25 Douglas, 'Diary of Mr Robert Douglas', p.59.

Upon Saturday the 8 ... in the morning a soldier of the Marquis of Newcastle was taken in the Earl of Manchester's leaguer: he was in a red suit he had pinch[ed], flax and other materials upon him for the firing of the suburbs there, as yet free from the wasting flames, Some more of the Marquis his soldiers were taken prisoner also; they had whitecoats (made of plundered cloth taken from the clothiers in these parts) with crosses on their sleeves, wrought with red and blue silk, an ensign as we conceive of some Popish regiment. Divers granadoes were cast from the city into the suburbs when the Earl of Manchester's men were about the firing of the gate, to make passage into the city.[26]

This sally was probably from either Bootham or Monkgate. Hildyard also records that:

a cannon bullet weighing 60 pounds, [was] shot from the Mill Hill above Saint Lawrence Leyes without Walmgate Barr, was shot through Saint Sampson's church steeple ... also in the time of the siege the spire of Saint Dionis church was shot through with a cannon bullet. During the leaguer the enemy shot well nigh 40 hot fiery bullets out of their mortar pieces, which providence so directed, as that most of them were quenched in the River Foss; only one slew a maid in Thursday's Market and a shell of that fell into Master Clarke's, the writing masters chamber there, which brake down a spar of the house, and cast down a couple of ling upon old Mistress Clarke, which knocked her under the table, being almost fourscore years of age, so that the table did preserve her from hurt.[27]

That evening Newcastle wrote to the Earl of Leven and to Lord Fairfax:

I cannot but admire that your Lordship hath so near beleaguered the city on all sides, made batteries against

Bootham Bar, York (Halfpenny of York, 1807)

---

26   TT E 51/19.
27   Torr, p.106.

it, and so near approached to it without signifying what your intentions are, and what you desire or expect, which is contrary to the rules of all military discipline and customs; therefore I have thought fit to remonstrate this much to your Lordship may signify your intentions and resolutions therein.[28]

Leven, replied that his 'intention [was] to reduce it to the obedience due to the King and Parliament, where unto if your Lordship shall speedily conform, it may save the effusion of much innocent blood'.[29] However, the two Parliamentarian generals realised that Newcastle had not sent Manchester the same letter so they refused any further negotiation until this oversight was corrected. Therefore on the following day Newcastle sent Manchester the copies of the letters he had sent Leven and Fairfax with a covering letter claiming that he did not know that he had arrived. With his pride soothed Manchester met with Leven and Fairfax later that evening to discuss what to do next. The result was that they would summoned Newcastle to surrender the city, in the name of 'King and Parliament', so that there would be 'no further effusion of blood … and that the City of York and Inhabitants may be preserved from ruin'.[30] Newcastle was given 24 hours to reply, who answered the following day (10 June):

> My Lords,
>
> I have received a letter from your Lordships, dated yesterday about four of the clock in the afternoon, wherein I am required to surrender the city to your Lordships within 24 hours after the receipt; but I know your Lordships are too full of honour to expect the rendering of the city upon a demand, and upon so short an advertisement to me, who have the King's commission to keep it, and where there are so many generous persons and men of honour, quality, and fortune concerned in it. But truly I conceive this said demand high enough to have been exacted from the meanest governor of any of his Majesty's garrisons: And your Lordships may be pleased to know, that I expect propositions to proceed from your Lordships, as becomes persons of honour to give and receive from one another; and if your Lordships therefore think fit to propound honourable and reasonable terms, and agree upon a general cessation from all acts of hostility, during the time of a treaty, then your Lordships may receive such satisfaction therein, as may be expected from persons of honour, and such as desire as much to avoid the effusion of Christian blood, or destruction of cities, towns, and countries, as any whatsoever; yet will not spare their own Lives, rather than to live in the least stain of Dishonour. And so desiring your Lordships' resolution.[31]

Newcastle chose as his commissioners to discuss the terms of surrender, Lord Witherington, Sir Thomas Glemham, Sir William Wentworth, Sir Richard Hutton, Sir Thomas Metham, and Sir Robert Strickland. Each of the three

---

28   TT E 51/19.
29   Ibid.
30   Ibid.
31   Ibid.

generals of the Anglo-Scottish army were each to choose two commissioners; Manchester chose Lieutenant General Hammond and Colonel Russell. Fairfax chose Colonels Sir William Fairfax and White, and Leven, the Earl of Lindsey and Lieutenant General Humbey, although according to Sir Harry Vane, who was at the siege, the Scottish commissioners were Lindsey and Lieutenant General Baillie, rather than Humbey.[32]

They were to meet 'in a tent between two forts: one lately taken by the besiegers, and in their possession, and the other belonging to the town'. The meeting was to take place at 3:00 p.m. the following day and each side was to have 100 musketeers to attend them. The meeting lasted until 9:00 p.m., and the Royalists presented the following propositions:

> That the City shall be rendered within twenty Days, in case no relief come to it by that time from the King or Prince Rupert, upon these Conditions:
>
> That the Marquis of Newcastle, with all his Officers and Soldiers therein, have free liberty to depart, with colours flying, and match lighted; and to take with them all arms, ammunition, artillery, money, plate, and other goods belonging to them: For which end, that carriages be provided them, and victuals, and other provision for their March.
>
> That they be convoyed to the King, Prince Rupert, or any other Garrisons of the King, where they please: And that they be not forced to march above eight miles a day.
>
> That they shall have liberty to stay, or appoint others to stay 40 days in the town, for the sale of such goods, or for conveying of them to other Places, which they shall not be able to carry away with them.
>
> That no oath, covenant, or Protestation be administered to any of them, further than is warranted by the known laws of the land.
>
> That the gentry therein have liberty to go to their Houses, and there be protected from Violence, and not questioned for what they have done: Nor any oath or covenant to be tendered to them, as aforesaid
>
> That the townsmen enjoy all their privileges and Liberty of Trade and merchandise as before, and not to be questioned for any thing they have done against the Parliament; and that no oath be tendered to any of them.
>
> That the garrison to be sent into York, be only Yorkshire Men.
>
> That all the Churches therein be kept from Profanation, and no violation offered to the cathedral church. That divine service be allowed to be performed therein, as formerly. That the revenues of the church remain to the officers thereof, as it hath done; and that the Prebends continue their Prebendaries and other revenues according to the laws.
>
> That all ministers and other ecclesiastical persons therein, of what county soever, have liberty to depart with the army, or to their own livings, there to serve God, and to enjoy their estates without disturbance. That no oath or Covenant be proffered to them, as aforesaid; nor they questioned hereafter for what they have done for the King's Party.

---

32   Hamilton, CSPD 1644, p.224.

> That good hostages be given, and to remain in custody; and that … the chief fort in York be still kept garrisoned by the King's party, until the articles above said be punctually performed: And then the said garrison, and all arms, ammunition and cannon therein, be safely convoyed to what garrison of the King's they please.[33]

However, these proposals were not acceptable to the Anglo-Scottish commissioners and after some debate three of them left the meeting to report to their respective generals. After about two hours they returned with their own conditions:

> That the City of York, and all the Forts, together with all Arms, Ammunition, and other Warlike Provisions whatsoever, in and about the same, be rendered and delivered up to us, for and to the use of the King and Parliament, upon the Conditions following: viz.
>
> That the Common Soldiers shall have free Liberty and Licence to depart and go to their own Homes, and to carry with them their Clothes and their own Money, (not exceeding fourteen Days Pay) and shall have safe Conduct and Protection of their Persons from Violence, they promising that they will not hereafter take up Arms against the Parliament, or Protestant Religion.
>
> That the citizens and ordinary inhabitants of the said city shall have their persons and houses protected from violence, and shall have the same free trade and commerce as others under obedience of King and Parliament; and that no regiments or companies shall be admitted or quartered in the town of York, except those that are appointed for the Garrison thereof.
>
> That the officers of all qualities shall have liberty to go to their own homes, with swords and horses, and shall have licence to carry their apparel and money along with them, (the money not exceeding one month's means for every several Officer.)
>
> Any officer that shall be recommended by the Marquis of Newcastle, shall have a pass from one of the generals to go beyond Seas, they promising not to serve against the Parliament and Protestant religion.
>
> That the gentry, and other Inhabitants of the county of York now residing in the city of York, shall have liberty to go to their own Homes, and shall be protected from violence.[34]

The generals wanted an answer to these demands by 3:00 p.m. the following day (15 June), and in the meantime the ceasefire was over. On reading these terms the Royalist commissioners refused to inform Newcastle about them and so the meeting broke up without agreement. However, the following day Leven sent a drummer to Newcastle with these conditions, who replied:

> 'I cannot suppose that your Lordships do imagine, that persons of honour can possible condescend to any of these propositions'.[35]

---

33 Rushworth,
34 Ibid.
35 Ibid.

During the truce the besiegers had not been idle, and had continued their work on several tunnels, or mines, to undermine the city's defences. Contemporary accounts differ as the number of mines there were, with some saying one, and other two and even three. One of these mines was sprung on 16 June under St Mary's Tower and possibly another under Walmgate Barr, which was near the sector besieged by Fairfax's army. According to Sir Henry Slingsby there was a second mine in this sector. Seeing the mine explode at St Mary's Tower, according to Rushworth, 'many townsmen and women were killed in the explosion'. Major General Crawford took the opportunity to attack the manor, now called King's Manor, which was one of the strong points in north western defences of the city, near Bootham Barr. Rushworth continues:

> about 200 of the besiegers entered, and having scaled two or three Walls, possessed themselves of the Manor. But the City being herewith alarmed, their forces flocked thither from all parts, and surrounded them, and blocked up the breach, the only way of retreat; yet they fought resolutely as long as their powder lasted, and then submitted; fifteen of them being killed, and sixty wounded, who, with about a hundred more, were made prisoners. There were also killed before they entered the breach about 20, and 40 wounded; so that in all that day the besiegers were computed to lose near 300 men.[36]

Hildyard also records this incident, saying that it was on Trinity Sunday that St Mary's Tower was blown up while the inhabitants were at prayer. On hearing that the Parliamentarians were attacking Newcastle's own regiment of whitecoats, Lieutenant Colonel Samuel Breary who commanded a company of '250 stout volunteer citizens' counterattacked. Breary was 'shot with a poison bullet' in an arm and died four days later.[37]

With the defeat of his men when he came report the events to the Committee of Both Kingdoms Manchester put a very a different slant to his attack:

> Within my quarters I sprang a mine, which did great execution upon the enemy, blowing up a tower which joined to the manor yard, and this mine taking so great effect my Major General commanded 600 men to storm the manor house, who beat the enemy and took 300 prisoners, but, being over confident, 2,000 of the enemy's best men fell upon them and beat them back. I lost near 300 men, but still maintain the breaches, and the enemy dare not make any sally out.[38]

Ashe and Good state that Manchester or Crawford had no option but to spring the mine because 'that work could not be longer delayed, in regard of waters which increase upon them in the chamber of the mine', and that the

---

36   Ibid.
37   Torr, pp.105–106.
38   W.D. Hamilton, *Calendar of State Papers Domestic*, (1644), p.246.

soldiers 'adventured too far through inconsiderateness, and hope of plunder', before their only way of retreat was blocked.[39]

According to Sir Henry Slingsby it was Sir Philip Byron, who led the counter attack, but 'leading up some of his men was unfortunately killed as he opened the door into the bowling green whither the enemy was gotten; but the difficulty was not much, we soon beat them out again, having taken 200 prisoners and killed many of them as might be seen in the bowling green, orchard and garden.'[40]

Colonel Edward Montagu's regiment is known to have taken part in this action, and possibly detachments of Major General Crawford's and Colonel John Pickering's regiments of foot since they were usually brigaded together, but unfortunately for them neither Manchester or Crawford had informed Leven or Lord Fairfax of their intentions, so they could not support this attack which might have diverted the garrison in their counter attack. Robert Baillie, who was then in London, went further putting it down to:

The foolish rashness of Major [General] Crawford, and his great vanity to assault … alone the breach made by his mine, without the acquainting of Leslie and Fairfax with it, and the killing of so great a number of his men … will force us to look on these walls till hunger make them fall, whereof as yet we hear not much.[41]

Since neither Fairfax or Leven were ready to attack the city this would suggest that there was only one mine which was sprung.

On hearing the news of this attack, Sir Henry Vane wrote to Sir Thomas Pelham that the three generals had possessed 'the manor and Abbey church upon the top of which they planted a battery, they have also taken all the hills round about the town that are within cannon shot and have made batteries so as it is conceived the town will be taken this week if it not be already'.[42]

The following day, records Ashe:

some of our soldiers betwixt nine and ten o'clock, approaching towards the place where the tower stood, heard in the rubbish a very doleful cry, some calling help, help; others water, water. This lamentable complaints moved our men to resolve their belief; so they dug one out dead in the rubbish, and brought two alive; but from the town such fierce opposition was made by the merciless enemy against our soldiers while they were labouring to save their friends lives, that they were compelled to leave many poor distressed ones dying in the dust.[43]

On Wednesday or Thursday a truce was agreed for an hour while the Parliamentarians buried their dead. The site of their grave has not been discovered, but in 2007 113 skeletons were found while excavating All Saints

39   TT E 51/19
40   Slingsby, p.109.
41   Baillie, pp.195–196.
42   BL: Add MS 33,084 f.46.
43   BL: TT E 2/1 *A Continuation of the True Intelligence … from the English and Scottish Forces in the North … now beleaguering York, from the 16 June to Wednesday the 10 of July 1644* by Simeon Ashe, (London: Thomas Underhill, 1644).

Church just outside the city's walls and near to Walmgate Barr. Originally they were believed to be all male skeletons, but on closer examination 87 of them were male, six female, and the sex of the remaining 20 was undetermined. Their ages ranged from 35 to 49, and showed evidence of physical activities and almost all had spinal joint disease. One skeleton even had both a leg and arm joint fused together so that walking without a crutch would have been impossible. Although carbon dating showed that their deaths occurred between 1480 and 1687, they were buried within the walls of the church sometime after it fell into disuse in 1580 and none showed signs of battle trauma. It is only circumstantial evidence that suggests that they died during the siege from disease, since there is no dating evidence. The media referred to the skeletons as belonging to 'Cromwell's Army', but if there are links to the siege then their position to the south of the city would suggest that they probably belonged to Fairfax's army. Isotope tests found a large part of their diet consisted of fish, many of his soldiers having been raised around the sea port of Hull.[44]

With sickness spreading through the besiegers and Crawford's repulse from the manor house, according to Baillie, this 'so discourage all the rest of the army, that they could not be brought to storm any more'.[45] Fairfax's and Leven's armies were also running low on ammunition, which caused Lord Fairfax to write to the Committee of Both Kingdoms on 18 June:

> I must solicit you for a speedy supply of gunpowder, match, and bullet for my own and the Scotch armies in very large proportions, otherwise the service of these armies will be much retarded, contrary to our desires and your expectations. For my own particular I must entreat a supply of muskets, pistols, and carbines, concerning which I have often written.[46]

The crisis was partly offset by Manchester lending the Scottish army 100 barrels of gunpowder, which would not be replaced until 26 August.[47]

However, the lack of ammunition was not all the problems that the besieging armies had to contend with, as Fairfax's letter of 18 June continues:

> my men are like to mutiny and many [have] run away, whom I cannot in justice punish having nothing to pay them withall, while Manchester's men are very well paid, and a considerable supply furnished to the Scots' army. I beseech you to consider what it is to have [the command of] an army and nothing to give them, while joined with other armies that are well paid. The pay of my army comes to £15,000 a month, and I have received only £10,000. for these four months past at least. I endeavour to struggle against all difficulties whatsoever to carry on

---

44 Lauren McIntyre and Graham Bruce, 'Excavating All Saint's, a medieval church rediscovered', in *Current Archaeology* (August 2010), pp.30–37. There were 10 graves altogether and each grave contained between four to 18 burials; BBC series Cold Case, series 2, 'The York 113'.

45 Baillie, p.200.

46 Hamilton, CSPD 1644, p.246.

47 TNA: WO 55/460 unfoliated.

this work, not doubting but that your Lordships and the two Houses will take the condition of my army into your speedy consideration.[48]

However, the garrison were also suffering. Hildyard says that:

a quarter of veal and mutton was sold for 16 shillings, a piece of beef at four shillings per stone; a pig at seven shillings; a hen at four shillings; eggs at three pence; and fresh butter at two shillings and eight pence a pound; yet the soldiers and citizens were well contented and courageous having no want of salt meat, nor of any sort of grain, which was sold at reasonable rates; and of wine and beer and ale there was plenty.[49]

Sir Henry Slingsby also wrote in his diary:

and [we] would have and end without … relief; therefore my lord would make trial to send to the prince [Rupert] to inform him of the condition the town was in; he chooseth out eight [who] undertake to go to the prince and either pass the Scots undescerned or else break through them; but all or most of them were taken; we made fires upon the minster which answered us again from Pontefract, but a messenger was hardly pass.[50]

The first incident appears to be recorded by Robert Douglas in his diary for 13 June, although he states that there were 'nine horsemen break out between Akham and Dring houses; six of them taken, two killed, [but] one escaped'.[51] While the garrison signalling to Pontefract Castle is recorded in a letter to the Committee of Both Kingdoms dated 18 June from the Earl of Manchester; 'I believe that the besieged cannot but be in straits, though they are not willing to express it, being in daily expectation of Prince Rupert's relieving them; these two last nights they have made fires upon the top of the Minster, and have been answered with the like signals from Pontefract'.[52]

With the situation on both sides deteriorating, the siege consisted more of 'daily small skirmishes, with some loss on both sides: cannon also playing frequently both night and day'. It was not until 24 June that the garrison sallied out of York in any force. About 600 men attacked the line where Manchester's men were, but after a 'sharp conflict were obliged to retreat with loss'. This sally seems to have been the last major incident of note made by either side.

But what of Prince Rupert? On 31 May the Committee of Both Kingdoms wrote to Manchester warning him:

We hear Prince Rupert, is upon his march for Lancashire with an army of 8,000, whereof most horse, and above 50 pieces of ordnance, where, if he be not

---

48   Hamilton, CSPD 1644, p.246.
49   Torr, pp.105–106.
50   Slingsby, p.110.
51   Douglas, p.59.
52   Hamilton, CSPD 1644, p.246.

hindered, he is like to double his forces by the power of the Earl of Derby, who hath invited him and the ill affected of that county, as is set down at large in the enclosed information.[53]

Such was the importance of stopping Rupert recruiting his army in Lancashire, the Committee again wrote to Manchester on the 1 and the 3 June ordering him to send forces into Lancashire to stop Rupert. It seems to have taken about four days to a week for a despatch to reach the besiegers at York from London, because it was not until 4 June that Manchester replied to the Committee of Both Kingdom's letters dated 28 and 30 May:

The relief of York is thought to be, the business which Prince Rupert aims at, and we have daily intelligence that they bend towards York … you give me to understand of Prince Rupert's march into Lancashire, which is most true, and he has done great spoil there. I am careful to have good intelligence of his movements, and though I am now quartered about York, yet I shall obey your commands in case he march southwards.[54]

On 8 June having received the Committee of Both Kingdom's letter of 3 June again appealing for Manchester to send forces into Lancashire, he replied:

I communicated to the [Earl of Leven,] General of Scotch army,' and to Lord Fairfax, who will certify you of the state of affairs, here. They consider this place [York] as of such consequence to the quiet of these parts that they consider themselves, both in duty to the public and regard to their own honours, engaged to bring it to some issue, before they attempt any other design. I trust the Lord will give us a speedy end of our endeavours here, and then we shall be ready for any service you may command … I hope you will not have cause to apprehend Prince Rupert's strength, for excepting plundering, at which his army is expert, no considerable places have been taken possession of by his army, the intelligence we daily receive assures us so.[55]

However, Manchester was wrong, Rupert had relieved Latham House on 25 May and then taken Bolton on 28 May, Liverpool on 7 June and Thornton Hall on 26 June. On 30 May he had been joined by Lord George Goring who commanded Newcastle's cavalry further increasing his strength. Meanwhile in the south of England the King's main Oxford army was being pursued by the armies of Earl of Essex and Sir William Waller. On 14 June fearing for his army, Charles wrote to Rupert:

I must give the true state of my affairs, which, if their condition be such as enforces me to give you more *peremptory commands* that I would willingly do, you must not take it ill. If York be lost I shall esteem *my crown little else*; unless supported by your sudden march to me; and a miraculous conquest in the South, before

---

53   Ibid., p.187.
54   Ibid., pp.202–203.
55   Ibid., pp.216–217.

the effects of their Northern power can be found here. *But if* York be relieved and you *beat the rebels' army* of both kingdoms, which are before it; then *(but otherwise not)* I may possibly make a shift (upon the defensive) to spin out time until you come to assist me, Wherefore I *command and conjure you*, by the duty and affection which I know you bear me, that all new enterprises laid aside, you immediately march, according to your first intention, with all your force to the relief of York. But if that be either lost, or have freed themselves from the besiegers, or that for want of powder you cannot undertake that work, that you immediately march with your whole strength to Worcester to assist me and my army; without which, or you having relieved York by beating the Scots, all the success you can afterwards have must infallibly be useless. You may believe that nothing but an extreme necessity could make me write thus unto you.; wherefore, in this case, I can no ways doubt of your punctual compliance with.[56]

Brigadier Peter Young in his book on Marston Moor records that a 'modern staff officer would be hard pressed indeed to make of this a direct order to fight a battle after York had been relieved'; but the key phrase is 'if York be relieved and you beat the rebels' army of both kingdoms'. Certainly on reading a copy of this letter Lord Culpepper asked the King whether it had been sent, when hearing it had, he replied 'why then … before God you are undone, for upon this peremptory order he will fight whatever comes on it'.[57]

This letter must have arrived on 26 June since according to a diary, which is often referred to as Rupert's Diary, although the author is not known, after the capture of Thornton Hall it reads; 'comes a peremptory order to go from thence to York'.[58] However, by the time Rupert received this letter he had no way of knowing that the strategic position in the south had changed completely, Essex having abandoned the pursuit of the King and had marched into the west to relieve Lyme, leaving Waller to pursue the King alone and that the Oxford army would defeat Waller at the battle of Cropredy Bridge on 29 June. Rupert stayed at Skipton Castle, between 26 and 29 June to prepare his army for the forthcoming encounter. On the evening of 29 June he quartered at Lord Fairfax's House at Denton, near Ottley and then on the following day he proceeded to Knaresborough near York.[59]

The sentinels of both sides are known to have talked to each other, whether this was a friendly chat or an exchange of insults is not known, but one day when the Royalists on guard duty called out to the Parliamentarian counterparts there was no reply. On 30 June, having received intelligence of Rupert's approach with an army of about 20,000 men, including Newcastle's cavalry, the allied generals had decided to abandon the siege the following day. Their aim was to withdraw to Tadcaster, via a place called Marston Moor.

---

56   Quoted in Young, *Marston Moor*, p.87. The italics are text inserted by Lord Wilmot.
57   Ibid.
58   Ibid., p.213.
59   Stephen Ede-Borrett, *The Iter Carolinum of Charles I (1642–1649)* and the *Journal of Prince Rupert's Marches, (1642–1646)* (Oxford: The Pike and Shot Society, 2013), p.40.

5

Marston Moor

Having abandoned the siege of York, the allied army quartered in the evening of 1 July in and around the town of Long Marston, where, according to Simeon Ashe, 'very few had either the comfort of convenient lodging, or food: our Soldiers did drink the wells dry, and then were necessitated to make use of puddle water'.[1] The allied generals held a council of war whether to fight or not. It is said that the English generals wanted to fight, but the Scottish commanders wanted to withdraw. Finally Leven got his way and the combined armies set off towards Tadcaster the following morning, while the cavalry, under the command of Sir Thomas Fairfax, Cromwell and David Leslie, would act as a rearguard on Marston Moor. Soon Royalist cavalry were spotted on the Moor, and soon after were joined by other forces; the Parliamentarians realised that this was no patrol and that there was a real danger that Rupert would catch the retreating army strung out on the march. Therefore, they decided to recall their forces, the forward elements of which were already within half a mile or a mile from Tadcaster. Fortunately for the allies, Rupert also had to wait for all his forces to arrive since Newcastle's infantry had decided to pillage their former besiegers' encampment.

While he was waiting, Rupert appears to have sent forward a cavalry detachment supported by artillery to occupy Bilton Bream, but they were soon forced to withdraw by a detachment of Eastern Association cavalry. Having failed to hold this position Rupert had no choice but to deploy his army on Marston Moor, both sides deploying their troops as they arrived. The allied army was drawn up on Marston Hill, which is described at the time of the battle, as 'a large field of rye, where the height of the corn, together with the showers of rain which then fell, prove no small inconvenience unto our soldiers; yet being on a hill we had the double advantage of the ground, and the wind'.[2] According to Lindsay, as the Scottish regiments arrived 'we drew them up on a corn hill up on the south west side of the moor in the best ways we could, so far as the straightness of that field and other disadvantages of the place could permit … before both armies were in readiness, it was near seven

---

1   BL: TT E 2/1 Simeon Ashe, *A Continuation of True Intelligence* (1644).
2   Vicars, *God's Ark*, p.27.

These hedges were lined with musketeers

Deployment of the Royalist Army at Marston Moor
from C S Terry's *Life and Campaigns of Alexander Leslie*, 1899 based on Bernard de Gomme's plan.

Sir Thomas Fairfax

Eglington

Cromwell

Leslie

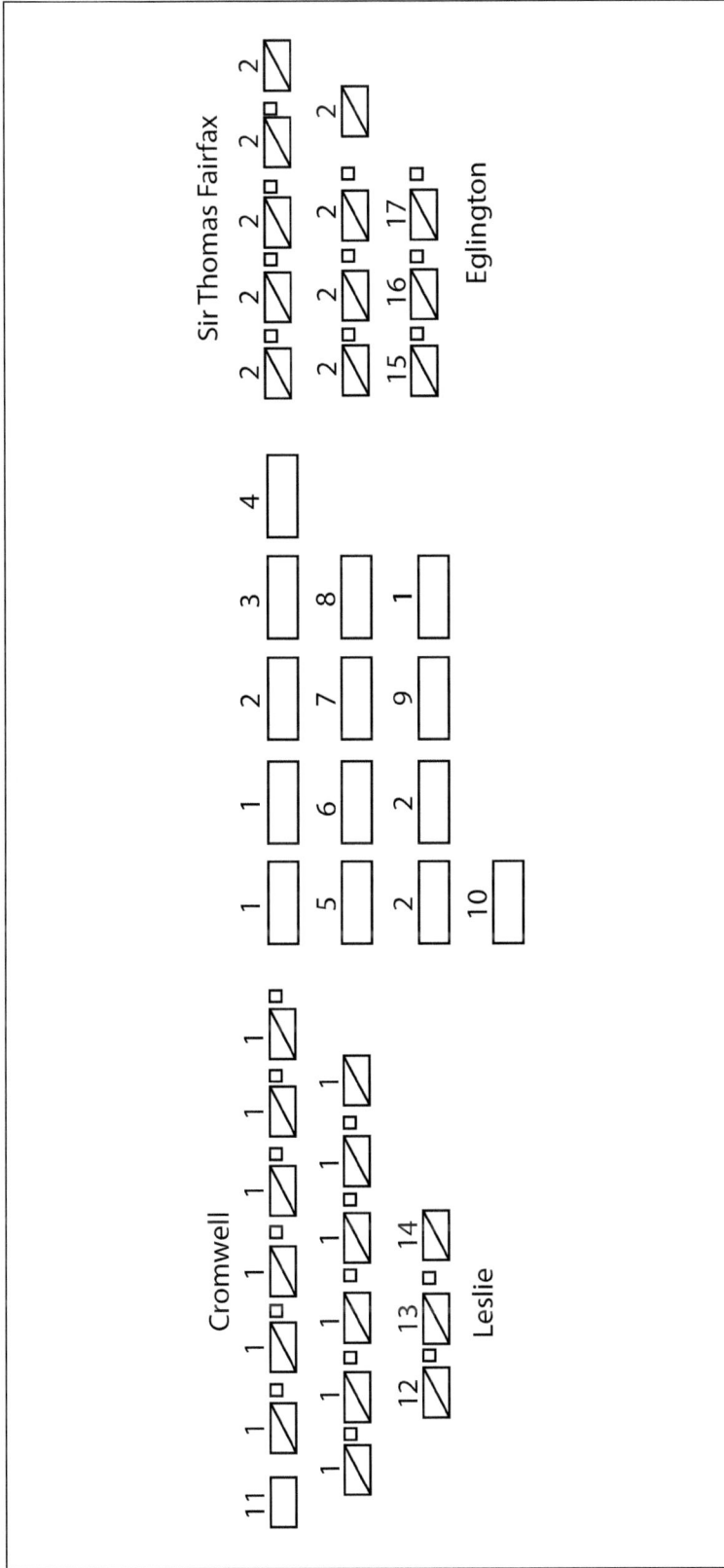

Map based on Major General James Lumsden's plan of the allied deployment at Marston Moor. Unfortunately he only knew of the exact deployment of the Scottish Army.

Key to Plans of Marston Moor

Allied Army Order of Battle

1 Eastern Association
2 Lord Fairfax's Northern Association
3 Colonel James Rae's and General Sir Alexander Hamilton's Regiments of Foot
4 Viscount Maitland's and Earl of Crawford-Lindsey's Regiments of Foot
5 Master of Yester's and Lord Livingstone's Regiments of Foot
6 Lord Coupar (or Cowper)'s and Earl of Dunfirmlane's Regiments of Foot
7 William Douglas of Kilhead's and Earl of Cassille's Regiments of Foot
8 Earl of Buccleach's and Earl of Loudon's Regiments of Foot
9 Sir Arthur Erskine of Scotscraig's and Viscount Dudhope's Regiments of Foot
10 unknown Scots [?Lord Sinclair's Regiment of Foot]
11 Colonel Hugh Fraser's Dragoons
12 Major General David Leslie's Regiment of Horse
13 Lord Kirkcudbright's Regiment of Horse
14 Earl of Balcarres' Regiment of Horse
15 Earl of Leven's Regiment of Horse commanded by Lord Balglonie
16 Lord of Eglington's Regiment of Horse
17 Earl of Dalhousie's Regiment of Horse

Royalist Order of Battle

A Prince Rupert's Regiment of Foot
B Lord Byron's Regiment of Foot
C Lord Byron's Regiment of Horse
D Colonel Sir John Urry's Regiment of Horse
E Sir William Vaughan's Regiment of Horse
F Colonel Marcus Trevor's Regiment of Horse
G Prince Rupert's Regiment of Horse
H Colonel Henry Warren's Regiment of Foot
Y Sir Thomas Tyldesley's Regiment of Foot
K Colonel Robert Broughton's Regiment of Foot
L Colonels Sir Michael Ernley's and Colonel Richard Gibson's Regiments of Foot
M Colonel Tillyer's Regiment of Foot
N Colonel John Freschesville's Regiment of Foot
O Colonel Rowland Eyres' Regiment of Foot
P Sir Charles Lucas' Brigade
Q Colonel Carnaby's Regiment of Foot
R Colonel Edward Chisnal's Regiment of Foot
S unknown
T Colonel Henry Chester's Regiment of Foot
V Sir Richard Dacre's Brigade
X Sir William Blakeston's Brigade
Z Seven Divisions of Lord Newcastle's Foot
AA Commissary General George Porter's Troop
BB Prince Rupert's Troop
CC Sir Edward Widdrington's Brigade
DD Colonel Thomas Leveson's Regiment of Horse
EE Colonel Sir Thomas Tyldesley's Regiment of Horse
FF Lord Molyneux's Regiment of Horse
GG Samuel Tuke's Regiment of Horse

o'clock at night; about which time both armies advanced towards each other'.[3] On the other hand Major General Sir James Lumsden refers to the battlefield as a 'plain field, three miles in length and in breadth, the fairest ground for such use that I had seen in England'.

As senior commander, the Earl of Leven 'exercised his martial abilities with unwearied activity and industry', recalls Simeon Ashe, 'He hastened from place to place to put all our forces in battle array, which he did to the satisfaction and admiration of all that beheld it: the other two generals [Manchester and Fairfax] acting also in their own armies'.[4] A Colonel James Somerville said that he had seen 'draughts' of the dispositions of the allied army 'taken upon the place'. Unfortunately these plans do not survive, which may have shone light on the allies' dispositions. Fortunately a plan by Sir James Lumsden has survived which although damaged in places lays out the allied army's order of battle, although in places it disagrees with some written sources.

Cromwell was to command the left wing, with the cavalry of the Eastern Association in two lines and a third line composed of Scottish cavalry commanded by David Leslie. Unfortunately the strength of Manchester's cavalry is not easy to estimate since many of the muster rolls have not survived, but it was probably less than 3,000 men plus Leslie's Scottish cavalry. Colonel Hugh Frazer's Scottish dragoons were ordered to secure the flank of this wing. The whereabouts of Manchester's regiment of dragoons, which was under the command of Lieutenant Colonel John Lilburne, is not recorded but may be the regiment of dragoons depicted on Lumsden's map on the right wing of the army.[5]

The right wing was commanded by Sir Thomas Fairfax, and composed of the cavalry of his father's Northern Association, and like the left wing had Scottish cavalry in the third line. As with the left flank about 500 dragoons protected its flank. The centre was composed of the infantry of the three armies, but there has been confusion of how it was formed. All written sources agree that the majority of infantry of the Eastern Association were on the left next to their cavalry, Watson referring to 'our three brigades of the Earl of Manchester's being on our right hand'.[6] However, Lumsden's plan clearly shows only two brigades of Manchester's foot on the left of the centre of the front line and a third brigade commanded by Manchester himself on the right of centre in the third line.

Since Manchester's regiment was composed of 18 companies, this must have formed one of the brigades; while Colonels Edward Montagu, John Pickering and Francis Russell's formed another brigade, leaving Crawford's and Sir Miles Hobart's regiments to form the third brigade. At a muster in June 1644 five of Manchester's six regiments of foot mustered just 3,145

3   Letter from Lord Lindsay to the Committee of the Estates of Scotland at Edinburgh, 6 July 1644 printed in *A Collection of the State Papers of John Thurloe*, vol.1, ed. Thomas Birch, (London: 1742), p.38.

4   BL: TT E 2/1.

5   C. H. Firth, 'Marston Moor', *Transactions of the Royal History Society* new series vol. XII (London: Longmans, Green and Co., 1898), pp.29–30.

6   BL: TT E 2/14, Leonard Watson, *A More Exact Relation of the Late Battell neare York* (1644).

men, so were drastically understrength. Unfortunately, the muster roll for Pickering's regiment for June has not survived, but on 8 May1644 the regiment mustered 738 men, but on 23 July it was only 524 men strong having been weakened by disease, the siege of York and Marston Moor. Therefore, the infantry of the Eastern Association must have numbered about 3,700 men, a figure suggested by C.H. Firth, although this might be a little too high since this accounts for just 45 soldiers being killed at the siege of York and that Pickering's was 600 strong. In addition to this strength since most companies had the standard number of officers and lesser officers no matter how understrength their company was, this would add a further 715 to this strength, or 4,415 officers and men.

Lumsden's plan also shows a battalion of Fairfax's infantry in the front line and two in the left of centre of the third line. The composition of theses brigades is not so easy to estimate since at least eight of Fairfax's regiments of foot were with him. Lumsden also places two Scottish brigades in the right of centre of the front line, four in the second line and one in the third line between Fairfax's two brigades and that of Manchester's.[7] Peter Young also places another brigade behind one of Fairfax's brigades, but too much of the plan is missing in this area to be certain.[8] The plan also shows that the Scots' brigades which were to support Manchester's two brigades were formed from Yester's, Livingstone's, Couper's and Dunfermline's regiments of foot, and Manchester's brigade in the third line, is supporting the brigade formed from Baccleuch's and Loudon's Scottish regiments. According to the tactics of the day the infantry in the second line should cover the gaps of the battalions in the first line, in a chessboard fashion, but Lumsden shows the infantry battalions drawn up behind each other and states 'the brigades drawn up here as we [three or four words missing] of haste. It is not so formal as ou[ght to be]'. Unfortunately, this sentence which is largely missing from his original letter was not printed in the Scottish newspaper. Since Leven was in overall command of the allied army, the remainder of the Scottish infantry were place on the right, the traditional place of honour. John Vicars, who was not present at the battle, places the allied artillery on 'top of the hill'. To keep themselves occupied the Parliamentarians sung psalms.[9]

The Royalists drew up on the Marston Moor which was open moorland, but was enclosed around 1766, and the area is now farmland. It is separated from Marston Hill, where the allied army drew up, by the Tockwith–Marston

---

7   The Scottish infantry was sometimes referred to by the name of its colonel or the area where it was raised so the following regiments which were at Marston Moor were: Viscount Dudhope's regiment, Angus; Viscount John Maitland, Midlothian; Sir Patrick Hepburn's, East Lothian; Earl of Lindsay, Fifeshire; John Earl of Cassilis', Kyle and Carrick; Earl of Loudon's, Glasgow; Colonel William Douglas of Kilhead, Nithsdale and Annandale; Lord Livingstone's Stirlingshire; Earl of Baccleugh's, Tweedale; Sir Arthur Erskine's, The Minster; Sir Alexander Hamilton, Clydesdale also known as the artillery regiment; Colonel James Rae's, Edinburgh; Earl of Dunfermline's, Fifeshire; Colonel William Stewart's, Galloway; Master of Yester, Linlithgow and Tweedale; Earl of Tullibardine's Perthshire; Lord Couper's, Strathearn; and Lord Sinclair's, the levied regiment.
8   Plan reproduced in Brigadier Peter Young, *Marston Moor 1644: The Campaign and the Battle* (Kineton: The Roundwood Press, 1970), plates 21 and 22.; David Cooke, *The Road to Marston Moor* (Barnsley: Pen and Sword, 2007), pp.111–114.
9   Vicars, *God's Ark*, p.271; Slingsby, *Diary*, pp.113–114.

Road. The moor rises from this road, but not as high as Marston Hill. There were three roads running along Marston Moor, Kendall Lane, which is where Byron deployed his cavalry, Moor Lane, which divided the Royalist's centre with their right wing, and Atterwick Lane which ran through the Royalist's left wing. At the end of Moor Lane it divided into three lanes, one going to the left and leading to what is now known as White Syke Close. However, according to Dr Peter Newman no contemporary source refers to a close by this name and no trace of its 'origin survives to relate it to the Whitecoats … the close today is altogether too vast to be defended stubbornly by a 1,000 or so men, let alone by a regiment of foot probably at half strength if that'.[10] The middle lane leads to Wilstrop Wood, where to west of the wood was a bean field. The third lane leads north east away from the battlefield. Also a stream, the Syke Beck ran to the west of the battlefield, which the allies and the Royalist used to protect their flanks.

The only plan we have for the deployment of the Royalist army is by the Royalist engineer Bernard de Gomme, although this plan has its critics: Alex Leadman, who wrote one of the first detailed histories of the battle in 1891 dismisses it as having been drawn during the reign of Charles II and that he had 'no reliance on Gomme's map, and its only value is in preserving the names of loyal men who found on the King's side'.[11] C. H. Firth on the other hand pointed out it was 'probably based on some sketch made at the time, either by de Gomme himself or by the Prince'. Certainly the plan is too neat to have been drawn in a hurry, so Firth is probably right that it is based on a rougher map which is now lost. What we do not know is whether it was based on a plan where Rupert wanted the army to deploy or whether it shows the Royalist army's actual deployment. Certainly if it is based upon the one shown to General James King (Lord Eythin) on the morning of the battle, this was before Newcastle's infantry had arrived, although they are depicted on the plan.

De Gomme's plan shows the front line of the Parliamentarians having six brigades rather than five as depicted by Lumsden. He also estimates the allied army to be about 27,000 strong. The plan portrays the Royalists' right wing being composed of 11 squadrons of cavalry in both the first and second lines, while the right wing's front line also had 11 squadrons, the second line was to be formed from the Newcastle's cavalry. The centre was composed of 22 battalions. Nineteen regiments of foot can be identified as making up Newcastle's infantry which were drawn up in seven divisions, so each division was about 430 strong, the remaining 15 being formed from the infantry of Rupert's army. Eight battalions formed the first line, mustering about 500 each, giving a strength of about 4,000. The second line was formed of seven battalions, again about 500 each and just forward of the Royalist centre was a brigade composed of Prince Rupert's own regiment of foot and that of Lord Byron's. A thousand musketeers had been withdrawn to support the cavalry wings further weakening the centre. There was also a reserve of cavalry

10   Dr Peter Newman, 'Marston Moor, 1644–1979, a study of a battlefield' in *Journal of Society of Army Historical Research* (Society of Army Historical Research, 1979), vol. 57 no. 231.
11   Alex D. H. Leadman, *Battles Fought in Yorkshire* (London: Bradbury, Agnew, 1891), p.177.

drawn up in seven squadrons. According to De Gomme the combined armies mustered 11,000 foot and 6,500 horse with 16 guns, although allied accounts record that they captured 20 guns in all, and one account states 25, but the figure of 20 might include the four pieces that the Royalists captured during the battle, only to be retaken later in the day. The number of guns the allies had is not recorded but since there were three armies combined it was probably at least the same amount as the Royalists and probably much more.

The plan also shows that the Royalists who were to confront Manchester's infantry were the regiments of Prince Rupert's (which formed in two battalions) and Lord John Byron's regiments of foot (which was formed in one). Rupert's regiment of bluecoats had been raised in 1642 and had seen service in many engagements, whereas Byron's regiment had been raised in late 1643. However, De Gomme shows these three battalions forward of the main position near a row of hedges and in front of the Colonel Marcus Trevor's and Rupert's regiments of horse. Colonel Henry Warren's and Sir Thomas Tyldesley's regiment of foot were also close enough to take on his infantry, who are shown by De Gomme as in the main line of the Royalist infantry.

As to the Royalist cavalry opposing the Eastern Association, the brigades under Lord Byron, Sir John Hurry and Sir William Vaughan formed the first line, while Lord Molyneux's, Sir Thomas Tyldesley's and Colonel Thomas Leveson's formed the Royalist second line on this wing, with Colonel Samuel Tuke's regiment of horse between both lines on the extreme right. It is estimated that the Royalists on this wing mustered about 2,600 horse and 500 musketeers.

Rupert was eager to attack and so when Newcastle arrived at about 9:00 a.m., he said to the Marquis 'my lord I hope we have a glorious day'. An anonymous account states that Newcastle tried to dissuade Rupert attacking then, but does not give the reasons why he was reluctant to attack, but Rupert exclaimed 'nothing ventured, nothing have etc'.[12] However, he did not attack that morning: according to Sir Hugh Cholmley it was Newcastle who 'dissuaded him telling him he had 4,000 good foot as were in the world,' which would soon join them.[13] Realising the sense in this argument Rupert decided to wait, but little did they know that the allied army was still strung out on its way back from Tadcaster. However, the hours ticked by and there was still no sign of Newcastle's infantry.

Finally, according to Cholmley, it was about 4:00 p.m. when Major General James King, Lord Eythin, arrived with Newcastle's infantry. King is said to have hated Rupert due to the latter's impatience at the battle of Lemgo in 1638, which led to the Prince's capture. Moreover, Newcastle had heard rumours that he was to be replaced by Rupert as the commander of the Royalist northern army, so if these stories are true it did not bode well for the Royalist hierarchy. The anonymous account records that:

---

12 Quoted in Margaret Duchess of Newcastle, *Life of William Cavendish, Duke of Newcastle*, ed. C. H. Firth (London: J. C. Nimmo, 1886), p.77.

13 C.H. Firth, 'Two accounts of the battle of Marston Moor' in *The English Historical Review* ed. Rev. Mandell Creighton, vol. V (London: Longmans, Green and Co, 1890), p.348.

> When Major-General King came up Prince Rupert, [he] showed the Marquis and the Earl a paper, which he said was the draught of the battle as he meant to fight it, and asked them what they thought of it. King answered, 'By God, sir, it is very fine in the paper, but there is no such thing in the fields'. The Prince replied, 'not so', &c.[14]

Cholmley also records that King criticised Rupert's deployment and told the Prince they were 'drawn too near the enemy, and in some place of disadvantage, then said the Prince, "they may be drawn to a further distance". "No sir", said King, "it is too late"'.[15] He continued, 'King dissuaded the Prince from fighting saying, "Sir your forwardness lost us the day in Germany, where yourself was taken prisoner," upon the dissuasions of the Marquis and King and that it was near night, the Prince was resolved not to join battle that day and therefore gave order to have the provisions for his army brought from York'.[16]

The anonymous account confirms that it was Rupert who decided not to attack that day: 'The Marquis asked the Prince what he would do? His Highness answered, "We will charge them to-morrow morning". My Lord asked him, whether he were sure the enemy would not fall on them sooner; he answered "No"; and the Marquis goes to his coach hard by, and calling for a pipe of tobacco'.[17]

Rupert appears not to have considered that the allies might themselves attack him. What the allied commanders were doing during this time is not recorded in any of the surviving accounts. According to tradition they held a council of war on a place called 'Cromwell's Plumb', which is now marked by some trees, but this is probably just another legend that has been handed down to us by Leadman. Although it is certain that as the regiments arrived they were ordered to a particular spot on the field and Leven is known to have ridden from unit to unit encouraging the allied army while it was watching the Royalists deploying below them.[18]

Cholmley was right about the distance of the Royalist army to that of the allied army, since other accounts also mention it; the Parliamentarian John Vicars records that the allies 'advanced 200 paces towards the enemy', while Ashe refers to the Royalists as being within 'musket shot' of the allied army, but were they referring to the main Royalist battle line or to the musketeers which Rupert is known to have placed in a ditch and/or hedge forward of his position? This position is shown on de Gomme's plan, running along the entire Royalist position and is marked 'These hedges were lined with musketeers'. The exact position of this hedge is unknown, Leadman describes the ditch as running parallel: 'about three to four hundred yards to the north' of the Long Marston-Tockwith Road:

---

14   Newcastle, *Life*, p.77.
15   C.H. Firth, 1890, p.348.
16   Ibid.
17   Newcastle, *Life*, p.77.
18   Vicars, *God's Ark*, p.271.

this ditch, long since filled up, seems to have contained very little or no water, and appears to have been of varying depth, as in some places it was for a short time defended, whilst in others it was easily passed … On the southern side of the ditch there was one continuous hedge of strong brushwood, which in several places can still be traced, and in my opinion this hedge was a far greater difficulty to the opposing armies than the ditch.[19]

The location of the ditch has been used by those writing the history of the battle ever since, but is Leadman right when he places the ditch and hedges so far north of the road? Despite having an impressive bibliography in his book, *Battles Fought in Yorkshire*, he tended to rely on hearsay rather than facts, which included the account of the ploughman being moved off Marston Moor before the battle, which is described in the introduction. He also refers to a cannonball entering an oven while a girl was baking bread, although it is hard to believe that she was doing this while a battle was raging outside her house.

In his articles on the battle which were published in 1978 and 1979 Dr Peter Newman dismisses the ditch depicted by Leadman and taken up by Brigadier Peter Young in his book on the battle, suggesting it to be running along the Long Marston–Tockwith, which is where S. R. Gardiner puts it in his history of the Civil War. However, by the time Newman published his book on the battle two years later, he used the Leadman/Young ditch. Unfortunately, he does not explain why he changed his mind.

The first edition six inches to the mile map of the area which is dated 1842, shows the ditch cutting across fields then when it reaches east field, where Byron is said to have drawn up it takes a diagonal approach towards the road and then makes a sharp turn so it runs almost parallel with the road itself. By the time of the second edition of the 25 inches to the mile map was published, part of this section had been filled in.[20] Whether this ditch was more extensive before 1842 is not known, but it is not shown on Francis White's 1785 map of the area, with Marston Moor stretching to the road. Whether this is an oversight by the cartographer or the ditch was a later feature is not known. Newman suggests that 'it may well be a post-enclosure ditch'.[21] This ditch still exists today so was Leadman mistaken and only part of the ditch was filled in or was he talking about a completely different ditch and hedge? Certainly Leadman is correct when he states that the ditch varied in depth because Captain William Stewart described it as 'a great ditch'; Watson and Rushworth call it 'a small ditch and a bank', and Ashe as a 'hedge and ditch',[22] while Fairfax refers to it as 'whins [furze] and ditches'.[23]

19 C.H. Firth, (1890), pp.17–79; Gardiner, vol. 1, p.375; Leadman, *Battles*, p.125.
20 Ordnance Survey 6″ to 1 mile sheet CLXXIII; 25″ to 1 mile CLXXIII.5 1892 and 1907 editions.
21 Map 1 in his article Newman (1779), which is based on White's map and the enclosure award of 1766, also shows the moorland stretching towards the road, although by the time he wrote his book on the battle published in 1981, on page 47 he shows a section of arable land straddling the road on both sides.
22 BL: TT E 2/1.
23 BL: TT E54/19 Captain William Stewart, *A Full Relation of the Late Victory Obtain (through God's providence) by the forces under the command of General Leslie, the Lord Fairfax and the*

Archaeological evidence shows a scattering of artefacts on both sides of the road where the arable field was. On De Gomme's plan it is written between where the allies drew up and the hedge, 'descending ground to the hedges', which would suggest that the hedges were nearer the road since the land begins to rise again after this. Watson recalls, that the Royalists 'drawing up with part of their foot close to our noses, so near that we had not liberty to take the moor … so that we … [had] to draw our men into a cornfield close to the moor'. Sir Henry Slingsby also refers to its position when he writes that some of the Royalist foot being 'drawn off to line the hedges of the cornfields, where the enemy must come to charge'.[24] The cornfields are known to have been south of the road, with the moor to the north of it.

While both armies were drawing up in their respective positions an artillery duel began, which according to Rushworth, 'The great ordnance on both sides began to play about three of the clock, but without doing any considerable execution on either part. All things being ready about five a clock, there was a general silence on each side, expecting who should begin the charge'.

Simeon Ashe mentions 'our cannon (which had played one or two hours before from the top of the hill) was drawn forward for our best advantage'.[25] Lumsden confirms that 'we advanced our cannon and entered to play on them on the left wing, which made a little move; which they perceiving brought up theirs and gave us the like'. How long this bombardment lasted depends on the sources. Lumsden says it 'continued not long', while Sir Henry Slingsby states that there was only 'four shots made'.[26] On the other hand others state that it continued several hours and lasted until about 5:00 p.m., although as Watson admits with 'small success to either'.

Ashe was impressed when he surveyed both armies drawn up, in what was to be the biggest battle of the Civil War and the second largest on British soil: 'How goodly a sight was this to behold, when two mighty armies, each of which consisted of above 20,000, horse and foot, did with flying colours prepared for the battle look each other in the face'.[27]

Rushworth continues 'In this posture they continued a considerable time, so that on each side it was believed there would be no action that night; but about seven a clock in the evening the Parliament's Generals resolved to fall on, and then the signal being given'.

Unfortunately, he does not say what this signal was, but it may have been the short bombardment mentioned by Lumsden and Slingsby. Robert Griffen records 'afterwards we all marched down to them, both horse and foot'.[28] As the allies began to advance a sudden thunderstorm broke out, but how widely the accompanying rain affected the soldiers' firearms is not known,

---

Earl of Manchester … (1644).
24   Slingsby, p.113.; Young, *Marston Moor*, p.228.
25   BL: TT E 2/1.
26   Quoted in Young, *Marston Moor*, pp.215–216, 229, 233, 267.
27   BL: TT E 2/1 A.
28   While speaking to a re-enactor, he mentioned that while his brigade was marching through a cornfield in June 'hundreds of insects' flew up into their faces, so the same thing might have happened at Marston Moor.

and on the left wing, Fraser's Scottish dragoons were sent forward to clear the hedge of the enemy's musketeers and presumably the dragoons on the right wing did the same. To distinguish between both sides the allied army chose as its field sign a white piece of paper or handkerchief in their hats and the words, 'God with us', whereas the Royalists' sign was without bands or scarves and their words were 'God and the King'.

Right Wing

The tactics of the day suggested that cavalry should attack at 'a good round trot', and Fairfax's cavalry advanced across the field in this way, but soon found their way blocked by the hedge and ditch which were occupied by the Royalists musketeers, as Fairfax's recalls 'the whims [furze] and ditches which we were to pass over before we could get to the enemy, which put us into great disorder … [in] the intervals of [their] horse … were lined with musketeers; which did us much hurt with their shot'.[29]

Captain William Stewart's accounts adds a little more details of this attack:

> The right wing of our foot [*sic*: horse] had several misfortunes, for betwixt them and the enemy there was no passage but at a narrow lane, where they could not march above 3 or 4 in front, upon the one side of the lane was a ditch, and on the other a hedge, both whereof were lined with musketeers, notwithstanding Sir Thomas Fairfax charged gallantly, but the enemy keeping themselves in a body, and receiving them by threes and fours as they marched out of the Lane.[30]

However, a large quantity of shot has been found on land between Moor Lane and Atterwick Lane suggesting that Fairfax's cavalry were able to deploy to meet their Royalist counterparts. Fairfax continues: 'I was necessitated to charge them. We were a long time engaged one with another; but at last we routed that part of the wing. We charged, and pursued them a good way towards York'.[31] In this account he continues that he had 400 horse at this time under his direct command, but in another account of the battle which Fairfax wrote '[It] being my lot to be cast upon many disadvantages, having command of the right wing, with much difficulty I could get but five troops in order; with which I charged the enemy's left wing; when the business was hotly disputed a long time at sword's point. We broke through; and had the chase of many of them'.[32]

The archaeological evidence suggests that Fairfax pursued the Royalists up Atterwick Lane, where a large amount of shot has been found, and even in 1891 Leadman marked on a plan of the battle, 'many relics found about

---

29   Quoted in Young, *Marston Moor*, pp.243–244. The square brackets are those given by Peter Young.
30   BL: TT E54/19.
31   Quoted in Young, *Marston Moor*, pp.243–244.
32   Ibid., p.245.

here'.[33] But, as Fairfax galloped off in pursuit of the routed Royalists he says that Colonel John Lambert 'should have seconded me …[but] charged in another place'.[34] However, Lambert had been met with a hail of musket and pistol shot, 'Major Fairfax, who was major of his [Lambert's] Regiment had at least 30 wounds; of which he died … [and was] deserted by his men'. Charles Fairfax, Sir Thomas' brother, would die a few days later.[35] This is probably when most of the shot mentioned above was fired, although the firefight was not one sided as Sir Philip Monckton, whose cavalry regiment was in the Royalists' front line, recalls:

> I had my horse shot under me as I caracoled at the head of the body I commanded, and so near the enemy that I could not be mounted again, but charged on foot, and beat Sir Hugh Bethel's Regiment of Horse, who was wounded and dismounted, and my servant brought me his horse. When I was mounted upon him the wind driving the smoke so as I could not see what was become of the body I commanded, which went in pursuit of the enemy.[36]

Here we see again the Royalist cavalry using the caracole, which is often referred to when one cavalry unit rides up to another and discharges their firearms. The smoke which obscured Monckton's view came from these firearms.[37] Finally under such pressure, and with Fairfax absent pursing part of the Royalist cavalry, the rest of his cavalry broke. One source says that while fleeing it rode through the allied infantry in a desperate attempt to escape, hotly pursued by the Royalist cavalry, some of whom found the allied baggage train too attractive to miss and set about plundering it. Although it was not just the Royalist cavalry that were tempted by the baggage train: according to Ashe, it was also 'the runaways, with other poor people who attended the Army'.[38] Even the Earl of Leven's coach was not safe. However, not all the Royalist cavalry set off in pursuit of Fairfax's cavalry: instead they wheeled to the right and plunged into the Scottish infantry, a manoeuvre usually associated with Cromwell's disciplined cavalry.

Oblivious of the disaster that had overtaken his command, Fairfax rode back to the battlefield, and recalls:

> returning back to go to my other troops, I was gotten in among the enemy, which stood up and down the field in several bodies of horse. So, taking the signal [a white handkerchief, or piece of paper] out of my hat, I passed through, for one of their own commanders; and so got to my Lord Manchester's horse in the other

---

33   Map from CD-ROM of Dr Peter Newman and P.R. Roberts, *Marston Moor, 1644, the Battle of Five Armies* (Pickering: Blackthorn Press, 2003).

34   Young, *Marston Moor*, p.244.

35   Ibid.

36   Firth (1898), pp.52–53.

37   In theory a trooper would have two pistols and a carbine.

38   BL: TT E 2/1.

wing; only with a cut in my cheek which was given me in the first charge, and a shot [which] my horse received.[39]

According to Captain William Stewart, Fairfax also took Colonel Lambert and Sir Thomas' brother, plus five or six troops of horse with him.[40] However, this seems unlikely since his brother had been mortally wounded, and the Northern horse were either chasing a detachment of Royalist cavalry towards York, or were being chased by Lord Goring's cavalry over Marston Hill. True there were still several Scottish cavalry regiments still on the right wing, but these appear to have made their own way to the centre. One of these regiments was Lord Alexander Balgonie's regiment, which were formed into two squadrons, one of which were armed with lances and charged an unidentified regiment of foot and 'put them wholly to the rout and after joined the left wing of horse, the other [squadron] by another way went also to the left wing'. The Earl of Eglinton's regiment of horse was also still in the field despite, as Lumsden says, 'not being well seconded' and had suffered heavy casualties including Eglinton's son who Stewart describes as 'deadly wounded', the Lieutenant Colonel, along with the Major and four lieutenants.[41] With these casualties the regiment appears to have had enough and did not follow Balgonie's regiment to the left wing, and what became of Dalhousie's regiment which was the other Scottish regiment on this wing is not recorded, so may have fled with Fairfax's cavalry.

Left Wing

Meanwhile on the allies' left wing the cavalry had met with better success, although they had to negotiate a rabbit warren on Bilton Bream. According to Watson, 'we came down the hill in the bravest order, and with the greatest resolution that ever was seen (I mean the left wing of our horse led by Cromwell)'. Ashe also states that it was 'the bravest sight in the world, for they moved down the hill like so many thick clouds'.[42] There is no archaeological evidence in the field traditionally associated with where Rupert deployed his right wing to show the struggle at the ditch or the subsequent cavalry melee. These artefacts may have been robbed out by battlefield scavengers over the centuries insomuch that if it was not for the written accounts we would presume that no fighting took place upon this part of the moor. Alternatively the frontage of both armies were much smaller than is usually

---

39 Young, *Marston Moor*, pp.243–244. The square brackets are those given by Peter Young. According to Ashe, 'our signal was a white Paper, or handkerchief in our hats; our word was God with us. The Enemies signal was to be without bands and scarves. Their word was God and the King'.

40 BL: TT E54/19.

41 BL: TT E54/19.

42 BL: TT E 2/1.

believed. Certainly the finds either side of the road suggests there were distinct engagements.[43]

One of these written accounts, *Full Relation,* states that Colonel Frazer's Scottish regiment of dragoons 'at the first assault they beat them [the Royalist musketeers] from the ditch, and shortly after killed a great many, and put the rest to rout'.[44] On seeing the rout of the Royalist musketeers, according to Rupert's diary 'Lord Byron … made a charge upon Cromwell's forces … [and] by the improper charge of the Lord Byron much harm was done'. There has been speculation why Byron made this charge when Rupert had given him strict orders not to do so. Was he carried away by seeing the musketeers driven from the ditch by Frazer's dragoons or was he ordered to do so? Certainly the *Life of James II* suggests the latter. Byron having been drawn up 'very advantageously behind a warren and a slough', but then Sir John Hurry 'persuaded' him to advance before the 700 musketeers which were to support his cavalry could have chance to fire at Cromwell's cavalry. Therefore, Byron's cavalry had to manoeuvre their way 'over the morass and charge them, by which inconsiderate action he gave them [the Parliamentarians] the same advantage which he had formerly over them; for they charging him in his passage over the ground already mentioned he was immediately routed'.[45] However, both Rupert's Diary and the *Life of James II* were written years later and Hurry had changed sides once more in August 1644, so he was an easy scapegoat. Another suggestion was that Byron, an experienced cavalry commander, wanted momentum when his front line met Cromwell's, or he advanced without orders. However, it is obvious that Rupert planned an offensive battle rather than a defensive one, so he may not have given any orders in the event that his army was attacked. Either way Byron's cavalry does not appear to have crossed the ditch itself, since it had already been occupied by Frazer's dragoons.

Soon both sides clashed, according to Cromwell: 'We never charged but we routed the enemy, the left wing which I commanded being our own horse saving a few Scots in our rear, beat all the Prince's horse, God made them as stubble to our swords'.[46] However this passage is from a letter of condolence rather than a detailed account of the action so that Cromwell could be paving the way to inform Colonel Valentine Walton of the death of his son and that his death had not been in vain. In reality the melee was probably more a kin to Leon Watson's account:

> Our front divisions of horse charged their front. Lieutenant General Cromwell's division of 300, in which himself was in person, charged the first division of Prince Rupert's, in which himself was in person. The rest of ours charged other divisions

---

43   Map from CD-Rom Newman and Roberts; David Keys, 'The fight to save battlegrounds from invasion of metal detectors', *The Independent* 22 September 2003; *Battlefield Archaeology: A Guide to the Archaeology of Conflict*, Guide 8, ed. Tim Sutherland, (BAJR Practical Guide Series), p.17.

44   BL: TT E54/19.

45   J. S. Clarke, *The Life of James the Second, King of England etc.* (London: Payne and Foss, 1816), vol. I, pp.22–23.

46   Carlyle, pp.152–153.

of theirs, but with such admirable valour as it was to be the astonishment of all the old soldiers of the army. Cromwell's own division had a hard pull of it; for they were charged by Rupert's bravest men both in front and flank; they stood at swords point a pretty while hacking one another; but at last (it so pleased God) he brake through them, scattering them before him like a little dust. At the same instant the rest of our horse of that wing had wholly broken all Prince Rupert's horse on their right wing, and were in the chase of them beyond their left wing.[47]

Manchester's regiment of horse was also involved in this melee: 'Colonel Sidney, son of the Earl of Leicester, charged with much gallantry at the head of my lord's regiment of horse and came off with much honour, though with many wounds to the grief of my lord, and many others, who is since gone to London for the cure of his wounds'.[48]

Hurry's regiment of horse is said to have been the first regiment to flee, while Byron's regiment for a time stood its ground, as probably did Vaughan's and Trevor's regiment, before crumbling under the pressure.[49] Seeing the situation on his right, Rupert galloped to the scene to stabilise the situation where he saw his own regiment, which had distinguished itself in many battles, also beginning to give ground. 'Swounds, do you run, follow me', Rupert is reported as saying:

So they facing about, he led them to a charge, but fruitlessly, the enemy having before broken the force of that wing, and without any great difficulty, for these troops which formerly had been thought unconquerable, now upon a panic fear, or I know not by what fate, took scare[?] and fled, most of them without striking a stroke, or having the enemy come near them, made as fast as they could to York. Those that gave this defeat were most of them Cromwell's horse to whom before the battle were joined David Leslie, and half the Scottish horse'.[50]

Rupert was separated from his lifeguard, 'and surrounded by the enemy, killed four or five with his own hands and at last he brake strangely [sic] through them'.

It was said that Hurry drew up the cavalry on this wing in small bodies, which were no match for the larger squadrons of the Eastern Association's cavalry. Robert Douglas, a chaplain in the Scottish army, records that Cromwell was wounded in the first charge, which is confirmed by John Vicars' *England's Worthies* who states that Cromwell 'behaved himself most bravely at the first onset ... but receiving (at the first charge) a wound in his neck, was fain to be conveyed out of the field, committing the further leading on of his brave regiment to Major General Crawford'.[51] Colonel Marcus Trevor, whose regiment was opposite Cromwell's claimed to have 'personally encountered that arch rebel and tyrant, Oliver Cromwell and wounded

47   BL: TT E 2/14 Leonard Watson, *A More Exact Relation of the Late Battell neare York* (1644).
48   Ashe, *Intelligence from the Armies in the North*, no.6.
49   Firth (1890), p.348.
50   Ibid.
51   John Vicars, *England's Worthies*, p.47.

him with his sword'.[52] While another cause is said to have been one of his regiment discharging his pistol and accidentally shooting him. Although it seems odd that Cromwell left the command of the cavalry to Crawford, who had a battle of his own to fight; or could this be a mistake for Major General David Leslie who was in a better position to take command of the situation? Certainly the Scots commissioner, William Baillie believed this was the case, since he later wrote that 'at the beginning of the fight Cromwell got a little wound on the craige which made him retire, so that he was not so much as present in the service; but his troopers were led on by David Leslie'. True, William Baillie was in London at the time he received this information from Colonel William Crawford of Nether Skeldon in Ayrshire, but as he claimed it was 'upon his oath'.[53]

However, if Crawford was in the vicinity during the battle then this fits in with an accusation made by Denzil Holles, a political enemy of Cromwell. Seeing that Cromwell was motionless with his cavalry, Crawford is said to have ridden up to Cromwell, who asked Crawford what he should do. To which he replied:

> Sir, if you charge not all is lost; Cromwell answered he was wounded and was not able to charge (his great wound being a little burn in the neck by the accident of one of his soldiers pistols), then Crawford desired him to go off the field, and sending one away with him (who very readily followed wholesome advice) led them on himself ...[54]

This incident has been questioned by some historians, but unlike Crawford and Leslie this was Cromwell's first major battle, in fact the biggest battle of the Civil War, therefore could he have frozen for some minutes while he pondered what to do next?

Another accusation levelled at Cromwell was that he left the battlefield at the moment of crisis and only returned once he discovered the Royalists were losing the battle. Although according to Robert Douglas, 'Cromwell charged very well but at the first charge he was lightly hurt, went off, and came not again'.[55] Douglas is mistaken here: Cromwell did return to the battle but how long he was away from the battle is not known.

Meanwhile, the battle of the allies' left wing was still to be won or lost, according to Captain Robert Clarke:

> after a little time the Earl of Manchester's horse were repulsed by fresh supplies of the enemy's, and forced to retreat in disorder ... [but] by the great courage and wisdom of the commanders our broken forces were rallied and made head against the enemies; in which service the Earl of Manchester and Lieutenant General

---

52   Terry Clavin, 'Marcus Trevor', *Dictionary of Irish Biography*.
53   Baillie, *Letters*, p.218.
54   Holles, *Memoirs*, p.16.
55   Douglas, *Diary*, pp.62–63.

Cromwell have merited most … at this second charge our men performed their duty with such resolution and courage as they utterly routed the enemy's army.[56]

Clarke was not the only one to record that the cavalry of the Eastern Association made at least two charges that day. However, it was not until Leslie's cavalry 'charged the enemy's horse (with whom Lieutenant General Cromwell was engaged) upon the flank, and in a very short space the enemy's whole cavalry was routed'.[57] Douglas also claimed that 'our Scots horse on that wing did good service, both in cutting off the foot and charging with Manchester's horse'.[58]

The Royalist cavalry fled north east between the River Nidd and Wilstrop Wood and were pursued by part of Cromwell's cavalry to York. Writing in 1809 a Mr E. Hargrove records that 'within these few years on cutting down the wood, belonging to Lord Petre, on one side of Marston Moor, the sawyers found many bullets in the hearts of the trees'.[59]

Centre

Although the allied infantry were said to have 'advanced in a running march' they would have been hard pressed to keep up with their cavalry, but they 'soon made their way over the ditch, and gave a smart charge'. Simeon Ashe recalls that:

> Upon the advancing of the Earl of Manchester's Foote, after short firings on both sides, we caused the enemy to quit the hedge in a disorderly manner, where they left behind them four Drakes. The Lord Fairfax his Brigade on our right hand did also beat off the Enemy from the hedges before them, driving them from their cannon, being two Drakes and one Demi Culverin.[60]

The Scottish infantry pressed home their attack with determination and also possessed themselves of the ditch, which according to Captain Stewart were held by:

> their best foot … upon the advance of our Battle were forced to give ground, being gallantly assaulted by the Earl of Lindsey's regiment, the Lord Maitland's, Cassilis', and Kilhead's. General Major Crawford having over winged the enemy set upon their flank, and did very good execution upon the enemy, which gave occasion to the Scottish foot to advance and pass the ditch.[61]

---

56 Firth, (1898), p.75.
57 BL: TT E54/19.
58 Douglas, *Diary*, pp.62–63.
59 E. Hargrove, *The History of the Castle, Town and Forest of Knaresbrough …* (Knaresbrough and Harrogate: Hargrove and Sons, 1809), pp.382–383.
60 BL: TT E 2/1.
61 BL: TT E54/19.

Rupert hiding in a bean field at Marston Moor (Contemporary pamphlet, *A Dog's Elegy or Rupert's Tears* (London, July 1644))

Once passed the ditch, the infantry of the Eastern Association met with Rupert's and Byron's regiments of foot in their exposed position and according to Thomas Fuller were 'impressed with unequal numbers, and distanced from seasonable succour, became a prey to their enemy'.[62] Among the soldiers of Rupert's bluecoats was William Stoakes, who at the Restoration petition for a pension having 'received many dangerous hurts' during the battle.[63]

According to the Parliamentarian newspaper, *A True Relation of the Late Fight*, 'what should I name the brigade of Colonel Russell, Colonel Montagu, and Colonel Pickering's who stood as a wall of brass and let fly small shot like hail upon the enemy, and not a man of their whole brigade [was] slain … I pity the enemy's common men who cried "pity us, pity us, we are array men"'. While the *Parliament Scout* records that, this brigade 'behaved themselves most gallantly'.[64] A Mr Ogden recalls Rupert's 'foot suffered much, they standing so stoutly to it, and the horse flying; most of Manchester's bluecoats which fought under the bloody colours are cut off.

---

62 Thomas Fuller, *Fuller's Worthies, Selected from the Worthies of England* (London: The Folio Society, 1987), ed. Richard Barber, p.436.

63 Somerset Heritage Centre (SHC): Q/SPET/1/106, Petition of William Stoakes, 23 April 1661. Stoakes served throughout the First Civil War with the regiment and was taken prisoner at Naseby.

64 BL: TT E 54/7 *A True Relation of the Late Fight, 8 July 1644* and; TT E 54/20, *Parliament Scout 4–11 July 1644*.

They have many of our colours and we of theirs'. These bluecoats almost certainly belonged to Crawford's regiment of foot, since the other regiments of the Eastern Association wore red coats.[65] Newcastle's infantry had also come to grips with the allied infantry, 'after thrice firing, [they] fell to it with the butt ends of their muskets'.[66] Newcastle's regiment of foot is said to have 'furiously assaulted' the brigade of Fairfax's infantry on the right of Manchester's infantry, which retreated in 'some disorder'.[67]

The Royalist infantry were not alone in the assault on the allied centre; after defeating Fairfax's cavalry Sir Charles Lucas and Lieutenant General Porter's cavalry brigades fell upon the Scottish infantry, and three of the brigades fled. According to Robert Douglas a brigade of Fairfax's foot were the first to flee, followed by the Edinburgh and artillery regiments, then the Chancellor and Maclaine's regiments.[68] According to Thomas Stockdale, who wrote on 5 July to John Rushworth:

Lord Fairfax's foot gaining ground of the enemy's foot in the main battle; after a little time … Lord Fairfax's foot and the Scots that were joined with them pursuing their advantage were charged by the enemy's horse and so disordered that they were forced to fly back and leave our ordnance behind them, and many of our horse were also repulsed by the enemy, which coming off in disorder on all sides did so daunt their spirits of the reserves that had not then engaged … that many fled away without ever striking a blow.[69]

This was Sir William Blakiston's brigade whose cavalry had been held in reserve behind the Royalist infantry, and may have been mistaken by an eyewitness for Fairfax's cavalry which had ridden down his infantry. Among the Royalist cavalry attacking the centre was Newcastle's lifeguard, who according to his wife:

[the Duke and his] troop of gentlemen volunteers … went on with the greatest courage; and passing through two bodies of foot, engaged with each other not at forty yards' distance, received not the least hurt, although they fired quick upon each other; but marched towards a Scots regiment of foot, which they charged and routed; in which encounter my Lord himself killed three with his page's half leaden sword, for he had no other left him; and though all the gentlemen in particular offered him their swords, yet my Lord refused to take a sword of any of them. At last, after they had passed through this regiment of foot, a pikeman made a stand to the whole troop; and though my Lord charged him twice or thrice, yet he could not enter1 him; but the troop despatched him soon.[70]

65   Firth, (1898), pp.71–72. The exception to this was Manchester's own regiment of foot, which had a division of greencoats faced red, and another division of redcoats faced green.
66   Fuller, *Worthies*, p.436.
67   BL: TT E 2/1
68   Charles S. Terry, *Life of and Campaigns of Alexander Leslie, First Earl of Leven* (Longmans: Green and Co., 1899), p.281.
69   Thomas Stockdale's letter to John Rushworth, 5 July 1644 printed in Firth, (1898), p.75.
70   Newcastle, *Life*, p.79.

According to Stockdale it was not just the Royalists that spread confusion in the allied ranks, many 'multitudes of people that were spectators ran away in such fear and confusion as more daunted our soldiers'.[71] A large quantity of artefacts have been found on both sides of the ditch, some of which came from the initial fighting for the ditch, but also certainly includes the debris of the fleeing infantry and their pursuers. With their right wing routed and their centre beginning to flee things looked bleak for the allies.

Fortunately, the infantry of the Eastern Association held firm as well as 18 regiments of Scottish infantry who were able to plug the gap, as Lumsden continues:

> Those brigades that failed on the van were presently supplied by Cassills, Killhead, Cowper and Dunfermline and some of Clydesdale's regiment who were on the battle, and gained what they had lost and made themselves masters of the cannon was next to them and took Sir Charles Lucas, Lieutenant General of the horse prisoner. Those that ran away show themselves most basely. I commanding the battle was at the head of your Lordship's regiment and Baccleach's but they carried not themselves as I would have wished neither could I prevail with them. For those that fled never came to charge with the enemies, but were so possessed with a panic fear that they ran for [an] example to the others and no enemy following, which gave the enemy occasion to charge them.[72]

A captain known only as W.H., who is believed to have served in Manchester's army, recalls 'it was hotly disputed between the two main bodies … but theirs at last perceiving their friends thus flying, began likewise for their own safety to betaken themselves to their heels'.[73] After leading the cavalry charges against the Scots, Sir Charles Lucas' horse was killed and he was captured.

By now the allied left wing had finally routed Rupert's cavalry and Cromwell was finally in a position to assist the allied centre, 'we charged their regiments of foot with our horse', he recalled, and 'routed all we charged'.[74] Captain W.H. also recalls that Cromwell led 'our brigade of horse [and] gave them a brave onset, that God seconding it with his blessing, in less than an hour we had totally routed their foot on the right wing [of the centre]'.[75]

However, not all the Royalist infantry fled. James Somerville's account also recalls Cromwell's charge:

> upon the naked flanks of the Prince's main battalion of foot, carrying them down with great violence; nether met they with any great resistance, until they came to the Marquis of Newcastle his battalion of white coats, who first peppering them soundly with their shot, when they came to charge stoutly bore them up with their pikes, that they could not enter to break them. Here the Parliament horse of that wing received their greatest loss, and a stop for some time to their hoped

71 Stockdale's letter in Firth (1898), p.75.
72 Lumsden's letter 5 July 1644 printed in Young, *Marston Moor*, pp.267–269.
73 TT E 54/11.
74 Carlyle, pp.152–153.
75 TT E 54/11.

Map showing the archaeological finds on Marston Moor,
Based on map in CD by Paul Roberts *Marston Moor, 1644* (Blackthorn Press, 2003)

for victory and that only by the stout resistance of this gallant battalion, which consisted near of four thousand foot.[76]

One of Cromwell's first biographers recalls that he, with:

> fury fell upon the Marquis' foot, whose regiment of white coats … yet stood and could not be broken till the field being almost cleared, the Parliament's infantry came up and then both horse and foot charged and broke them, Cromwell here made a very great slaughter and carnage, especially in the rout and pursuit … gaining here the title of *Ironsides*, from the impenetrable strength of his troops, which could by no means be broken or divided.[77]

Since they had arrived late on the field, Newcastle's infantry deployed in the second line of the Royalist infantry. The archaeological evidence shows that some infantry retreated to north of the lane which branches off from Moor Lane to the area which is now known as White Syke Close.[78] What made the other Royalist infantry run, and Newcastle's stay is not known, possibly they were covering the Royalists' retreat, but also in other accounts Newcastle's army were referred to as the 'Popish Army', so they may not have had an option but to fight on whether they were Catholics or not. Whatever the reason they put up a stiff resistance. Although not present at the battle, William Lilly writing during the Commonwealth period describes the scene:

> There was one entire regiment belonging to Newcastle called the lambs, because they were all new clothed in white woollen cloth, two or three days before the fight. This sole regiment after the day was lost, having got into a small parcel of ground ditched in, and not of easy access of horse, would take no quarter; and by mere valour, for one whole hour, kept the troops of horse from entering amongst them at near push of pike: when the horse did enter, they would have no quarter, but fought it out till there was not thirty of them living; those whose hap it was to be beaten down upon the ground as the troopers came near them, though they could not rise for their wounds, yet were so desperate as to get either a pike or sword, or piece of them, and to gore the troopers' horses as they came over them, or passed by them. Captain Camby, then a trooper under Cromwell, and an actor, who was the third or fourth man that entered amongst them, protested, he never in all the fights he was in, met with such resolute brave fellows, or whom he pitied so much, and said, he saved two or three against their wills.[79]

The Duchess of Newcastle recalls that it was her husband's 'white coats [who] showed such an extraordinary valour and courage in that action, that they were killed in rank and file'.[80] The infantry could easily defend themselves

---

76 James Somerville, *Memoire of the Somervilles, being a history of the baronial house of Somerville* (Edinburgh: James Ballantyne and co., 1815), pp.346–349.

77 James Heath, *Flagellum: or the Life and Death, Birth and Burial of Oliver Cromwell* (London: LR, 1663), p.29.

78 Map from CD-ROM, Newman and Roberts.

79 William Lilly, *History of His Life and Times* (London: Charles Baldwin, 1822), pp.178–180.

80 Newcastle, *Life*, p.79.

against cavalry, with the pikemen giving protection to the musketeers, but when Frazer's dragoons and two other unnamed regiments were 'brought to open them [up] which at length they did; when all their ammunition was spent, having refused quarter, every man fell in the same order and rank wherein he had fought'.[81] According to Thomas Fuller, they had brought their 'winding sheets', or shrouds with them to the battle.[82] Rushworth also admired 'The Marquis of Newcastle's Regiment of white coats [who] were almost wholly cut off, for they scorned to fly, and were slain in rank and file'.

Traditionally the last stand of Newcastle's whitecoats marks the end of the battle. However, according to Captain William Stewart after dealing with Newcastle's men, they 'charged a brigade of green coats, whereof they cut off a great number, and put the rest to the rout'.[83] Stewart is the only one to refer to this attack, although in his book on the battle Brigadier Peter Young suggested that this might have been at an earlier stage of the battle. Young also suggests that it was either Robert Broughton's or Henry Tillier's regiment of foot, who had arrived from Ireland, and both are known to have worn green coats, and Tillier was among those captured during the battle.[84]

Stewart also mentions after the stand of the greencoats came the clash between Cromwell and the Royalist cavalry of the left wing. According to Watson:

> The enemy seeing us come on in such a gallant posture … left all thoughts of pursuit, and began to think that they must fight again for that victory which they thought had been already got. They marching down the hill upon us, from our carriages, so that they fought upon the same ground, and with the same front that our right wing had before stood to receive our charge.[85]

Peter Newman puts this cavalry melee south west of Long Marston, where a large quantity of artefacts have been found, but this means Cromwell would have had to return to Marston Hill where the allies had been drawn up that morning. However, it is more likely that this is the debris left behind by the fleeing infantry and the cavalry of Fairfax's wing, along with their Royalist pursuers. In 2003 a metal detector rally found many objects further south than this, which is said to have included musket and pistol balls, parts of gunpowder flasks, spurs and a halberd or pike head. Unfortunately, despite being a legal event many of these artefacts and their exact location were not identified so their historic value to the battle was lost, insomuch that the rally was discussed in the House of Lords.[86]

It is more likely that the last cavalry melee was between Cromwell's cavalry and the Royalist horse which attacked the allied centre, as a *Full Relation* suggests, they 'met with the enemy's horse (being retreated upon the repulse

81   Somerville, pp.346–349.
82   Fuller, *Worthies*, p.436.
83   BL: TT E54/19:
84   Young, *Marston Moor*, p.137.
85   BL: TT E 2/14.
86   Keys, *The Independent* 22 September 2003; Sutherland, *Battlefield Archaeology*, p.17.

they had from the Scottish foot) at the same place of disadvantage where they had routed our horse formerly'.[87] How long this cavalry melee lasted is not known, but Cromwell was victorious once more. However, not all the Royalist cavalry were driven from the field since Monckton recalls seeing a large body of Royalist cavalry:[88]

> I retired over the glen, where I saw a body of some two thousand horse that were broken, which as I endeavoured to rally, I saw Sir John Hurry … come galloping through the glen. I rid to him and told him that there were none in that great body, but they knew either himself or me, and that if he would help me to put them in order, we might again regain the field. He told me, broken horse would not fight, and galloped from me towards York.[89]

The location of the glen is not known, but it is believed to have been somewhere north of where the Royalist left wing drew up that day. According to Cholmley, Rupert wanted to withdraw the remainder of the garrison from York and, along with these cavalrymen, renew the fight that evening, but decided against it.

Conclusion

It was not just Cromwell that had left the field: there were reports that Manchester, Lord Fairfax and Leven had also fled. Newspapers accused Leven of fleeing to Leeds, Hull, Wetherby and Bradford. Even a coward cannot be in four places at the same time.[90] While other accounts place him on the battlefield, Simeon Ashe saw both Leven and Manchester rallying soldiers:

> The Earl of Manchester with much labour did rally five hundred of the soldiers who were leaving the field in great disorder, and brought them back again to the battle. The worthy General Leslie [Leven] was much offended with the soldiers who shrunk from the service of the day: and having endeavoured both by words and blows to keep them in the field, with much wisdom and affection he pressed this argument; "Although you run from your enemies, yet leave not your General, though you fly from them, yet forsake not me".[91]

This has been seen as Manchester returning to battlefield after fleeing, but since Leven was in overall command and his subordinates had control of their part of the battlefield, he did not really have anything to do, until he saw

---

87   BL: TT E54/19.
88   Another possibility is that they were the remnants of Byron's cavalry who had not abandoned the field after being routed by Cromwell.
89   Young, *Marston Moor*, pp.222–223.
90   S. Murdoch and A. Grossjean, *Alexander Leslie and the Scottish Generals of the Thirty Years War, 1618–1648* (London: Pickering and Chatto, 2014), pp.126–134.
91   BL: TT E 2/1.

the fleeing soldiers and tried to rally them. Lord Ferdinando Fairfax is said to have fled to his bed at his nearby estate, but even this cannot be verified.

However, it was not just the allied commanders whose conduct that day can be criticised. Prince Rupert also had questions to answer. No accounts of the battle mentions him after the part he played in the cavalry melee, just that he retired to York that evening, although Parliamentarian propaganda says he hid in a bean field after his cavalry had been routed on his right wing. Also whether he should have fought the battle at all, an accusation made by Sir Edward Hyde in his *History of the Great Rebellion*, when he states:

> There was irreconcilable differences and jealousies between the officers and indeed the nations; the English resolving to join no more with the Scots, and they, on the other side as weary as their company and discipline. The prince had done his work, and, if he had sat still, the other great army would have mouldered to nothing, and been exposed to any advantage his highness would take of them.[92]

True, Hyde hated Rupert and this criticism was written years later when England and Scotland had twice gone to war with each other. However, Lieutenant Colonel James Somerville also writes in a similar vein: 'Prince Rupert would not content himself with what he had done, but would needs over act in forcing the Parliament's armies to a present engagement, whereas a few days want of forage and bread would have sent them far enough a packing, and forced these three armies to have separate'.[93]

That night Manchester thanked the soldiers for 'the exceeding good service which they had done … [and] that although he could not possibly that night make provisions for them, according to their deserts and necessities, yet he would without fail endeavour their satisfactions in that kind in the morning'. This was appreciated by the soldiers who 'told his Lordship with much cheerfulness that though they had long fasted, and were faint, yet they would willingly wait three days longer, rather then give off the Service, or leave his Lordship'.[94] However, the soldiers were not too faint to seek plunder from the battlefield, as Ashe continues: 'Many of our soldiers (the horse-men especially) met with much gold and silver, and other commodities of good worth: And indeed they deserved such encouragements, by their excellent service and brave adventures'.[95]

Captain W.H. probably echoed many on both sides when he wrote to his friend, 'By God's blessing I can tell you I am alive'.[96] While many of the soldiers thanked God for the victory, including Cromwell, many of the Independents in Parliament thanked Cromwell for leading the army to victory, which was echoed in the Parliamentary press. Denzil Holles would also later write:

---

92   Clarendon, p.217.
93   Quoted in Young, *Marston Moor*, pp.259–60.
94   BL: TT E 2/1.
95   Ibid.
96   TT E 54/11.

Cromwell had the impudence and boldness to assume much of the honour of it to himself, or rather, *Herod* like, to suffer others to magnify him and adore him for it (for I can scarce believe he should be so impudent to give it out himself, so conscious as he must be of his own base cowardliness) those who did the principal service that day, were Major General Leslie, who commanded the Scots' horse, Major General Crawford, who was major general to the Earl of Manchester's brigade, and Sir Thomas Fairfax who, under his father, commanded the Northern Brigade.[97]

Holles was not the only one to be infuriated by the praise showered on Cromwell: Robert Baillie, wrote about the 'vanity and falsehood of their disgraceful relation', which forgot to mention that it had been the Earl of Leven who had commanded the army.[98] The Scotsman Sir Thomas Hope ascribed the victory to 'the general of the Scots' army, the Earl of Leven, assisted with Sir Thomas Fairfax and Lord Manchester; where our army by the blessing of God was victorious and Prince Rupert defeated'.[99]

However, many were also not so lucky as Captain W. H. According to the allied commanders' official report to the Committee of Both Kingdoms:

There were killed upon the spot about 3,000 of the enemy, whereof many were chief officers, and 1,500 prisoners taken, among whom there are above 100 officers, in which number is Sir Charles Lucas, Lieutenant General to the Marquis of Newcastle's horse, Major-General Porter, and Major-General Tillier, besides diverse colonels, lieutenant colonels, and majors. Our loss is not very great, being only one lieutenant colonel, a few captains, and 200 or 300 common soldiers.[100]

Among those who were killed on the allies' side was Captain Valentine Walton who served in Cromwell's own regiment. On the 5 July Cromwell sat down to write to his friend Colonel Valentine Walton about his son's death. After a preamble of the events of the battle he says:

Sir, God hath taken away your eldest son by a cannon shot, it brake his leg, we were necessitated to have it cut off, whereof he died.

Sir you know my trials this way [having also lost a son], but the Lord supported me with this, that the Lord took him into the happiness we all pant after. And live for. There is your precious child, full of glory to know sin nor sorrow any more. He was a gallant young man, exceeding gracious. God give you his comfort. Before his death he was so full of comfort, that to [Colonel] Frank Russell and myself he could not express it, it was so great above his pain. This he said to us. Indeed it was admirable. A little after he said one thing lay upon his spirit. I asked him what that was. He told me that it was, that God had not suffered him to be no more the executioner of his enemies. At his fall, his horse

97   Holles, p.15.
98   Baillie, p.203.
99   Sir Thomas Hope, *A Diary of the Public Correspondence of Sir Thomas Hope of Craighall, Bart, 1633–1645* (Edinburgh: 1893), p.207.
100 CSPD 1644, p.311, 5 July 1644.

being killed with the bullet and as I am informed three horses more, I am told he bid them open to the right, and left, that he might see the rogues run. Truly he was exceedingly beloved in the army of all that knew him, but few knew him for a precious young man, fit for God. You have cause to bless the Lord, he is a glorious saint in heaven, wherein you ought exceedingly to rejoice. Let this drink up your sorrow, seeing these are not fain words to comfort you, but the thing is so real and undoubted truth. You may do all things by the strength of Christ, seek that, and you shall easily bear your trial. Let this public mercy to the church of God make you to forget your private sorrow. The Lord be your strength, so prays your truly faithful and loving brother … My love to your daughter and my cousin Percival, sister Desbrow and all friends with you.[101]

This letter gives mixed emotions, on the one hand we see a different side to Cromwell, of a caring nature trying to reassure a father over the death of his son and reminding him that he knows what he is going through since he also had lost a son in the war. On the other we see Captain Walton, who allegedly wished that he had killed more Royalists before he died, and to the reader it shows these two were not one dimensional historical figures, but people who had feelings. However, how much of this letter is true? As C. H. Firth points out it was not meant to be a despatch reporting the events of the battle but a letter of condolence between two fathers who had both lost sons saying that the son had not thrown his life away needlessly.[102]

As the regimental surgeons and their mates set to work treating the wounded, on 11 July the following sums were distributed to the following troops and companies to assist their treatment:[103]

101 Carlyle, pp.152–153.
102 C.H. Firth, *Oliver Cromwell and the rule of the Puritans in England* (London: and New York: G. P. Putnam's Sons, 1929), pp.109–110.
103 TNA: SP 28/17 ff.162–174.

Death of Rupert's dog at Marston Moor (Contemporary pamphlet, *A Dog's Elegy or Rupert's Tears* (London, July 1644))

Troop or Company	Regiment	Amount
Lt Gen. Cromwell's	Cromwell's Horse	£22 01s 00d
Captain Bethel's	Cromwell's Horse	£8 15s 00d
Captain Walton's	Cromwell's Horse	£5 05s 00d
Captain Browne's	Cromwell's Horse	£14 00s 00d
Captain Margery's	Cromwell's Horse	£5 05s 00d
Captain Swallow's	Cromwell's Horse	£5 05s 00d
Captain Lawrence's	Cromwell's Horse	£5 05s 00d
Major General Crawford's	Fleetwood's Horse	£0 17s 00d
Captain John Moody's	Fleetwood's Horse	£1 15s 00d
Captain Abbot's	Manchester's Dragoons	£4 14s 6d
Lt Col. Lilburne's	Manchester's Dragoons	£2 02s 00d
Major Ewer's	Manchester's Dragoons	£2 01s 00d
Captain Beaumont's (later Langridge's)	Manchester's Dragoons	£2 01s 00d

On 13 July a further 17s was paid to Samuel Daby, a wounded trooper of Captain Margery's troop for his care.[104] However, these appear to have been initial payments since on 17 July a further £24 was paid for 12 'sick and wounded' troopers of Captain Swallow's troop and on 19 October 1644 Dr Edward Webb presented his bill for 'curing of wounded and maimed soldiers', including:[105]

---

104 Ibid., f.166.
105 TNA: SP 28/19 f.370.

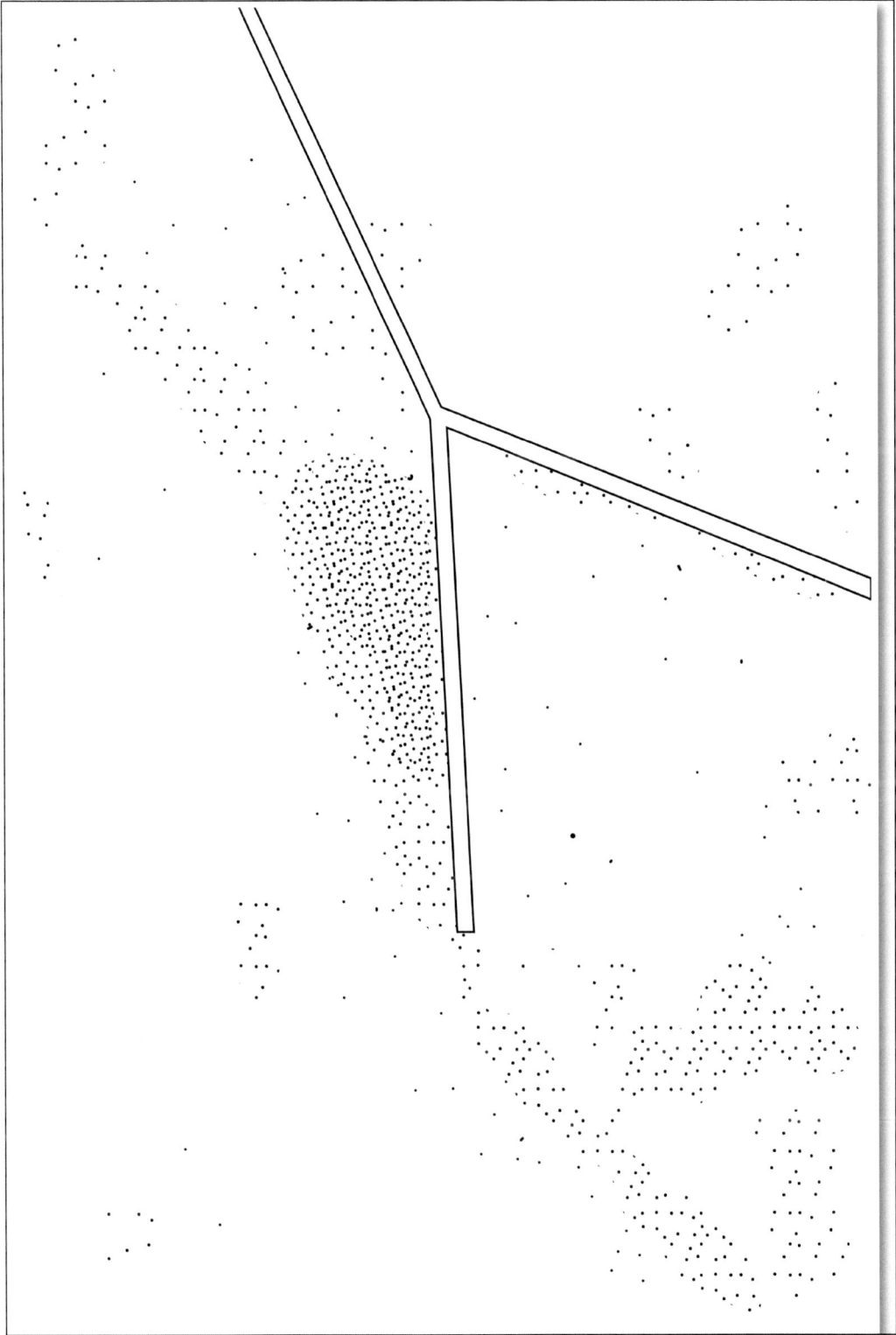

Map showing the archaeological finds around White Syke Close.
Based on map in CD by Paul Roberts *Marston Moor, 1644* (Blackthorn Press, 2003)

Captain Mercer's Soldiers

John Tison, shot in the face with a bullet at York fight for his cure, £1 00s 00

John Gash, had his elbow cut at York for his cure, £1 00s 00

Major General Crawford's Soldiers

Abraham Castle, for wounds in his head and fractures in his skull for his cure, £1 00s 00

Captain Lawrence's Soldiers

Thomas Coope, shot through the foot at York and the bones broke all to shatters for his cure, £6 13s 4d

Samuel Mayhew, for wounds in his legs for his cure, £0 10s 00d

Captain Meredith's Soldiers

William Parker, shot at York and the bones of his hand shattered all to pieces and eleven tents goeth in it every day and every night, for his cure, 6 13s 4d

It is clear from this warrant that the surgeons only received money for the patients they treated if they survived. Payments were also paid to individual soldiers, such as Thomas Cave of Great Okeley, Northampton, who was a trooper in Cromwell's own regiment who had lost both eyes during the battle. On 17 February 1648 he was granted £100 as compensation, but on 9 December 1652 he was described as 'in a very sad and perishing condition', having only received £20 of this sum.[106] In one way Cave was lucky in that usually a maimed soldier received just £2 a year.

As to the Scottish army, Robert Douglas recalled 'many officers hurt … Lieutenant Harrison was killed; Ensign Murray, Frances Hart, very ill. Dudhope was taken, and after a space (of about?) some 20 days, took a fever and died'.[107] Lieutenant Colonel James Bryson of the minister's regiment was also killed. Sir Thomas Fairfax recalls about this battle that he escaped:

> only with a cut in my cheek, which was given me in the first charge, and a shot which my horse received. In this charge many of my officers and soldiers were hurt and slain: The captain of my own troop was shot in the arm, my cornet had both his hands cut, so as rendered him ever after unserviceable. Captain Micklethwait, an honest stout gentleman, was slain: And scarce any officer who was in this charge but received a hurt … But that nearest if all concerned me was the loss of my brother, who being deserted of his men, was sore wounded, of which in three or four days after he died. Buried at Marston aged 23. In this charge as many were hurt and killed as in the whole army besides.[108]

---

106 *Calendar of the Committee for the Advance of Money*, part 2 1645–1650 (London: HMSO, 1888), pp.849–862.

107 Colonel Sir James Scrimgeour, 2nd Viscount Dunhope commanded the Angus regiment of foot.

108 Sir Thomas Fairfax, *A Short Memorial of the Northern Actions in which I was engaged, during the war there, from the year 1642 to the year 1644* (*Yorkshire Archaeological Journal*, vol. VIII 1884), pp.88–89.

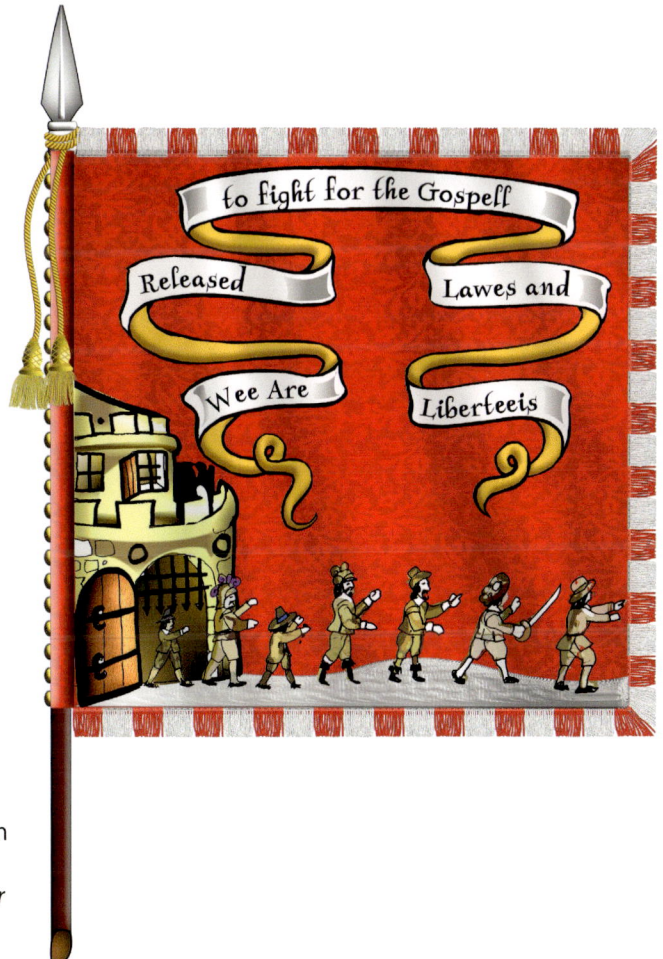

Plate A
A.1 Captain James Berry
Lieutenant-General Oliver
Cromwell's Regiment of Horse
1644–1645
A.2 Captain William Dingley
The Earl of Manchester's
Regiment of Horse 1643–1645
(Illustrations by Dr Lesley Prince © Helion
& Company)
*See Colour Plate Commentaries for further
information.*

Pro Rege et Lege Parati:

to fight for the Gospell
Released
Lawes and
Wee Are
Liberteeis

Plate B
B.1 Captain John Disbrowe
Lieutenant-General Oliver
Cromwell's Regiment of Horse
1643–1645
B.2 Captain John Grove
Lieutenant-General Oliver
Cromwell's Regiment of Horse
1644–1645
(Illustrations by Dr Lesley Prince © Helion & Company)
See Colour Plate Commentaries for further information.

NESCIT ✠ VIRTVS ✠ STARE ✠ LOCO

PRO Reformatione PVGNANDVM.

Plate C
C.1 Captain Thomas Hammond
The Earl of Manchester's
Regiment of Horse
1644–1645
C.2 Captain Ralph Knight
The Earl of Manchester's
Regiment of Horse
1644–1645
(Illustrations by Dr Lesley Prince ©
Helion & Company)
See Colour Plate Commentaries for
further information.

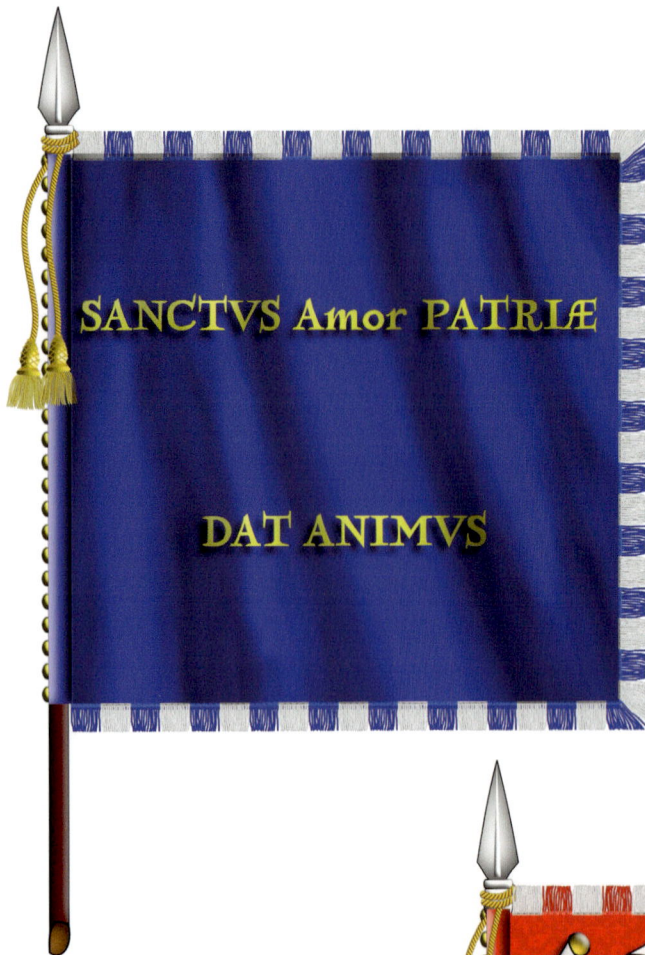

Plate D
D.1 Colonel Algernon Sidney
Earl of Manchester's Regiment
of Horse
1644–1645
D.2 Captain Henry Ireton,
Francis Thornhagh's Regiment
of Horse, then Oliver Cromwell's
Regiment of Horse
1643–1645
(Illustrations by Dr Lesley Prince ©
Helion & Company)
See Colour Plate Commentaries for further
information.

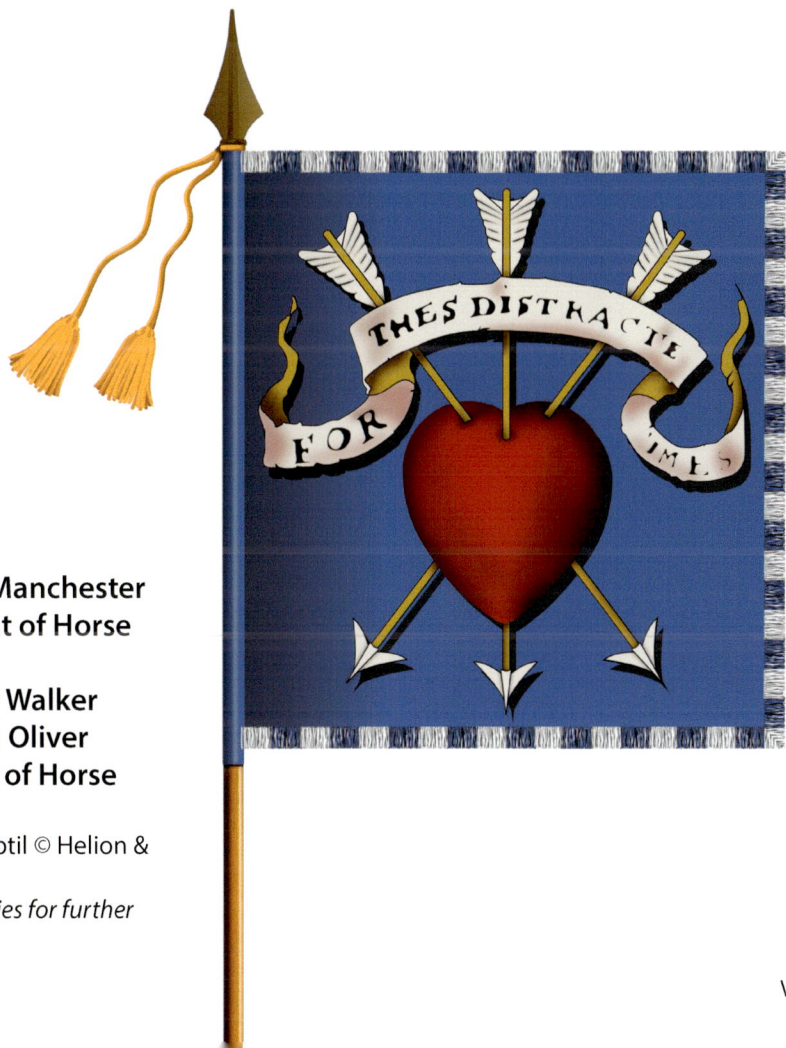

TRVTH AND PEACE:

THES DISTRACTE

FOR

IMES

Plate E
E.1 General the Earl of Manchester
Colonel, own Regiment of Horse
1643–1645
E.2 Captain Zachary Walker
Lieutenant General Oliver
Cromwell's Regiment of Horse
1643–1644
(Illustrations by Anderson Subtil © Helion &
Company)
See Colour Plate Commentaries for further
information.

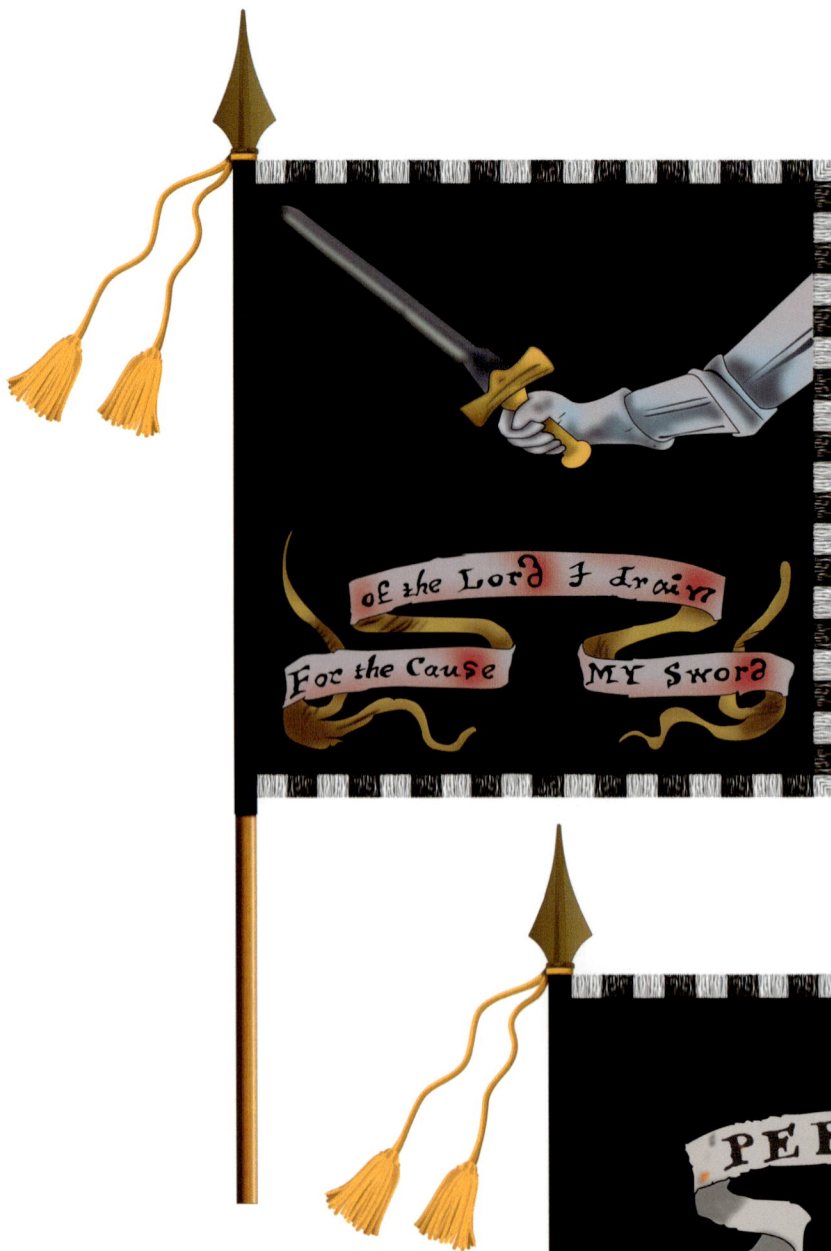

Plate F
F.1, F.2 Captain Anthony Markham
Edward Rossiter's Regiment of
Horse
1644–1645
(Illustrations by Anderson Subtil © Helion &
Company)
*See Colour Plate Commentaries for further
information.*

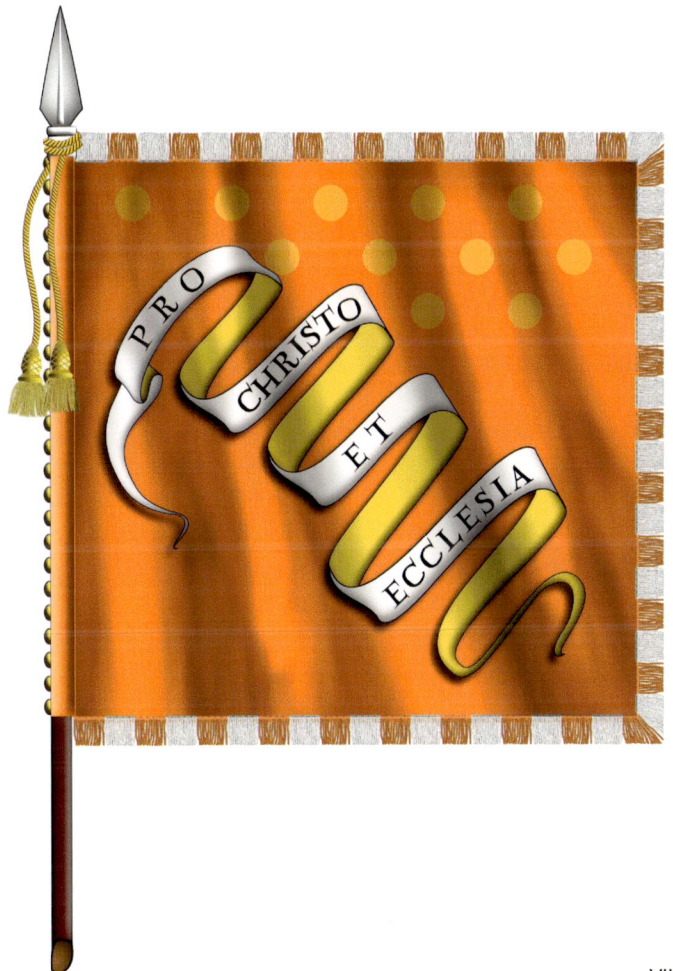

Plate G
G.1 Captain Thomas Moulson
Sir John Norwich's Regiment of Horse
1643–1644
G.2 Colonel Sir John Norwich's Regiment of Horse
1643–1647
(Illustrations by Dr Lesley Prince ©
Helion & Company)
*See Colour Plate Commentaries for
further information.*

Plate H
H.1 Captain William Packer
Lieutenant General Oliver
Cromwell's Regiment of Horse
1644–1645
H.2 Captain Robert Sparrow
Lieutenant General Oliver
Cromwell's Regiment of Horse
1644 (–1646?)
(Illustrations by Dr Lesley Prince ©
Helion & Company)
See Colour Plate Commentaries for
further information.

No doubt the casualties among the regiments that fled must have been higher than those that stood their ground, since fleeing soldiers were easy prey to the pursuing cavalry, but unfortunately no returns have survived for either armies.

On the Royalist side, James Moore of Letwell in Yorkshire would petition that he served under Newcastle and during the battle 'he received many wounds in his head, especially one by a pistol shot, which bullet doth sit in his neck which is very apparent to be seen, which is both painful and very troublesome to him being very near 80 years of age'. Since it was not until 17 January 1699 that he applied for a pension, it must have been due to old age rather that his wound which he received 55 years previously that prompted him to do so. Nevertheless, he received 40 shillings per year.[109] Also among the dead was Rupert's dog, 'Boy', who had been shot by a Parliamentarian musketeer. As at Newark, the death of 'Boy' was celebrated in the Parliamentarian newspapers, but this time it was no rumour.

In 1859, it was reported in the newspapers that workers laying a drain while digging a pit 12 yards long and eight feet wide, found about 20 to 25 skeletons about four feet deep, 'laid one over the other … the form of many were left in the clay'. Despite it being over 200 years since they were buried, 'the smell at first was intolerable and could be felt at some distance; it was so bad that the men could only work short spells'. As for the skeletons:

> the skulls had preserved their shape but crumbled away when exposed to the air … [the foreman] is reported as saying, "there was a bullet in one skull, which dropped out when the skull fell to pieces; the bones especially the large ones, did not crumble away, but were very brittle when touched with the spade. The teeth were quite perfect, and many of them taken away by the drainers".

Such was the interest in this mass grave that it was reported in the *Hobart Town Daily Mercury* in Australia on 5 April 1859.[110] The site of this grave is not recorded, but the Ordnance Survey map shows a burial site just where White Syke Close is located. As to the teeth, one reporter warned his readers that they would probably be sold to dentists so that they could make them into dentures, 'so that some London beauty or neuralgic Guardsman may sport [them] next season'.[111] The reporter was not warning against this practice since 'Waterloo teeth' were being sold even before 1815, the date of the battle where they get their name, and the practice was still known up to the end of the nineteenth century when cheaper (and more hygienic) forms of dentures were introduced. What he was warning his readers about was that these teeth were over 200 years old.

Ashe records that:

---

109 West Yorkshire History Centre (WYHC): QS1/38/3/6. Petition of James Moore of Letwell in Yorkshire, 1699.
110 *Yorkshire Gazette*, 8 January 1859; *Windsor and Eton Express*, 8 January 1859.
111 *The Leeds Intelligencer*, 19 February 1859, reprinting an article in the *Daily Telegraph*.

That night we kept the field, when the bodies of the dead were stripped. In the morning, there was a mortifying object to behold, when the naked bodies of thousands lay upon the ground, and many not altogether dead. We judge that about three thousand of the enemies were slain; but the countrymen (who were commanded to bury the corpses) tell us they have buried four thousand one hundred and fifty bodies.[112]

Most sources agree that all of the Royalists' artillery of 20 guns were captured and Captain William Stewart of the Scottish army had the honour of bringing the 100 captured standards and colours to London. Although a Parliamentarian newspaper describes just 21 cavalry cornets, most of which were probably captured by Cromwell and Leslie's cavalry and 'some torn ensigns'. These included Rupert's own standard which was said to have born 'the Arms of the Palatine, near five Yards long and broad, with a Red Cross in the middle'.[113]

According to *A Full Relation of the Victory*: 'There are likewise sent by him [Stewart] all the cornets and colours which could be got from the Soldiers, who esteem it a great glory to divide them in pieces and wear them, and before Proclamation was made for delivery of them had disposed of the most part of them'.[114]

An account book for the Eastern Association records that a Mr Zinzan paid £3 15s to soldiers for the colours they had captured. In addition 'Lieutenant Colonel Rich, his man' was paid £2 for two cornets that were captured during the battle.[115]

On 7 July the Scottish army held a thanksgiving for the victory and on 13 July the Commissioners of the General Assembly in Scotland sent out a letter to all parishes requiring them to also hold a thanksgiving on the next Sabbath, and the 'Sabbath thereafter'.[116] It was not just in Scotland that these services were held: Kingston upon Hull also held a service and no doubt other towns in England besides.[117]

Only three regiments had been left to garrison York, who watched as their fellow soldiers streamed back towards the city after the battle. According to Slingsby, these fugitives 'made a great confusion; for at the Barr none was suffered to come in but such as were of the town, so that the whole street was thronged up to the Barr with wounded and lame people, which made a pitiful cry among them'.[118] However, either the governor of the city relented or the guards were overwhelmed by the fleeing mass, because the following

---

112 BL: TT E 2/1.

113 BL: TT E54/19.

114 Ibid.

115 Alan Everitt, *Suffolk and the Great Rebellion, 1640–1660* (Suffolk Record Society, 1960), p.92; SP: 28/24 part III f.337; SP: 28/152 f.8.

116 Anon, *Extracts from the Presbytery Book of Strathbogie 1631 to 1654* (Aberdeen: Spalding Club, 1893), p.59; William Stevenson, *The Presbytrie Book of Kirkcaldie* (Kirkcaldy: James Burt, 1900), p.272.

117 *A Sermon preached at Kingston upon Hull upon the day of Thanksgiving after the battle and that marvellous victory at Hessem Moore, near York* (London: Grays Inn, 1644).

118 Slingsby, *Diary*, p.114.

day Prince Rupert with the remains of his army marched out of Monk Barr heading north, while Newcastle and some of his senior officers went to Scarborough, from where they sailed for Hamburg leaving the remnants of his army behind. 'Thus we were left at York', recalls Sir Henry Slingsby, 'out of all hope of relief, the town much distracted, and everyone ready to abandon her … many left us not liking to abide another siege'. To raise morale reports were made saying that Rupert had fallen upon the enemy once more and had routed them, but the truth was soon known when the allied army appeared before the walls of York two days after the battle.[119]

The allies began to repair their siege lines and construct new batteries. Knowing the garrison had been severely weakened, they began making scaling ladders to storm the city. About 12 July, as was traditional before an assault on a town, the besieging commanders sent the governor a last chance to surrender. The governor, Sir Thomas Glenham, replied that he was willing to negotiate the surrender of the city and negotiations began the following day. Finally on the 15 July articles of surrender were drawn up and signed. According to Slingsby, 'we yield[ed] the town and that upon very good conditions'.[120] Simeon Ashe agreed with Slingsby that the Royalists had been given better terms than expected, writing that:

> If any upon the perusal of those articles, do imagine that too much favour was granted to the enemy, we desire that this may be considered for their satisfaction. That the benefit which could be expected for our armies, or the kingdom, by taking the town by storm, could not possibly in any measure counter-veil the miserable consequences thereof, to many thousands. Who knows how much precious blood might have been split upon so hot a service? How few in the town could have preserved their houses and shops from spoil, if more than 20,000 soldiers had broken in upon them with heat and violence? How many of our good friends in other places who drive trades with citizens here, would have been pinched in their estates, by the impoverishing of their debtors?[121]

Glenham had not only surrendered the city, but also the north to the Royalist cause. Despite losing their commander, Newcastle's cavalry would still play a major part in the war effort, but his infantry had been decimated on the field of Marston Moor, and with the loss of the north and its vast recruiting areas it was impossible to bring these regiments up to strength again, and Fairfax's Northern Association was able to mop up the remaining Royalist garrisons.

Among the prisoners that were released were 28 soldiers of Russell's regiment, nine from Captain Sands, and 12 from Major Knight's company and 16 soldiers from Colonel Pickering's regiment and 13 soldiers of an unidentified company.[122] Also on 15 July Pickering's regiment held a muster covering the period 11 June to that day and 59 were found to be sick or wounded. On 18 September they received £69 2s 8d for their maintenance.

---

119 Ibid., pp.114–115.
120 Ibid., p.116.
121 BL: TT E 2/1.
122 TNA: SP 28/17 f.155.

Pickering's own company mustered just 36 soldiers, plus five sick and wounded, plus 11 are described as 'dead and runaway'. Captain Cromwell's Company mustered just 22 men, with six dead.[123] This is unusual because only those with the colours and the sick or wounded are usually mentioned, those who had been killed or runaway were usually not recorded, so a regiment or company may appear on paper to have suffered heavy casualties, but in fact many may have just deserted.

The following day Ashe watched as the Royalists marched out of York with the honours of war:

> Upon Tuesday the enemy went out of the town, according to Articles, our soldiers were set on both sides [of] the way, where they were to pass for the space of a mile from Micklegate; and the officers according command, went from place to place, to prevent the doing of any wrong to the enemies, as they marched away … The fourth part of them, at least, were who marched out of the town were women, many very poor in their apparel, and others in better fashion. Most of the men had filled, and distempered themselves with drink; the number of the soldiers, as we conjectured, was not above a thousand, besides the sick and wounded.[124]

Under the articles of surrender the Royalists were to have safe passage to Skipton Castle or another Royalist garrison, and detachments from each of the allied army appear to have taken it in turns to guard the Royalists on their journey. This article was observed until they came to the soldiers of the Eastern Association, when according to Ashe:

> In their march through the horse quarters of my Lord of Manchester, the day after they went from York, some of the troopers remembering how they had been pillaged at Newark of all they had, contrary to the agreement, fell upon their carts and wagons, and pillaged them very deeply, taking away both clothes, plate and some money, which when some of our officers had notice of, they presently rode from their quarters and restrained them.

Ashe excused this violation as follows:

> This miscarriage which casts dishonour upon us, and hath been as occasion of much grief to my noble Lord, and to many others, was occasioned through negligence of the officers, who were appointed to publish the agreement through the army, that the enemy's goods should be protected from violence, but had not done it. And one reason of that omission may be in regard of the shortness of time from the sealing of the articles by the generals, and the marching out of the enemy; the one being on Monday noon, and the other to be eleven a clock the next day, and our horse quarters lying dispersedly many miles distant. Upon examination of the business, the troopers do all plead ignorance of the agreement, which (if true) may in some measure lessen the offence. These things coming the next day after to the knowledge of the generals, there were all filled with

---

123 TNA: SP 28/25 ff.3, 60.
124 BL: TT E 2/1.

indignation against such unworthy carriages, abominating and being ashamed of [the] breach of faith (even with the enemies) though formerly and false and unfaithful in their covenants. Hereunto my Lord (whose soul abhorred the thoughts of this wickedness, being contrary to his profession and disposition), sent commands to Lieutenant General Cromwell, and some other officers of horse, presently to sit and make diligent enquires who were the actors and confederates in so horrid a crime, to the end that not only restitution might be made of the goods so plundered, but also that the offenders might be punished according to their deserts. These gentlemen sat divers days in the pursuance of his Lordship's commands; and upon examination they found divers troopers deeply guilty, some whereof they committed to the Provost Marshal, others (upon their captain's engagements for their forthcoming) enjoyed liberty for the present; they causing to be delivered in to them all the goods they had so taken. A perfect return of which proceedings being made to my Lord, his Honour resolved for better finding out of the rest of the goods unjustly taken and that full restitution of them (if possible) might be made.[125]

This declaration read as follows:

Being informed that divers soldiers and troopers under my command, did plunder divers wagons and carriages belonging to the enemy, when they came out of York, and were by the generals articled with, to have safe conduct for their persons, arms, and baggage: And forasmuch as Endeavours having been used to discover in whose hands the goods so plundered are, the success is without any considerable effect hitherto: I do hereby declare, that if any person who hath had a hand in this Action, so much to be abhorred by all honest Men, (being a breach of faith, which being once given, ought by all professing, Christianity inviolably to be observed) and shall, out of a true remorse for their offence, within two days after publication hereof, bring into the hands of the several captains respectively of his or their said troops respectively, to which he or they belong, all such money, plate, horse, arms, or other goods so taken, as aforesaid; they shall be freed from Punishment for such his or their offence. But if any trooper or other soldier, shall, through obstinacy, wickedly again any of the things before mentioned, beyond the time hereby limited for them to be brought in; or shall not at least acquaint his captain, lieutenant, or other officer with his resolution so to do, in case the said goods be not now in his or their hands, and by reason thereof cannot be restored within the time appointed; the said person or persons so offending, shall expect no favour or mercy at all, but the uttermost Severity, being death by the Articles of War, published by his Excellency the Earl of Essex in that behalf. Given under my Hand, 25 July, 1644. Manchester.[126]

Manchester's own regiment of horse seems to have been responsible for this violation and when the court martial was held at Doncaster, sixteen officers made up the judging panel including Crawford, Vermuyden and Pickering, but as the senior officer present Cromwell was appointed president. Some

---

125 BL: TT E 2/1.
126 Ibid.

troopers claimed that they did not know about the agreement, while others said that they had been encouraged to plunder some of the wagons by the Royalists themselves who pointed out to them which ones belonged to Catholic soldiers. Moreover, since some of the Scottish soldiers had found some weapons hidden in these wagons they claimed this had violated the terms of surrender.[127] Unfortunately, the minutes of the meeting do not survive so we have no way of knowing if any of the soldiers were found guilty, and if they were what punishment they received, although according to the Laws of War, this should have been death. Certainly they appear to have received some sort of punishment because a lieutenant who was 'highly guilty of the robbery with all the rest … having the name of a Godly man, being an Independent, was set at liberty by Cromwell, which highly incensed our enemies for our falsehood against them'.[128]

With York having surrendered, there was no longer a need for the three armies to remain together. A large detachment of Fairfax's army would form the garrison of York, while 1,000 horse would rendezvous with the Parliamentarian forces of Lancashire, Cheshire and Derbyshire to observe Rupert's movements and the Scottish army would march north to besiege Newcastle-upon-Tyne. The Earl of Manchester was to march back into the counties of the Eastern Association to recruit his army, leaving Major General Crawford to reduce various local garrisons.

---

127 BL: TT E 4/6, *A Continuation of True Intelligence from the armies in the North, from 10 day to the 27 of this instant* (London: Thomas Underhill, 1644). There were also four lieutenant colonels, 6 majors and a captain, plus Mr John Weaver advocate.
128 Bruce and Masson, *Quarrel*, pp.60–61.

6

Crawford's Campaign

After the capture of York, Manchester's army marched south and on Saturday 20 July his infantry quartered at Tadcaster, where they rested the following day. On Monday they marched to Ferrybridge, deciding not to besiege the Royalist garrison at Pontefract Castle, and continued their march to Doncaster, where they arrived on 23 July and remained until 1 August. However, during this time they were not idle: on 23 July Lieutenant Colonel John Lilburne with his regiment of dragoons was sent to capture Tickhill Castle, whose garrison was a 'great oppression and injury to the country thereabouts, both by laying heavy burdens and taxes upon them'. The dragoons appear to have surprised some of the Royalists in the town who were captured. Despite being well fortified and garrisoned by 80 musketeers and a troop of horse, it does not appear to have put up much resistance and surrendered the following day. On 26 July the garrison marched out without their arms and returned to their homes 'unplundered and not molested'. Only the governor and his officers were allowed to ride out with their arms and Manchester even gave the officers horses for their baggage, and those who had brought their wives with them were given a horse for them.[1]

Edward Montagu, Earl of Manchester (Public Domain)

---

1   Rushworth, *Historical Recollections*.

On 27 July Manchester wrote to the Committee of Both Kingdoms, 'the place is of consequence, lying so as to hinder all commerce betwixt Derbyshire and these parts. I have sent to inform Lord Fairfax so that he may dispose of the place as he pleases'.[2] Certainly the garrison had intercepted many convoys of cloth travelling from 'Leeds, Halifax and other parts of the north to Hull, Lincoln, Boston and other southward parts'.[3] However, Cromwell would later claim that Manchester 'was very unwilling to the summoning of Tickhill Castle, and expressed much anger and threats against him that (being sent to quarter in the town) did summon it, though upon the bare summons it was surrendered'.[4]

On 1 August Manchester resolved to return to the counties of the Eastern Association, but first 'I was further moved by the Committee and gentlemen of Nottingham for the reducing of the garrison in Welbeck to the obedience of the Parliament, because it was a great annoyance to those parts'.[5] Welbeck House was part of the Marquis of Newcastle's estate, and the following day as was customary he demanded the garrison to surrender. Fortunately they accepted since 'I was not in a condition to besiege a place so well fortified as that was'. Unlike at Tickhill Castle the garrison was permitted to march out with the honours of war, 'but when I came to take possession of the house', Manchester records, 'most of the soldiers came to me to lay down their arms, desiring tickets of me to return to their own homes, the which I granted them'.[6]

After this success Manchester continued his march south with a large part of his army, leaving Crawford to take Sheffield Castle. Crawford's force consisted of his own regiment along with those Colonels Pickering and Montagu's regiments of foot, which mustered about 1,200 men, plus Manchester's own regiment of horse and a detachment of dragoons. His artillery consisted of 'three of our biggest guns', but travelling 'through very rocky and almost inaccessible country' Crawford was forced to press ahead without them.[7] His force quartered that night at Rotherham, where his artillery and baggage train managed to join him at about midnight. To assist him in the siege Lord Fairfax sent his own regiment of horse, 300 foot and some pieces of artillery under the command of Colonel John Bright.

That day Crawford, accompanied by Bright, went to view Sheffield Castle. An anonymous pamphlet records that the castle was:

> very considerable in strength, both for natural situation, being in a triangle with
> two rivers, the water deep in the west and east sides of the castle, flanked on all
> sides, a strong fort before the gate pallisadoed, a trench 12 foot deep and 18 broad

---

2   CSPD 1644, p.380.
3   Rushworth, *Historical Recollections*.
4   Bruce and Masson, p.80.
5   CSPD 1644, p.404.
6   CSPD 1644, p.404.
7   BL: TT E 6/17, *A Continuation of the True Intelligence*, no. 7 (London: Thomas Underhill, 1644); Anon., *A Journal or true and exact relation of each days passage, of that party of the Right Honourable the Earl of Manchester's Army, under the command of the ever honoured Major General Crawford from the 1st August to the end of the same month* (London: Hugh Perry, 1644).

about the fort, and the other parts of the castle, and a breastwork pallisadoed within the trench, betwixt it and the castle.[8]

William Good, Manchester's chaplain, who accompanied Crawford, adds that the walls of the castle had 'a troop of horse and 200 foot, strongly fortified with a broad and deep trench of 18 foot deep, and water in it, a strong breast work pallisadoed, a wall round of two yards thick, eight pieces of iron ordnance and two mortar pieces'.[9]

After surveying the castle's defences Crawford rejoined his forces that night at Rotherham and sent a message to Manchester asking for advice. The messenger returned the following morning with a despatch leaving it up to Crawford what he should do next, although he should not 'endanger' his men. Upon this advice Crawford held a council of war, which decided that they should try and take the castle. According to the anonymous pamphlet a Culverin was placed in the park, which 'did discharge three great shot with great dexterity into the castle, one whereof shot through the governor's chamber'. During the day Crawford had sent a trumpeter to the castle to demand its surrender in the name of 'King and Parliament', but he was shot at three times, which was against the laws of war. According to John Vicars' *Burning Bush Not Consumed*, two of these shots 'came very near and hardly missed him: and they flourishing their swords cried out, "they would have no other parley". Whereupon ours advanced into the town.'[10]

The Parliamentarians occupied the upper park closer to the castle and entered the upper end of the town. Despite the castle being held for the King, the townsfolk appear to have supported Parliament, so that when the soldiers entered Sheffield:

> the townsmen with great joy drew down the ordnance to the market place …
> [and] all this night all degrees and sexes with all cheerfulness cut sods [of earth],
> and brought them to make the battery across the street within forty yards of
> the castle, where the careful and vigilant major general was himself working,
> encouraging others with his presence, cheerful words and example, the battery
> was well nigh perfected this night.[11]

William Good mentions that the day after their arrival, 'we raised two batteries within 60 yards of the enemy's outworks, whereon our ordnance fell to play, and did much execution on the walls as pieces of their bigness could do, the greatest being but a Demi Culverin'.[12] After firing for 24 hours it was decided to send Colonel Bright to York to obtain some additional artillery pieces from Lord Fairfax. However, according to the anonymous account, Bright was sent to Fairfax before Crawford decided to besiege the castle, but

---

8   Anon., *A Journal or True and Exact Relation.*

9   BL: TT E 6/17.

10   When writing the *Burning Bush Not Consumed*, John Vicars appears to have plagiarised William
     Good's account of this part of the campaign.

11   Anon., *A Journal or True and Exact Relation.*

12   BL: TT E 6/17.

the Parliamentarians did not have it all their own day that day (3 August) because Crawford's master gunner and a captain of pioneers were mortally wounded while surveying the best place to erect the battery. The Royalist musketeers were probably armed with fowling pieces or rifles and must have been somewhere in the town since they were hidden from view of the castle itself. Crawford, who was with them, escaped unhurt.

Crawford also 'by threats, promises and money' summoned some miners to undermine the castle but this was found to be impracticable since it was built on rock, and he also wrote to Manchester for more supplies of ammunition. While he was waiting for these supplies, Crawford also went to the surrounding iron mills and persuaded them to cast iron shot for the artillery pieces. That night the besiegers tried to break a sluice to let the water out of the ditch on the east side of the castle by an orchard, but without success. However, they did succeed in erecting another battery and platform that flanked the drawbridge of the castle, in an attempt to destroy it and prevent any reinforcements or supplies reaching the garrison.

Fearing that Manchester might order Crawford to abandon the siege, the inhabitants of Sheffield sent a petition to him stating that if he did so 'their consciences would be overburdened, their estates plundered and themselves [would] become subject to all slavery and misery, or otherwise they would be necessitated to follow the army'.[13] The townsfolks' fears were eased when Manchester replied to them that he had no intention of abandoning the siege.

On 7 August the besiegers received the supplies of ammunition from the Earl of Manchester and the local iron works and their morale was raised by the arrival of Colonel Bright with 800 horse and foot with two large pieces of artillery. According to the anonymous newspaper one of these was a demi-cannon which fired a 32 lb ball, although William Good refers to it as a 'whole Culverin', which fired a 19 lb ball. The second piece, known as the 'Queen's Pocket Pistol' and which had been captured the year before at Hull. These guns arrived at the siege on either the 8 or 9 August, depending on the source, and during the evening these two pieces were formed into a battery with a demi-culverin that Crawford already had. These opened fire early the next morning, 'which did very great execution on one side of the house, brought the strong walls down into their trenches and made a perfect breach'.[14] While this battery was firing at the breach, a battery of sakers bombarded the castle's battlements, but the garrison did not remain silent, since they shot some 'great grenadoes' into the town and churchyard, 'which did no execution'. Although, two gunners had their fingers shot off by members of the garrison using fowling pieces which were fired through the portholes of the battery's platform.

During the siege the besiegers had been preparing scaling ladders and made faggots to be thrown into the ditch to block it up for the storming party, but since the ditch was reported to be 12 foot deep and 18 foot wide the soldiers would have to have made quite a few. Nevertheless, Crawford held a council of war, which resolved to send a final summons to the governor,

---

13   Anon., *A Journal or True and Exact Relation*.
14   BL: TT E 6/17.

Major Thomas Beaumont, before the Parliamentarians attempted to storm the castle. This time the governor was more accommodating and agreed to a parley. Colonel Pickering, Lieutenant Colonel Grimes of Montagu's regiment and Major Hamilton of Crawford's regiment where commissioners for the Parliament's side and Captain Heinsworth, Mr Samuel Saville and a Mr Robson, acted on behalf of the governor, but the parley dragged on until 6:00 p.m. when the meeting broke up so that the Royalist commissioners could advise the governor on how the negotiations were going.

When the commissioners did not return after the appointed period of time, six more shots were fired into the castle which brought about the desired effect, and it was agreed that the garrison would march out of the castle at 3:00 p.m. the following day, 11 August. Only the officers were to keep their arms, drums and colours and the garrison along with their wives and children were to march to Pontefract Castle. A special clause was granted to Lady Savile and her family, whose husband had been killed earlier that year and she was heavily pregnant, which allowed her to keep her coach and horses and was given an escort to the destination of her choice, so she chose Woodhouse.

According to Montagu's journal, 468 great shot had been made against the castle between 1 and 10 August. For the most part the garrison laid down their arms, apart from about 30 who were to be escorted to Pontefract by Captain Gothericke, a captain of horse of Lord Fairfax's army. However, when they did appear they were so 'drunk, that they were not apprehensive of [any] danger, nor capable of anything but evil and raising speeches, whereof they were very lavish, which lost some stragglers their clothes, who went not with the convoy'.[15] The besiegers found a large quantity of food in the castle which they sold to the local population for £250, and the majority of the ammunition they probably left for Colonel John Bright who became the castle's governor while the men he had brought with him formed the garrison.

Once Crawford had settled his affairs at Sheffield, he set his sights on Bolsover Castle, but on his journey he decided to face Colonel John Fretchville's house. Fretchville was serving with the Parliamentarian army under Sir John Gell, the commander of the local Parliamentarian force, when his house was occupied by the Royalists. On 12 August Crawford summoned the garrison to surrender, which it did without resistance. The strength of the garrison is not recorded, but within the house there were found 11 iron guns, which included a demi-culverin, 300 arms and a 'considerable quantity of powder'. Before his force left the house Crawford had its fortifications slighted.

Two days later Crawford's force arrived at Bolsover Castle and he immediately ordered a battery to be erected close to a fort in front of the castle gate, and another battery was set up on the Sheffield side of the castle. It was while these fortifications were being erected that a drummer from the castle arrived requesting a parley. After a little debate according to the

---

15   Anon., *A Journal or True and Exact Relation.*

anonymous pamphlet an 'old gentleman' appeared with a letter for a Colonel Barmundin, the local Parliamentary commander, who he presumed to be the commander of this force. When he discovered his error, the old gentleman returned to the castle to discuss the situation with Major Edward Muschamp, the governor of the castle. He agreed to surrender the castle if the garrison could march out with the honours of war, that is, colours flying, drums beating and the officers and soldiers carrying their arms and be conducted to Newark. Although technically the garrison did not deserve this honour since it put up no resistance, Crawford agreed. The garrison marched out of Bolsover at 3:00 p.m. on 15 August, but using the excuse that he had broken the terms of surrender by straying from the convoy, the soldiers plundered Muschamp of his belongings and so Pickering gave him a horse and arms as fitting his status as an officer. When the Parliamentarians entered the castle they found plenty of arms and ammunition, but the garrison had stored little to no provisions for a siege. Crawford left Captain Christopher Mercer with his company of dragoons and the artillery pieces he had captured at Colonel Fretchville's house to garrison the castle.

The same day that Bolsover Castle surrendered, Manchester, who was then at Lincoln, wrote to Crawford congratulating him on the taking of Sheffield Castle for so little loss of life and promising him £100 for the upkeep of his regiment of foot and £50 each for Montagu's and Pickering's regiments, plus an additional £60 for shoes and stockings for these regiments.[16]

After settling affairs at Bolsover Castle on Saturday 17 August Crawford set out for Wingfield Manor in Derbyshire, which was situated on top of a hill with three very steep sides and the other fortified with a breastwork and a deep ditch. Crawford arrived during the evening of the following day, where he found Sir John Gell besieging the house with about 500 foot and 600 horse. Unlike Bolsover Castle, Wingfield was prepared for a long siege and the 'men full of resolution' and 'resolved to die rather then to surrender it to Sir John Gell'. Nevertheless that evening after a sermon, Crawford ordered a battery to be erected within 80 yards of the house, which was finished the following night. Crawford ordered that his artillery should be drawn up with Gell's 'brass and iron Culverins', which opened fire on the morning of 20 August. All day the Parliamentarian artillery pounded Wingfield until a breach was made in the walls. As was customary, Crawford sent a summons for the house to surrender, and despite their previous boast that they were prepared to die, agreed to negotiate and hostages were exchanged. The Royalist hostage, Major Eyre, wanted to send a message to Sheffield and Bolsover castles for advice, and when he was informed of their surrender, Eyre did not believe it. Therefore Eyre was returned to the house and with the truce over the Parliamentarian artillery once more opened fire. Once again the governor, Colonel Roger Molyneux, beat a parley 'which for the noise of the ordnance was not heard for a long time'. Negotiations began once more and this time the articles of surrender were agreed and that the manor would be surrendered at 12:00 p.m. on 21 August. The terms were similar to those of the other strongholds that Crawford had already captured, but this time the garrison were to march to Lichfield, without arms, and were to be protected from 'plundering, pillaging or any let or molestation whatsoever'. When they entered the manor the Parliamentarians found 500 arms, four barrels of powder, eight pieces of ordnance and a good quantity of provisions.

News of the surrender of Wingfield Manor reached the Earl of Manchester that day since on 21 August he wrote to the Committee of Both Kingdoms: 'I received to-day news of the surrender of Wingfield Manor upon composition, so as I hope I shall now have my forces together to refresh and recruit themselves, and be ready for any further service you shall command.'[17]

After this success Crawford's force was ordered to rejoin Manchester and on 2 or 3 September the journal of Montagu's regiment recalls 'We met with our army and train of artillery again and then we advanced to Ashby and the headquarters [were] at Digby.'[18]

The anonymous pamphlet boasted that Crawford had lost fewer than six men during this campaign, and 'some' were sick. However, the regimental returns do not confirm this, in July Crawford's regiment had mustered 608 soldiers, but in September this had fallen to 396; likewise Pickering's mustered 524 and 362 men respectively and Montagu's 418 to 307 men, or a loss of 485 men.[19] Of course not all were deaths through violence, others were from sickness and desertion. One of these sick soldiers was George Hancock, who a member of Captain Dennis Taylor's company in Montagu's regiment. Despite being described as the company's clerk he had been at the storming of Lincoln and had scaled the walls of the manor yard at York, before being present at Marston Moor. He had taken part in all the actions of Crawford's campaign, but:

> Ever since August your supplicant has been carried upon a cart after the army, until such time as he was so weak that he and another sick soldier, one Robert Fawcett, were brought from Baldock upon a cart to Cambridge, where now he lies both sick and lame, not having the wherewithal to relieve himself.

His pay was 18 weeks in arrears, being 10s. 6d and so he was ordered to be paid 20 shillings.[20]

The success of this campaign disproves one of the charges levelled against Cromwell and 'his junta', in that they absolutely refused or obey orders from Major General Crawford, especially Colonel Pickering's and Montagu's regiments.[21]

---

17 CSPD 1644, p.444.
18 BodLib: Carte MS 74, ff.159–160. Journal of Colonel Edward Montagu's regiment of foot. The person who wrote this journal claims that Crawford arrived at Wingfield Manor on 21 August and that it surrendered on 22, rather than 20 and 21 respectively.
19 Holmes, *Eastern Association*, p.238.
20 TNA: SP 16/503/6.
21 Bruce and Masson, p.61.

7

Manchester's Campaign

While Manchester's army was besieging York, other elements of the Eastern Association were besieging Greenland House near Henley-on-Thames. The house was owned by Sir John D'Oyley and overlooked the Thames, so a garrison could cut the traffic between Reading and London. At the end of May the Earl of Essex had reconnoitred the house, but his army, along with Sir William Waller's were pursing the King's Oxford army, so it was left to the local forces to besiege it. The precise composition of this force is unknown, but included Colonel John Venn's regiment of foot from Windsor Castle and on 5 June the Hertfordshire regiment was ordered to join the forces at Greenland House, but by the beginning of July the regiment was eager to return home, so on the 3 July the Committee of Both Kingdoms wrote to the Committee of Hertfordshire 'The service your forces are now engaged in at the siege of Greenland House we conceive to be of so great importance that it cannot without very great prejudice be deserted. We therefore desire that they may be continued there till we can replace them by others'.[1] The Hertfordshire forces included Colonel Mitchell's regiment and the three regiments of the Essex trained bands were also embroiled to take part in the siege.

On 5 July Major General Sir Richard Browne, who had been commissioned to command the forces of Oxfordshire, Berkshire and Buckinghamshire, wrote that it was also his intention to march to the siege of Greenland House, but it was only on 11 July that Browne finally arrived at the house, since the Committee of Both Kingdoms had ordered him to take Boarstall House first, only to change their minds a few days later. Despite Browne describing it as being 'strongly fortified', he hoped it would not be a long siege and 'firing a few shots with our gun ... did good execution'.[2] Despite referring to his artillery in the singular, he seems to have had more than one gun at his disposal since on 14 June, Venn had been ordered to send three sakers and four drakes to the siege.[3] On the evening of 11 July the garrison sounded a parley and agreed to surrender, since according to Hyde, 'the whole structure being beaten

---

1   CSPD 1644, p.304.
2   Ibid., p.341.
3   *Journal of the House of Commons*, vol. 3, pp.529–530.

down by the cannon'.[4] However, he must have been exaggerating since the Committee of Both Kingdoms had wanted Browne to garrison the house, but the letter does not appear to have arrived because on 15 July he wrote: 'not having received any commands from you to the contrary, I thought fit, according to the desire of the country, to slight the works and fortifications of Greenland House'.[5]

The surrender of Greenland House was a mixed blessing for Browne, because he added:

> The Committee of St. Albans send me word that they can no longer pay their regiments and desire they may be sent home, [or] at least one regiment, and bid me to take care for the payment of the other. Since the taking of Greenland House, I understand the Hertfordshire, and Essex men will not stay any longer with me. I desire your advice what to do in the premises, however, [there shall be] no want of my endeavours to stay them.[6]

With the surrender of the house, on 10 July Sir Thomas Honeywood, who appears to have been the overall commander of the Essex Trained Bands, wrote to the Committee of Both Kingdoms for permission to return home. Unfortunately, this letter does not appear to have survived, but on 12 July the Committee replied:

> we understand your desire to return with your forces into your county. We know that your soldiers belonging to the trained bands cannot, without great inconvenience, be long absent from their employments, especially at harvest time. As they were not drawn forth without a pressing necessity, so we desire not to continue them longer under those difficulties which they are unaccustomed to than there is need. We take their willing rising as a very good service to the public, besides their own safety assured thereby against an enemy who was resolved to have fallen into the bowels of the Association had not your readiness to meet him abroad prevented it. We thank you for your good service in this expedition, and think fit that your trained bands may now go home into their countries.[7]

On the same day, the Committee also wrote to Browne of their decision and excusing them since 'the men are mostly of that quality and course of life as cannot well bear the difficulties of a soldier's life'.[8]

On 22 July 1644, while besieging York, Manchester wrote that:

> I am upon my march, and hope to be at Doncaster to-morrow night, where I intend to stay till I shall receive your commands. My men through want of clothes and other necessaries fall sick daily. I hope the Lord will preserve us from

---

4   Clarendon, p.411.
5   CSPD 1644, p.350.
6   Ibid., p.341.
7   Ibid., p.346. Unfortunately, Honeywood's letter of the 10 July does not appear to have survived.
8   Ibid.

any pestilential disease, yet the Scotch Army and mine is very much weakened through sickness'.[9]

Four months later he would again report that his infantry were 'so weakened and wasted that I may truly say they are not sufficient ... to guard the train of artillery here with me'. The regiments were said to be suffering from a 'fever and flux'.[10]

As early as the 5 July Parliament had published an ordinance calling upon 'all men well affected ... [between] the age of 16 to 60 (being of ability of body)' to enlist because of 'these times of imminent danger ... from the invasion and fury of the Irish rebels, Popish and ill affected persons'. Those who had £100 or more in lands and goods were to give up their 'horses and mares above four years of age'.[11] The members of the trained bands were exempt from being conscripted and so enlistment into the militia was much sought after, but were usually only open to the 'middling sort' of person such as merchants. Even then they could pay a substitute to serve in their place if or when the trained bands were called out. Those who failed to supply either arms or turn up to their appointed rendezvous were to be fined not more than £20.[12]

On 1 August Manchester was at Blyth when he wrote to the Committee of Both Kingdoms demanded the arrears of pay that was due to his army, adding 'I do acknowledge it as a blessing from God, that both the officers and soldiers have never yet refused any marching or duty for want of pay, and I hope they never will'.[13] After successfully capturing Welbeck House, he continued his march south, but on 4 August about 200 or 300 Royalist horse from Newark under Colonel Eyre, bypassed some Parliamentarian outposts and during the night attacked some troops which were quartered at Tuxford in Clay, about 10 miles from Newark. According to Rushworth, Eyre's force killed a lieutenant, a quartermaster and some troopers and took about eight prisoners and some horses.[14] The following day Manchester arrived at Gainsborough, where he quartered his infantry in the surrounding villages before travelling onto Lincoln, from where on 6 August he wrote to the Committee of Both Kingdoms that he hoped to give his army some rest 'after the great hardships they have endured', but complained that despite his numerous letters to the various counties which made up the Association they had done little to raise the recruits demanded of them, which 'puts me into an unserviceable condition'.[15] The same day that he wrote this letter, the Committee of Both Kingdoms fearing that Rupert – who had retreated into

---

9   Ibid., p.366.
10   Holmes, *The Eastern Association*, pp.168–169.
11   *An Ordnance of the Lords and Commons assembled in Parliament for putting the Associated Counties of Suffolk, Norfolk, Essex ... in to a Posture of defence. By the better regulating of the trained bands and raising other forces of Horse and Foot...* (London: Edward Husbands, 5 July 1644).
12   Ibid.
13   CSPD 1644, pp.388–389.
14   Rushworth, *Historical Recollections*.
15   CSPD 1644, pp.404–405.

Cheshire after Marston Moor was recruiting his army once more – wrote to Manchester that they considered the 'necessity of hindering the recruits of Prince Rupert and breaking up his army if it be possible … and attend his movements. You are to follow him which way soever he shall go and secure any advantages that may be offered'. To achieve this end Manchester could call upon the forces of Nottinghamshire, Derbyshire, and Lancashire and all those which made up Sir William Brereton's and Sir Thomas Middleton's armies.[16] Manchester received this letter on 9 August and replied the following day: 'This appeared to me so large a commission and a work so difficult, considering the weak condition of the forces which are here with me, who are now under great indispositions and infections'. Nevertheless, he summoned a council of war and sent the Committee the following conditions why this was impossible:

1. That they could not expect force Prince Rupert to a second engagement and that besieging Chester was 'not a work for a month in the latter end of summer';
2. That the army of the Eastern Association was not strong enough to undertake such a task, because of:

> our present want of ammunition and equipage of all sorts for the train [of artillery] … [and] Our regiments, too, are in great need of recruits, so many being sick and wounded, so that if we should now march we must leave a third part of our forces behind, added to which our arrears of pay are intolerable, and there is no money in the treasury to take with us for better encouragements in the future.

3. That he could not march north again while Belvoir, Newark, Bolsover and Tutbury Castle were still in Royalist hands. If these garrisons were 'taken or blocked up it would gain … Parliament the advantage of raising new forces and maintenance for them out of five or six counties';
4. While he was absent this would give the counties of the Association 'cause to withdraw or slacken their hands from our further recruiting or maintenance, and seek for some other body and head to protect them, and the same only to be maintained by them'.[17]

Cromwell almost certainly attended this council of war, but this did not stop him accusing Manchester being lethargic in his movements by not besieging Newark despite having 'no other employment or impediment to hinder his army … although the forces he had there with him all the while were sufficient for the service'.[18]

The Committees of Lincolnshire and Nottinghamshire also appealed to the Committee of Both Kingdoms for assistance in reducing Newark, who replied on 12 August that they sympathised with their sufferings, but had 'given other orders to the Earl of Manchester which cannot be altered, but they will take it into consideration in due time'.[19] Despite the urgency that

---

16   CSPD 1644, p.406.
17   Ibid., p.417.
18   Bruce and Masson, pp.80–81.
19   CSPD 1644, p.421.

the Committee of Both Kingdoms placed on the situation, Manchester was still at Lincoln on 2 September, but he did despatched a party of horse and dragoons to Cheshire, but they were recalled when he received intelligence that Rupert had now left that county and was heading for Bristol.[20]

True the counties of the Eastern Association had been slow to raise their allocated number of recruits, but at least two infantry regiments were raised that spring. The first was raised in Lincolnshire and was commanded by Colonel Thomas Rainsborough. The exact date of his commission is not known but appears to have been either in April or May. A warrant dated 2 June 1644 was for payment for arms, drums and colours for a total cost of £363 12s. It is clear from this warrant that the regiment had 10 companies, although it was to muster just 600 men. At least two of its company commanders, Lieutenant Colonel Israel Stoughton and Major Nathaniel Bourne, had estates in America and Rainsborough himself had been a captain of a ship before receiving a commission to raise this regiment.[21]

Thomas Rainsborough (Public Domain)

The second regiment was raised in Essex and commanded by Colonel John Sparrow. Despite the commission stating that it should muster 1,000 men, by 7 September it was reported to be just 400 strong and part of the garrison of Abingdon.[22] There appears to have been little discipline within this regiment and even its colonel and Lieutenant Colonel, St John Holcroft, were absent for long periods.[23] Since the officers appeared to care little for their men and the soldiers were unpaid, many deserted, so that at the beginning of October it was even suggested by the Committee of Essex that it should be broken up and used as their quota of recruits for Manchester's army, or placed under a different commander, but this was rejected by the Committee of Both Kingdoms. The situation went unresolved and in January 1645 Browne again suggested that it should be placed under different officers or reduced into another regiment.[24] The lack of pay appears to have been a major cause for desertion, which was not unique to Sparrow's regiment, since Browne also complained about the Hertfordshire regiment: 'It will not be believed how many run away daily, including the Hertfordshire forces, to Aylesbury, where they are constantly paid, and to other places'.[25]

Finally on 1 April it was decided that Sparrow's regiment was to be reduced to a company and placed in Browne's own regiment.[26]

On 7 August the Committee of Both Kingdoms agreed that a further ordinance calling for a further 1,800 foot to be raised for Manchester's army.[27]

---

20 Ibid., p.468.
21 Spring, *The Army of the Eastern Association*, pp.158–160.
22 Ibid., pp.173–175; CSPD 1644, p.528.
23 CSPD 1644–1645, p.180.
24 Ibid., p.233.
25 Ibid.
26 Ibid., p.379.
27 Ibid., pp.410, 412, 414.

Essex was to be exempt since they had already raised Colonel Sparrow's regiment. On 14 August Manchester wrote that:

> I had arranged for the counties out of which these regiments were first raised to supply their defects, as I found this plan to give the best satisfaction to the counties and made the soldiers more united. My own regiment being raised in Essex, I thought to have recruited it from thence. But, as you have otherwise ordered it'.[28]

If this was not enough during the middle of August it was also decided that Manchester should also reinforce the garrison at Abingdon by 1,000 men. Therefore on 15 August the 300 men who formed Colonel Ayloffe's regiment of foot, which had formed part of the garrison of Newport Pagnell, were ordered to march to Aylesbury where they were to rendezvous with 200 foot from Manchester's army and then proceed to Abingdon. The other 500 men were to be newly levied men from Hertfordshire.[29] The three troops of Sir John Norwich's regiment, who 'had been long without employment', were chosen to escort the Hertfordshire recruits, but Norwich disobeyed saying since his regiment belonged to Manchester's army, it was up to Manchester to order him to do so. On 29 August the Committee wrote to Manchester, asking him to order Norwich to escort the Hertfordshire men and 'if he neglects to do so, you are to cashier him and take such course as you shall think fit to secure the horse under his command and their arms for the service of the State'.[30] The outcome of this is not known, but this force seems to have come to nothing because on 21 August Ayloffe was again ordered to march to Abingdon to replace remnants of Waller's army who were quartered there.

Further afield, after defeating Waller at Cropredy Bridge on 29 June, Charles set off in pursuit of the Earl of Essex's army, who had relieved the town of Lyme and recaptured Taunton. Faced with the King's Oxford army and Prince Maurice's western army, Essex was driven back to Lostwithiel. After his defeat Waller had retired to Abingdon, from where during the third week of August he was ordered to advance into the west to assist Essex's army, but he was in no condition to do so. On 27 August when Colonel Ayloffe's regiment, reportedly 600 strong, arrived at Abingdon they found Waller still there so had to quarter at Marcham two miles from the town.[31] Soon Manchester was also ordered into the west, but on 7 September the Committee of Both Kingdoms again wrote to Manchester to speedily 'march that way with all the forces you can according to our former orders'. The following day Manchester acknowledged the receipt of this letter and replied:

> which gives a very sad account of his present condition, of the which I have a very deep sense. The Lord's arm is not shortened though we be much weakened. I trust He will give us a happy recovery. I shall march with all speed according to your former orders, but cannot expect to have any recruits by reason of my sudden

---

28 Ibid.
29 Ibid., p.429-431
30 Ibid., p.461.
31 Ibid., pp.445, 454.

departure from these parts; this will be a great disappointment to me considering the weakness of these forces … I hope you will find that I shall take such care as, by the blessing of God, nothing of the public service shall be retarded.[32]

On 12 September Manchester's horse were reported to be at Luton on their way to Abingdon.

According to Cromwell, Manchester's army arrived at St Albans on 13 September having taken 'four nights or more' from Lincoln. On 14 September Major Gabriel Holmes and Captain George Montgomery of Manchester's regiment of foot wrote to Manchester:

> We are now come to St Albans were Colonel Montagu and Colonel Pickering's Regiment with the train [of artillery] were quartered which greatly did straighten your honour's regiment. But we procured the quarter master general to send Colonel Montagu's Regiment into the adjacent villages whereby our quarters are now indifferently enlarged; yet notwithstanding we find a general indisposition in the inhabitants to accommodate the soldiers with victuals (that last money which was received from the treasurer being already expended and the people for the most part unwilling or unable to to trust although we have engaged ourselves for paying [for] all quarters. We have hereby made bold to represent our condition unto your Lordship and think it very requisite (if it may stand with your honour's pleasure to give order) that our debentary for six weekly pay might be made and issued forth according to our last muster whereof five weeks pay at least are already in the money borrowed from the treasurer [are] exhausted, so that there will be scarce one week's pay forthcoming to the regiment. And then in regard of our late recruits (if your Lordship think fit, we may forthwith muster and be paid as your Lordship shall please.[33]

This letter seems to have prompted a muster where the soldiers appear to have received at least some of their arrears. At this time Manchester's infantry mustered as follows:[34]

Regiment	Number
Manchester's	1,111
Crawford's	396
Pickering's	362
Hobart's	400
Montagu's	307
Russell's	771
Hoogan's (formerly Palgrave's)	633
	3,980

---

32 Ibid., pp.469, 481.
33 PA: Wil/2/51.
34 Holmes, *Eastern Association*, Appendix 8. Manchester's regiment had mustered on 26 August rather than in September.

As with April we do not have a complete list of musters for the cavalry, but of the eight troops whose strength are known they mustered between 43 and 122 troopers, or an average of 3,397 troopers, which unlike the infantry is an increase in their equivalent strength since April.[35] This figure is about the same number that Manchester was reported to have had on 20 September: '2,000 horse and dragoons and 4,000 foot, besides 1,500 horse and dragoons remaining near Oxford for the security of his Association'.[36] Furthermore, the condition of the horses made many unfit for service as Quarter Master General Henry Ireton pointed out to Manchester on 13 September:

> Having at several rendezvous taken special notice of the condition of the horse, I find … that it is in a very miserable state, and as such … it does really indispose and disable them for the service without the some supply of money. Of divers troops the officers soberly and calmly profess they having lent all their own and borrowed all they could find their troops to supply them that have wanted for mere necessaries (as shoeing horses, etc.), they had at present many horses marching back for want of money to shoe them.[37]

Ireton also mentions that he had ordered Cromwell's and Fleetwood's regiments to quarter at Beaconsfield, while Vermuyden's were ordered to quarter at Amersham. The whereabouts of Manchester's own regiment of horse is not recorded; Manchester himself is known to have been at Chelsea at this time.

The army remained around St Albans for a further eight or nine days, since Manchester was torn between obeying the Committee of Both Kingdoms, or his paymasters the Committee of the Eastern Association. The Committee at Cambridge were ordering him to return at once since there were rumours that Sir Thomas Glenham 'with 21 colours of horse and dragoons' might sally out Newark

Henry Ireton (Public Domain)

---

35   Holmes, *Eastern Association*, Appendix 9. The overall figure is based on the average number per troop multiplied by 36 or the number of troops which made up Manchester's regiments at this time. By consulting the warrants that he used, he only records the troopers rather than all the troop, so a further 10 combatants should be added per troop since troops (and companies) always had the correct strength of officers no matter how many troopers there were. Many of the troops were paid their salary on 26 August, rather than in September as Holmes suggests.
36   CSPD 1644, p.521.
37   PA: Wil/2/50.

once more and attacked the counties of the Eastern Association or that he might relieve Banbury.[38] Nevertheless, Manchester arrived at Reading on 29 September, where he found some shoes for his men.[39] That day he again wrote to the Committee of Both Kingdoms:

> I do not think it advisable that I should march further [westward] with so inconsiderable a strength as I have. Since I came hither I have inquired into the strength of Abingdon, which I hear is in such a condition as I much fear it will not be a place for you to rely upon. This town [Reading] is of very great consequence, and it is a great prejudice that the fortifications have been so neglected. I am much troubled to hear of the enemy's overrunning most part of Lincolnshire; it cannot but much distract, and distress those Associated counties … if the King should march into these parts, Abingdon will not be able to resist him, but the garrison will be a prey to him.[40]

Despite almost daily orders for him to march into the west and appraising Manchester of the situation, he would not budge. On 3 October he again wrote to the Committee of Both Kingdoms:

> I have since received other letters from Norfolk remonstrating against their forces being carried so far away from them as they heard was intended. They request me to improve my interest in effecting their desires, otherwise they feared they should be disabled as to further recruits or payments of money. I should fail in my duty both to them and you if I were not to declare this to you.[41]

To appease the Committee he continued:

> As to my marching further westward, which I conceive is to Newbury, that place being appointed for a rendezvous for the Lord General's [Essex] foot and mine, I have ordered two regiments of foot to lie in Newbury, which is more than the town can well accommodate in addition to those forces of Major-General Browne that are there already. The rest of my foot are quartered in this town and the villages hereabouts, and they shall be within a day's march of the rendezvous. I confess I have ordered it in this manner because it gives some satisfaction to the counties which entrust me, and it refreshes the foot for whom I have not as yet money nor clothes which I expect in a few days. As for the horse which you direct me to send to Marlborough they are thus disposed at this present, 4 troops at Basing and 9 near Newbury, so that they may be assistant either to Newbury or Abingdon if there be occasion. The rest of those troops that are with me lie quartered about this town. There are 20 troops of horse and dragoons with Lieutenant General Cromwell about Banbury according to your command … Tomorrow I go to Newbury, but shall be here again by Saturday.[42]

---

38 CSPD 1644, pp.541, 542.
39 Ibid., pp.495, 498, 507.
40 Ibid., p.542.
41 Ibid. (1644–1645), pp.9–10.
42 Ibid.

On 29 September Colonel Jeremy Horton, who was Browne's Adjutant General lay siege to Donnington Castle, near Newbury with elements from Abingdon, Windsor and Reading. He summoned the castle to surrender, the governor Lieutenant Colonel John Boys said 'we do resolve to maintain this place [to] the uttermost of our powers'.[43] Manchester sent Colonel Montagu's and Hobart's regiments of foot to the siege and arrived himself on 4 October. He summoned Donnington Castle to surrender, but Boys sent a similar answer as before. Therefore according to Clarendon 'He resolved to storm the castle the next day. But his soldiers, being well informed of the resolution of those within, declined that hot service'. Therefore, Manchester and Horton had little choice but to bombard the castle, although according to the Royalist newsletter, *Mercurius Aulicus*, Manchester got Captain Vincent Boys, who was an officer in his army to write a letter to his brother, John Boys, to try and persuade him to surrender the castle on 'honourable conditions' and preserve his estate at Bonnington in Kent. John Boys is said to have replied that nothing could 'deter him from his fidelity and loyalty to his sovereign'.[44]

On 9 October Manchester returned to Reading and the day after, Clarendon continues:

> they plied it [the castle] with their artillery until the next night; and then removed their battery to the other side of the castle and began their approaches by saps. Then the governor made a strong sally and beat them out of their trenches, and killed a lieutenant colonel, who commanded in chief, with many soldiers, shot their chief cannoneer through the head, brought away their cannon baskets and many arms, and returned with little loss. Yet the next night they finished their battery, and continued some days their great shot, till they heard of the approach of the king's army, and thereupon they drew off their ordnance.[45]

According to Walter Money in the 19 days of the siege the Parliamentarians fired over 1,000 shots at the castle. On 18 October the siege was raised and Horton and the besieging force returned to Abingdon, while Montagu's and Hobart's regiment proceeded to West Sherbourne.[46]

Meanwhile, Waller, with the remnants of his army, had finally marched into the west to support Essex, having sent a brigade of cavalry under Lieutenant General John Middleton beforehand, but he could not save Essex's army. Essex's outer position on Beacon Hill had been quickly overrun and with Castle Dore about to fall, Essex saw that there was no option but to abandon his army. On 31 August most of Essex's cavalry, under the command of Sir William Balfour, broke out of Lostwithiel and Essex escaped in a fishing boat, leaving his regiments of foot and a regiment of cavalry to their fate. These surrendered the following day being forced to lay down their arms and

---

43   Quoted in Walter Money, *The First and Second Battles of Newbury and the Siege of Donnington Castle During the Civil War* (London: Simkin, Marshal & Co. 1884), p.147.

44   Money, *Donnington Castle*, p.150. Captain Vincent Boys was a captain in Manchester's own regiment of foot.

45   Clarendon, p.239.

46   Money, *Donnington Castle*, p.149; BodLib: Carte, MS 74 f.74.

take up white sticks, an ignoble sign that they had surrendered without the honours of war. Their condition was made even worse by being plundered by the western Royalists and their women. By the time they reached Plymouth, Essex's infantry had been reduced to 2,000 men, just a third of those who had been at Lostwithiel.

On 9 September Essex's 2,000 cavalry joined with Middleton's force, but unfortunately he and Balfour hated each other, which had caused the former to transfer to Waller's army earlier that year, so three days later both forces had separated: Balfour reportedly going to Dorchester, while Middleton went to Sherborne.[47] Waller would later join Middleton but their movements are obscure at this point.

Hearing of these events in the west on 5 or 6 September 1644 Cromwell wrote to Colonel Valentine Walton:

> We do with grief of heart resent the sad condition of our Army in the West, and of affairs there. That business hath our hearts with it, and truly had we wings, we would fly thither. So soon as ever my Lord and the Foot set me loose, there shall be no want in me to hasten what I can to that service … We hope to forget our wants, which are exceeding great, and ill-cared for … [but] we find our men never so cheerful as when there is work to do.[48]

Despite wishing he had 'wings' to fly to Essex's assistance on 6 September he returned to Peterborough in Lincolnshire, and the following day to Huntingdon. On 11 September he went to London, where on 12 September he was congratulated by the Commons for his part in the battle of Marston Moor. He left London on 17 September for Banbury, where since the beginning of August the Parliamentarian forces from Northamptonshire and Warwickshire, along with 1,000 foot, a troop of horse and a company of dragoons from Abingdon had been besieging the castle. The town had quickly fallen, but by 3 September the Committee of Both Kingdoms believed 'there is little likelihood of carrying Banbury Castle, and having intelligence that Prince Rupert's forces are about Worcester, we have given orders for removing the siege'. However the Committee left it to the local commanders whether they wanted to abandon the siege or not. Colonels John Fiennes and Nathaniel Whetham decided to continue and on 26 September Cromwell arrived at the siege with his regiment of horse and three troops of dragoons.

On 7 October he was ordered to join Manchester at Reading, but he seems to have ignored this because on 11 October he was again ordered 'immediately to give order to the horse of your regiment that are left behind at or about Banbury that they march up with all expedition to the rest of your horse … according to [our] former directions.'[49] This time he seems to

47 BL: TT E 256/2, *Perfect Occurances of Parliament, 6–13 September 1644* (London, September 1644): Andrew Coe, September (1644); TT E 256/3, *A Perfect Diurnal of some passages in Parliament and other parts of this Kingdom, 9–16 September 1644* (London: Samuel Peck, September 1644); CSPD 1644, pp.495–496, Sir William Waller and Sir Arthur Heselrige to the Committee of Both Kingdoms, 12 September 1644.

48 Carlyle, p.180.

49 CSPD 1644–1645, pp.32–33.

have obeyed and joined Manchester on 14 October. The siege appears to have been raised shortly afterwards.

The same day Waller and Sir Arthur Haselrigg wrote from their quarters at Winterbourne Stoke in Wiltshire: 'This day there have come to us ten troops of the Earl of Manchester's horse and two of dragoons'.[50] On 15 October despite this reinforcement Waller was still not strong enough to take on the combined Oxford and western armies and so fell back to Andover, arriving that evening. He was still there on 18 October, when the Royalists 'beat up his quarters' and forced him to abandon the town.

Hearing that the Royalist army were marching eastward, on 14 October Manchester was finally ready to leave Reading and wrote:

> I intend to be about Basingstoke on Wednesday, the foot lying between Newbury and Basingstoke, where I expect to meet with the Lord General. Lieutenant General Cromwell arrived here this night, but his troops are yet at Henley. I have given order that they shall march forward tomorrow, according to your directions. I heard today from Waller, who remains still in his same quarters, and the King remains at Blandford. I hear that Prince Rupert is bringing up the remainder of his forces from Bristol to join the King.[51]

By his dallying at Reading, it allowed the infantry and cavalry of Essex's army and those of Waller to retire on him rather than heading off into the west as he had been originally ordered. On 20 October Waller was able to rendezvous with Manchester's army. A brigade of London trained bands and Essex's cavalry were also close by. Manchester had arrived three days beforehand and his movement had been observed by the nearby Royalist garrison of Basing House:

> Past noon from off our tower, we see the van of Manchester's Army marching to Basingstoke and Sherfield; next day some of his horse visit the leaguer, and by our marksmen two of them are shot, the following day eight regiments of foot and some horse with all their carriage and artillery, drawn on the south of Basingstoke facing the house, make halt; some hours and towards night return into the town, most of their horse which all the day had stood at two miles distance near Rooks' Down, at night with haste enough troop to their quarters towards Farnham.[52]

The siege diary is incorrect: rather than marching to Farnham, which was Waller's headquarters, the combined Parliamentarian armies moved towards Newbury along with the Royalist armies.

---

50 Ibid., p.41.
51 Ibid., pp.40–41.
52 Printed in John Adair, *They Saw it Happen: Contemporary Accounts of the Siege of Basing House* (Hampshire: Hampshire County Council, 1981), p.54.

8

Newbury Campaign

From Basingstoke the combined armies marched to Aldermaston Park, from where on 24 October they heard the King had arrived at Newbury, so they moved to Bucklebury Heath, five miles from Newbury and the following day to Thatcham, where the diary of Montagu's regiment recalls 'where we lay in the field all night'.[1] On 26 October they marched to Newbury and began to deploy on Clay Hill overlooking the village of Shaw, to the north-east of Newbury, where they found the Royalist army had fortified the position.

Front view of Shaw House
(Author's collection)

Although points of the battle are still visible such as Donnington Castle and Shaw House, which was known as Dolman's House at the time of the Civil War, much of the battlefield had changed with the expansion of Newbury and so much of it has been lost to housing development. However, Charles' Secretary of State, Sir Edward Walker describes the field as it then was:

The greatest part of our army was placed toward the Rebel quarter and Mr Dolman's house, at Shaw, in the village near it defended by the river that runs under Donnington Castle, in a house between that village and Newbury, about which a work was cast up, and at a mill upon the River Kennet all which lay almost

---

1   BodLib: Carte, MS 74 f.159.

east from the town. Directly north from thence are two open fields where most of our horse stood, and our train of artillery, and about a mile west in the village of Speen and beyond it a small heath. In this village all Prince Maurice's Foot lay, with some Western horse. At the entrance of the heath between two hedges we cast up a work, which cleared the heath and all the fields to the north even to the river, to the south within the hedge there was one narrow field; and from thence a perpendicular descent into a marsh, between that and the River Kennet.[2]

On 5 May 1879 the London Geologists Association visited Newbury and undertook what we would today call a battlefield tour. Their tour guide was Walter Money who published a book on both battles of Newbury and the local newspaper reported their tour: 'having ascended the highest point of the [Clay] hill from which a splendid view of the town and neighbourhood could be seen'. The party then went to Shaw House where on the lawn stood four Civil War cannons and inside the house was a display 'consisting of ancient armour, helmets, cannon balls, a Puritan's preacher hat, and a cloak left behind after the second battle of Newbury, traditionally said to have belonged to Oliver Cromwell'. The party then went to Donnington Castle, where they were able to climb the castle's spiral staircase, 'and from the elevated battlement a magnificent panorama opened, amply rewarding those that had made the toilsome effort'. Finally the tour came to Speen Moors, which are described as being of chalk and gravel which in large areas was covered with peat.[3]

On 26 October there were skirmishes between the armies on Clay Hill and the Royalists near Shaw Village. Unfortunately, little has been recorded of the events of this day, although two Parliamentary commissioners, Sir A. Johnstone and John Crew, reported 'Our dragoons and theirs fired upon each other for two hours, 20 of our horses are killed, but not one of our men lost. A captain of our horse who came up in the van was shot in the thigh'. Colonel Edmund Ludlow recalls, there was:

Plaque allegedly marking the spot where a musket ball narrowly missed the King at Shaw House. However, it is believed that Charles was not in the house at the time of the battle. (Author's collection)

---

2   Sir Edward Walker, *Historical Discourses, upon several occasions: vol 1 The happy progress and success of the arms of King Charles I* (London: Samuel Keble, 1705), pp.110–111.

3   *The Newbury Weekly News*, Thursday 8 May 1879. Today there are four artillery barrels outside the house, but these are later than the Civil War

skirmishing in small parties, as they thought fit to come to us. On our side we had the advantage of a hill, which served in some measure to cover our men, here we plated some of our field pieces, and fired upon the enemy who answered us in the like manner from the town. In the afternoon they drew two of their guns to the other side of the river, and with them fired upon that part of ours that lay on the side of the hill, who were much exposed to that place where their guns were planted: my Regiment being that day on the guard, received the greatest damage.[4]

Among those hit by the Royalist artillery was Ludlow's cousin, Cornet Gabriel Ludlow. His smashed body was taken to the rear, 'his belly broken, and bowels torn, his hip bone broken all to shivers'. The artillery piece must have been of a small calibre because when a surgeon examined him he found the ball still inside him. He recovered his senses for a short time. 'In this condition he desired me to kiss him', wrote Edmund Ludlow, 'I kissed him; and soon after having recommended his mother, brothers and sisters to my care, he died.'[5]

According to Cromwell when the three armies rendezvoused at Basingstoke, they had 'near 11,000 foot and about 8,000 horse and dragoons'.[6] If these figures are correct for the combined Parliamentarian armies, the Eastern Association is believed to have had about 3,700 foot and 2,700 horse and Essex's army had between 2,930 and 3,538 foot and 1,994 horse. Waller had left most of his infantry in the West to reinforce the garrisons there or converted them into dragoon regiments. No return of the strength of Waller's cavalry has survived, but if Cromwell is correct then this leaves 3,306 horse and dragoons which is probably about right for Waller's cavalry. On 19 October Sir James Harrington's brigade, which had left London two days previously mustered 3,000, although he hoped 'in a day or two our companies, which are yet thin, will be 4,000 complete, if our Committee in London force out our defaulters'. The Southwark trained bands were left at Reading to reinforce the garrison which further weakened Harrington's brigade by about 600 men, so possibly it consisted of about 2,000 men, since on 26 October Sir A. Johnstone and John Crew urged the Committee of Both Kingdoms 'being informed by such as come from London that they meet many soldiers going homewards, we renew our desire that some exemplary punishment may be inflicted upon them'.[7]

Cromwell also estimates the strength of the Royalist to be, 'not above 10,000 horse and foot', while the *True Informer* states about 13,000 'whereof 7,000 foot'.[8] However, this figure comes from his evidence against Manchester

---

4   CSPD 1644, p.73.; Edmund Ludlow, *The Memoirs of Edmund Ludlow, Lieutenant general of the Horse in the Army of the Commonwealth of England*, Vol.1, ed. C. H. Firth (Oxford: Clarendon Press, 1894), pp.102–103.
5   Ibid.
6   Bruce and Masson, p.83.
7   Ibid., p.85.; Simon Marsh, 'The Disarmed Multitude: The impact of the Lostwithiel Campaign on the Earl of Essex's Army and its Reconstitution for the Second Newbury Campaign', in Serena Jones (ed.), *Home and Away: The British Experience of War, 1618–1721* (Warwick: Helion & Co. 2018), pp.64–66; CSPD 1644, pp.56, 73.
8   Bruce and Masson, p.83.; Entry in *True Informer* quoted in Money, p.151.

and so he probably altered the facts to suit his own ends. Certainly the Royalists seem to have been optimistic in the forthcoming battle, insomuch as in a letter written by Lord Digby to Prince Rupert, he said 'We may promise ourselves a very happy conclusion of this summer's war', and Charles was able to send 800 horse under the Earl of Northampton to relieve Banbury.[9] According to the diary of Richard Symonds, who served in Charles' lifeguard 'When the King's Army was in Cornwall, the infantry was divided into three tertias and every tertia consisted of three brigades'. The first tertia was under Sir Thomas Blagge was composed of the King's old army and was formed of nine regiments. The second tertia was under Colonel George Lisle and was also composed of nine regiments which had formerly comprised the garrison of Reading. While the third tertia was under Sir Bernard Astley, and was formed from eight regiments of Sir Ralph Hopton's old army which had been reduced into the King's Oxford army after Hopton's defeat at the battle of Cheriton on 29 March 1644. On 26 July 1644 when the King reviewed Prince Maurice's army it also consisted of three tertias, two were 1,500 strong and were formed from four regiments of foot, and the third was 1,580 strong and composed of eight regiments. These regiment included the remnants of Hopton's Cornish infantry which he had led early in the war up to the fall of Bristol to Prince Rupert in July 1643.[10]

As to the Royalist cavalry there were five brigades of the Oxford army, which Symonds states were commanded by the Earl of Northampton, the Earl of Cleveland, Lord Wentworth, Colonel Sir Humphrey Bennet and Colonel Thomas Howard. The latter brigade was formerly commanded by Lord Wilmot, who had been dismissed from his command in August due to secret peace negotiations he had undertaken without Charles' knowledge with the Earl of Essex. Maurice's western army was always short of cavalry, so possibly mustered just one or two brigades. The number of guns on each side is not known.

At a Council of War it was resolved that the Royalist army was too strong to attack frontally, so a large part of the combined armies under the command of Sir William Waller, including the majority of the Eastern Association's horse under Cromwell, should by a night march move around the Royalists' left flank and attack them from the village of Speen, north-west of Newbury. While this march was taking place Manchester would occupy the Royalists' attention by drawing up the remainder of the army on Clay Hill. According to Manchester's chaplain, Simeon Ashe his force was composed of the Eastern Association's infantry, and 'a small body of horse', or roughly 3,000 to 3,700 foot, and 1,500 to 1,800 horse.[11] The horse included Colonels Edmund Ludlow and Richard Norton's regiments, which formed part of Waller's Southern Association. It is fortunate that the Royalists had not planned an offensive battle otherwise Manchester would have found himself isolated without the assistance of a large part of the Parliamentarian army.

---

9   Money, p.144.
10   BL: Harl MS 6804 f.199 Prince Maurice's Army, 27 July 1644.
11   Money, p.161.

In his account of the battle Ashe refers to the 'hardship' that the Parliamentarians met with during the night of 26/27, although he does not elaborate on this, but it was almost certainly due to the wet weather. Ashe continues that it was decided 'that so soon as he [Manchester] heard the engagement of our friends on Speen hill (by the discharging of the cannon) he should fall on the enemy on this side [of] the river [Lambourn], that he might divert the strength of the battle, from them there'. Manchester's objectives were the Royalists in the village of Shaw and Mr Dolman's House, both of which had been fortified with earthworks which according to the Royalist John Gwyn:

> By the great contrivance of Major General Lord Astley and [the] great performance of 800 foot, commanded by Colonel Thelwall; 400 foot commanded by [Lieutenant Colonel] Sir Richard] Page, at Dolman's House; 200 horse commanded by Sir George Lisle, in the interval between Dolman's House and the field Thelwall was in.[12]

According to Rushworth, it was early in the morning of 27 October that Waller's force 'were on the march and in four hours' time … made their approach towards the west side of Newbury'. However, Waller's force had to march 12 or so miles around the Royalist's flank and then to deploy in their rear, so Manchester would have to wait not knowing when Waller would be in a position to attack. During this wait Manchester appears to have ordered a bridge to be built over the Lambourne to make access to the south bank easier.

Waller's flank march was meant to be a secret, and according to Ashe, Manchester launched a diversionary attack on the morning of 27 October:

> A party of about 400 musketeers to fall on, over the little river, on the left hand of Shaw, that he might soon enough divert the enemy's strength from Speen hill: This party of ours took two of the enemy's works, one captain, and several prisoners: but marching too far, contrary to order, they were beaten back with some loss; by this service, the greatest part of the King's foot were drawing towards us, and so the work to which we were designed, was accomplished long before our friends on Speen hill did engage.[13]

Sir Edward Walker also mentions this attack:

> Early of Sunday morning being the 27 October, about 1,000 of Manchester's forces and the London Trained Band, came down the hill, and passed the river that was by Shaw, and being nor discovered forced some of our foot from a pass not far from the house we had entrenched, where Sir Bernard Astley lay, who instantly drew out 400 musketeers, fell upon the body, and not only routed them, but caused them to do the like to two other bodies that were coming to second

---

12   Gwyn, p.58.
13   BL: TT E 22/10; Simeon Ashe, *A True Relation of the Chief Occurrences at and since the late battle of Newbury* (London: Edward Brewster, 1644).

them. In the pursuit many of them were slain, divers drowned in the river and about 200 arms gained, The action was ended soon after the rising of the sun.[14]

According to Money, Astley's brigade formed up near a house in Shaw Park 'between Shaw and Newbury', which had also been fortified by entrenchments. This was not Shaw House, because Money refers to it as having been 'pulled down many years since'.[15] After this attack, Richard Symonds recalls 'they lay quiet until 3 [in the] afternoon, only our cannon and theirs played'.[16]

However, the Parliamentarians could not hide such a large flanking force and they were observed by the garrison of Donnington Castle and several Royalist pickets, so word soon got back to the King and his Council of War, which had Maurice's army re-deploy to cover Speen village. Here the Royalists began digging fortifications so that when Waller's force finally arrived it was the Parliamentarians, and not the Royalists, who were surprised to find a force ready for them. In the meantime, Manchester 'with the forces remaining under his command, were in readiness to assault the enemy, expecting from hour to hour, to hear of the engagement at Speen hill'.[17]

When Waller finally began to deploy his army ready for battle is not known, since some sources put it at midday while others at about 4:00 p.m. Cromwell commanded the left wing, which included the Eastern Association's cavalry and those of Waller's army, while Lieutenant General Sir William Balfour commanded the right with Essex's cavalry. Major General Phillip Skippon of Essex's army commanded the centre, which were composed of Essex's infantry which were divided into two brigades commanded by Colonels Henry Barclay and Edward Aldrich, each composed of three regiments and a third brigade was commanded by Sir James Harrington and consisted of the four regiments of London trained bands.

On the western approaches of Speen, both the right wing and the centre made headway against the Royalists. Waller recalls:

> After arriving on the heath about a mile and a half from Newbury at two, we fell into the lanes and hedges and marched not above one quarter of a mile before we came into sight of the enemy who had blocked up our way with a strong breastwork and in it five pieces of cannon, and for their better advantage they were under the favour of Donnington Castle, their best pieces being there. Upon our approach their cannon played hard upon us, the place being a narrow heath gave no leave to bring up our body. The hedges hindered our horse very much. Their cannon made our ground very hot. There was no way left but to fall on with horse and foot and without delay, which put in execution...his Excellency's [Essex's] foot … went on undauntedly.[18]

---

14   Walker, p.111.
15   Money, p.153.
16   Richard Symonds, *Diary of the Marches of the Royal Army during the Great Civil War kept by Richard Symonds*, ed. Charles E. Long (London: Camden Press, 1859), p.145.
17   BL: TT E 22/10.
18   BL: Harl MS 166.

Sir Edward Walker also mentions these fortifications:

> At the entrance of the Heath, between two Hedges we cast up a work which cleared the Heath and all the fields to the North even to the river [Lamborne]; to the South, within the hedge, there was one narrow field, and from thence a perpendicular descent into a marsh [Speen Moor] between that and the River Kennet. This was our position, wherein, had the traverse been finished and made down to the Marish, although' we were inferior in number, yet we should have sufficiently provided to have withstood their force.[19]

Due to their treatment by Maurice's army in Cornwall, Essex's infantry were eager for revenge as Colonel Ludlow recalls, they charged 'with such vigour, that some of them ran to their cannon, and clapped their hats upon the touch-holes of them, falling so furiously upon the enemy'.[20] Skippon described the actions of the infantry as follows:

> The forlorn hope, consisting of about 800 musketeers, was led by Colonel Aldridge's Lieutenant Colonel Lloyd, a worthy man who was shot in the arm, and my Lord Robert's Major, Hurry; and lodged themselves (fighting) close to the enemy's forlorne hope: His excellency's Regiment fell upon the right hand of them with great boldness; Colonel Aldrich, with his brigade consisting of his own, Colonel Davis', Colonel Fortescue's and Colonel Ingoldsby's Regiments, fell on directly on their main work with undaunted resolution. His Excellency's Regiment coming upon the right hand of them, they both fell pell-mell into the same work. The Two Red and Yellow Regiments of the Citizens held the enemy [in] play on the right hand; Colonel Barclay and his brigade alone, wherein was his own, my Lord Robert's and my Regiment, most resolutely repulsed three violent charges of the enemy's horse in a plain field and after that did farther good service; The Blue City Regiment were the reserve. The sum is, (after a very sharp fight for the time) the enemy were quite driven out of all their works and the village of Speen.[21]

Six sakers which they had lost by Essex's Army during the Lostwithiel campaign were recaptured, along with a further three guns.

Meanwhile Balfour had to contend with the King's lifeguard of horse and Sir Humphrey Bennet's brigade, which he forced to retire. According to Sir Edward Walker seeing the lifeguard retreat made 'many of our horse then in our rear fled disorderly to Newbury'. The situation was saved for the Royalists by two troops of the Queen's lifeguard attacking Balfour's cavalry and the 'King's Lifeguard rallying and renewing their attack prevented a total rout'.[22] Richard Symonds, who was a member of the King's lifeguard, adds:

---

19 Walker, p.111.
20 Ludlow, p.103.
21 Major General Philip Skippon at Newbury to the Committee of Both Kingdoms, 30 October 1644, printed in Rushworth's *Historical Collections*.
22 Walker, p.112.

[At] 4 of the clock, their bodies of horse approached towards our field at the bottom of the hill near the church called (Shaw) and one body came into the field, (and) charged Sir John Campsfield's Regiment [also known as the Queen's Regiment] which stood them most gallantly. The King's Regiment being near, drove at them, which made them wheel off in confusion, and followed them in the chase, made all their bodies of horse run in confusion, killed many, besides musketeers that lined the hedges and played upon us in the chase until we cut their throats.

Meanwhile on Waller's left flank the attack had stalled, according to Ashe 'My Lord of Manchester's horse commanded by Lieutenant Colonel[sic] Cromwell (from whom very much was expected) did little service, gained no honour in this work this day'. Several Parliamentarian accounts are silent of the action on this wing, while others accuse Cromwell of doing nothing even when the centre was being attacked by Royalist cavalry:

If Cromwell had played the part that became him, then enemy had been totally routed; all the horse under his command stood still when Colonel Barclay['s] Brigade was charged three times. Notwithstanding all that they stood still … General Lieutenant Middleton came seeing so great absurdities and oversights, and desired the said Cromwell's horse to charge, who refused him till he went with one of the squadrons and charged the enemy, who was routed and left on seconded to fly for his life, being in the middle of his enemies, so that day there was no service performed at all by Cromwell.[23]

Later Cromwell in a speech to Parliament would claim that it was Manchester who gave him the order to charge, even though he was on the other side of the battlefield, and that:

I refused to obey his direction and order; for this it was his Majesty's horse being betwixt four or five thousand in a large common, in good order, he commands me … to charge them; we having no way to come at them but through a narrow lane, where not above three horse could march abreast, whereby had I followed his order, we had been all cut off ere we could have got into any order.[24]

Sir Edward Walker does mention the Parliamentarian's left attack, but it is unclear whether it was led by Cromwell or Middleton:

At the same time the Rebel's horse of the left wing were advancing towards the North side of the wheat field, but before they were got thither Colonel Goring put himself into the head of the Earl of Cleveland's Brigade, consisting of the Earl of Cleveland, Colonel Howard, Hamilton, Culpepper and Stuart's Regiment of Horse) and being accompanied by the Earl himself, he fell upon them, and forced them back in great confusion, and then got over the hedge, where he was again charged by another body, but he quickly defeated them also, and slew diverse of

---

23   Bruce and Masson, pp.63–64.
24   Lily, pp.182–184.

the rebels on the place. In this charge the courageous Earl of Cleveland engaged himself so far and by the illness of his horse which fell under him prisoner. This charge was the more gallant, because this brigade not only went over the ditch to meet the Rebels, but passed by three bodies of the Rebels foot, who shot at them both when they pursued the Rebels and as they came back.[25]

Mercurius Aulicus continues:

Thus the Rebels were repulsed on the west side of Speen, but those others on the east side were more confident of success, who having settled three bodies of foot in certain enclosures and ditches, advanced over a ditch, with a good body of horse, hoping thereby to break through his Majesty's guards; but this was as soon discerned and prevented by General Goring, who instantly drew up the Earl of Cleveland's brigade, put himself in their head of it … The general told them they must now charge home, and thereupon suddenly advanced up to the gap, where about fourscore of the rebels were now already come over, the rest hastening after. These he soon fell upon, and forced them back again in much confusion; As soon as he got part of the brigade over the ditch, he hastened to order them as fast as they came over, but the eager Rebels would not grant him so much leisure, and therefore a new body came to second the former, whom the general received with those horse he had already over the ditch, and then charged so home, that he made them quickly scatter and shift for themselves, many whereof were killed in the place … This charge was the more gallant, because this brigade of horse not only went over the ditch to meet the Rebels, but passed by three bodies of the Rebels' foot, who were placed in the ditches and enclosures; two of which bodies shot at his Majesty's horse as they pursued the Rebels, and as they came back.

However, another Royalist, Richard Symonds, gives a very different account: 'The Earl of Cleveland before our charge was taken prisoner, and most of his officers hurt and killed, his men beaten, being overpowered with horse and foot'. One of those wounded was Thomas White of Sherfield in Hampshire, who 'served under Lord Wentworth [and] was wounded in his right arm.'[26]

Meanwhile, across the fields from Speen what was happening at Shaw? According to Colonel Richard Norton, 'About 3pm the great guns with the Parliament's forces [at Speen] open fire'.[27] However, Manchester remained motionless, despite Norton's and several other officers pleading with him to attack. The situation had changed since the council of war the previous evening. The Parliamentarians had expected the sudden appearance of Waller's force in their rear would spread panic through the unsuspecting ranks of the Royalist army, but instead there was no element of surprise and the Royalists were able to not only stabilise the situation in their rear, but

---

25   Walker, pp.112–114.
26   Hampshire Record Office (HRO): Quarter Sessions 30 September 1662, Petition of Thomas White. The churchwardens and overseers of the poor were ordered to provide him with a house and maintain him.
27   Colonel Richard Norton's evidence against Manchester, undated [1 January 1645?] printed in CSPD 1644–45, p.159.

they were ready for any onslaught that Manchester might throw at them. Nevertheless, Crawford attacked. According to Ashe:

> You must not imagine that my Lord of Manchester's foot were all this while idle spectators on this side [of] the river (although as I told you before, the enemy's best foot were diverted from Speen hill, which might have extenuated the seeming fault of some delays) for while our Drakes (before mentioned) were at work, a commanded party of 500 musketeers was drawn forth as a Forlorn hope. To assault the enemy, who being seconded with the several brigades of foot, continued in hot service, until for want of daylight to direct our soldiers wounded and killed one another. The undaunted valour of our foot was admirable, they were indeed too forward too adventurous, overrunning their commands, unwilling to be called off. And here this is notable, that when one company of our foot had taken one of the works of the enemy, another company (through overmuch forwardness and mistake) did beat them out again.[28]

An anonymous account, believed to be written by William Dodson, who was an opponent of Cromwell, records:

> So that time the Earl of Manchester did continue in his very great toiling to prepare the falling upon the enemy in and near Dolman's house, and above 500 commanded musketeers, commanded for the falling on first as forlorn hope, which to the amazement of the enemy were several times drawn on and off, and at last they fell on, seconded by the several brigades of foot. If the forwardness of Major General Crawford's regiment had been seconded the house and garden had been gained, but they were beat off with the loss of one of Major General Crawford's colours and two drakes, lost for want of looking unto being carried headlong on; the fault of the losing of the drakes was Captain Hammond.[29]

It was only 'towards three or four o'clock', according to Rushworth:

> hearing the cannon play from Speen Hill, Manchester drew forth two Drakes to play on Mr Dolman's House, and commanded out a party of 500 musketeers, as a forlorn hope, to attack the said House, and beat those that sallied out from thence into their works; and the reason why they did not more was said to be because night came on.[30]

Clarendon recalls that the soldiers of the Eastern Association advanced 'with great resolution upon Shaw House and the field adjacent. They came signing psalms'.[31] Sir Edward Walker also refers to them signing psalms as they advanced, recalling that:

28 BL: TT E 22/10.
29 Bruce and Masson, p.65.
30 John Rushworth, *Historical Collections*.
31 Clarendon, p.242.

In the meantime the Earl of Manchester's Forces came down the hill near Shaw, being 1,200 horse and 3,000 Foot, and at the same time that the others got Speen, they advanced towards the Guards, which the Lord Astley disposed, under the command of Colonel George Lisle, who appointed Lieutenant Colonel Page to keep Mr Dolman's House, placed some dragoons in the hedges and lane near it, and Colonel Thelwall with his own regiment and others of the Reading Brigade top be a reserve. The Rebels came signing of psalms, and at first gave a great shout, but they were presently charged by Sir John Browne with Prince Charles' his Regiment of Horse and very good execution done upon them, who instantly received another charge of 1,000 of the Rebel's horse, and then retreated to the foot in Mr Dolman's garden which flanked that field and killed many of the Rebels. Whereupon their horse faced about, and Sir John Browne fell on their rear, and cut off many of them, and kept the ground all that day. At the same time the reserve commanded by Colonel Thelwall came on, being about 400 men, and after they had galled the Rebels with several volleys, they fell on with the butt end of their muskets and beat the rebels not only from the hedges, but quite out of the field, the Rebels running off in great confusion, leaving two drakes, some colours, and many dead bodies behind them. In the meantime another great body of the Rebel's foot fell on those in Mr Dolman's House, where they were so stoutly opposed by Lieutenant Colonel Page that they began to run, and were pursued up the hill, with the notable execution of near 500 in a small compass of ground, which done, we had leisure to draw off two drakes of the Rebels that were formerly engaged.[32]

As darkness descended on the battlefield Sir George Lisle is said to have taken off his coat to reveal his white shirt so that his men could see him better; according to tradition, as the Parliamentarians advanced they thought he was a witch flying about the Royalist lines. Among those present was the Royalist John Gwyn who records that:

Colonel Thelwall was making up of the gaps in the quickset hedge, which he was to maintain, and making of the ditch under it deeper and wider; Sir George Lisle and Sir Richard Page were fixing of themselves, as well as they could, at their posts. Then orders were given to Thelwall not to give fire upon the enemy until they came within a pike's length of him. Sir Richard Page needed no such orders, for they came near to him as they moved by: nor could they come to charge Sir George Lisle but through the enemy's fire, for Sir Richard Page with his leather guns, loaded with keyshot [case shot], and 400 musketeers in the dry moat, played between the pailes [pailings] upon the flanks of them; and Thelwall, which his body of musketeers, likewise played through the quickset hedge in their teeth, that made a heavy slaughter among them, maimed and so disabled them, that they came in disorder to charge Sir George Lisle, which made him the better able to defend himself against so powerful an opposition: and it is observable, that sometimes great commanders have miscarried, in too much slighting of an enemy, and trusting to their own strength: and it is very like those two

---

32   Walker, pp.112–114.

commanders were under the same mistake, deceived as presuming too much in their exceeding number of men, which in all probability, might fairly promise them victory, having on their side more than six to one the odds of it: and withal knew, that at the same instant the King was hotly engaged in [a] close fight.[33]

The leather guns that Gwyn refers to were probably those which had been captured from Waller at Cropredy Bridge.

But what time did Manchester launch his attack? According to Cromwell it was 'almost half an hour after sunset'. Sunset has been estimated at about 4.26 p.m. Whereas in a letter sent to the House of Lords, it states that 'The Earl of Manchester, about four of the clock endeavoured to force a passage through Shaw, a village on the other side of the field'.[34] John Weaver, the Judge Advocate stated the forces attacked 'about sunset', and Leon Watson, Scoutmaster-General to the Earl of Manchester states 'the Earl fell on about a quarter of an hour after sunset'.[35]

A. Johnston and J. Crewe record that:

The Earl of Manchester about 4 o'clock endeavoured to force a passage through Shaw, a village on the other side of the field, where the King's forces lay. Prince Maurice was on that side and many of the King's best foot, who maintained those passages, although they were bravely assaulted. The Earl of Manchester for want of daylight and by reason of the great guards did not take the passages; but his employing so many of the King's forces on that side was of great advantage to our other forces.[36]

Only part of George Lisle's tertia had been committed to the battle in and around the village of Shaw and Dolman's house, leaving at least two tertias of Sir Bernard Astley's and Colonel Thomas Blagge (apart from the Duke of York's regiment) uncommitted waiting for Manchester to descend the hill. Ashe records that Lisle's men were 'seconded with the several brigades of foot', rather than tertias, of course he could have been mistaken, but the only reference to elements of Sir Bernard Astley's tertia taking part in the battle were by Walker during Manchester's initial attack that morning.

Likewise only two of Charles' brigades of cavalry are known to have been committed to the battle so far. There is no plan to show where these brigades were formed up, but the Parliamentarian newspaper *Mercurius Civicus* states that the King's general's believed that the attack on Speen was just a feint and that Manchester's main thrust was yet to come.[37] If true then the main body of the Royalist army had remained uncommitted for the entire day. Only Walker claims that Manchester had committed all his infantry and cavalry; but other sources state that only part of his force had attacked Shaw House: the rest remained on Clay Hill. This force was by no means strong enough to

33   Gwyn, p.60.
34   *Journal of the House of Lords*, vol. 7, p.41.
35   CSPD 1644–45, pp.149–150.
36   *Journal of the House of Lords*, vol. 7, p.41.
37   BL: TT E 14/14.

take on the King's main strength, so that to a large extent he had achieved his aim in distracting the Royalists from attacking Speen, whether he intended to do so or not. Unfortunately, this may have been the aim in the morning, but now the intention was the destruction of the Royalist army. Nevertheless, Manchester was congratulated for the victory he had obtained.

However, by now it was dark and Ashe continues:

> For want of daylight to direct our soldiers wounded and killed one another. The undaunted valour of our foot was admirable, they were indeed too forward too adventurous, overrunning their commands, unwilling to be called off. And here this is notable, that when one company of our foot had taken one of the works of the enemy, another company (through overmuch forwardness and mistake) did beat them out again. So that our greatest loss, both in regard of men wounded and slain, was from ourselves.[38]

Johnston and Crewe records 'the battle lasted about three hours; they fought at least an hour by moonlight'.[39] Cromwell also recalls 'having gained most of the hedges toward Newbury field, did cease and draw our men together to avoid confusion in the dark by that scattered way of fighting', but added:

> his Lordship going on so late, his men presently fell fowl one upon another, and were put to assault Dolman's house on that only side where it was inaccessible (whereas twas open on the other), by which means he lost two pieces of ordnance and many gallant men; whereas had he fallen on by daylight and according to agreement he might, on the open side, have taken that house with the men and ordnance in it.[40]

With night having put a stop to the fighting Manchester looked to his soldiers believing that the battle would resume the following day.[41] But the King had other ideas and slipped away under cover of darkness for Wallingford, leaving his artillery in Donnington Castle. The Parliamentarians made little effort to pursue the retreating Royalists. Leon Watson would accuse Manchester that if he:

> had sent forth a party of horse he might have gained intelligence of the King's movements upon the flight of his army. That the Earl and his forces were much nearer and lay better to gain intelligence of the King's motions than the other party of the Parliament's army who were on the other side of the river at Speen. That the forces of the Cavaliers at Dolman's house marched away westward little more than musket shot of the Earl's forces, and this examinant doth not know that any party of the Earl's were sent after them upon their retreat.[42]

---

38   BL: TT E 22/10.
39   *Journal of the House of Lords*, vol. 7, p.41.
40   Bruce and Masson, pp.86–87.
41   BL: TT E 22/10.
42   CSPD 1644–45, p.150.

Captain John Hooper also believed that:

> if the Earl had sent forth a party of scouts to discover which way the King's army fled, that the Parliament's Army might then have pursued the former 7 or 8 hours sooner than they did; also that the Earl might have immediately pursued, being on the same side of the river, and only a little more than a quarter of a mile from the King's army at the time of its flight.[43]

On the other hand many Parliamentarians probably were glad to see the back of the Royalists, many of whom would likely be exhausted by their night march and subsequent battle. The Parliamentarians began looking to the wounded of both sides. On 28 October Johnston and Crewe wrote to the Committee of Both Kingdoms 'We earnestly entreat you to take care that the want of surgeons may be supplied. It is a miserable thing to see men want means of cure who have been wounded in the defence of the public'. Unfortunately, there are no casualty returns for either side and in the various reports on the battle none offered an opinion to the number of killed and wounded. True, there is a list published in Money's book, but this is for the first battle of Newbury rather than the second as he implies. Among those wounded was

The remains of Donnington Castle (Author's collection)

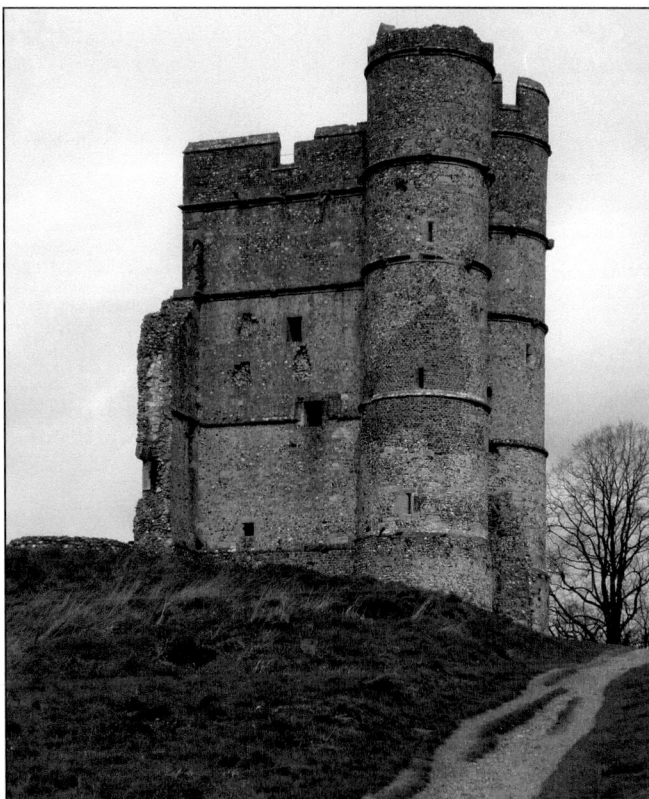

Trooper Bonden of Springfield, Essex, whose father petitioned for a pension for 'a bruise which he got by a fall from his horse [when it was] slain under him at Newbury fight … he hath gotten a grievous fistula in his back of which he hath now line these 18 months and upwards under the surgeon's hands'. Unfortunately, his petition does not name the regiment he belonged to.[44]

While the combined armies remained at Newbury, Charles met with Prince Rupert and together they decided to return to Newbury and offer battle once more, and retrieve the artillery that had been left at Donnington Castle. On 9 November they arrived back at Newbury and Rupert's engineer, Bernard de Gomme, drew up a plan of the Royalist battle array which shows that the Royalists had 4,200 horse and 5,000 foot on this occasion, the Earl of Northampton's brigade having also rejoined Charles. The plan also shows that the Royalists deployed their army in four bodies of infantry in the front

43   CSPD 1644–45, p.149.
44   ERO: Q/SBa2/61.

line in the centre, supported by Sir William Blakeson's brigade of horse. In the second line were a further three bodies of infantry, with two regiments of cavalry drawn up behind them. Seven bodies of cavalry formed the left and seven the right, with 100 musketeers supporting each body of cavalry. Four bodies of cavalry and one of foot formed the reserve. The Parliamentarians are just represented by a hedge lined with dragoons of the Parliament, which ran directly north of Newbury towards the River Lambourne and two bodies of cavalry and two of infantry at the end of the hedge closest to Newbury with 'the Lord Manchester and the rest of Parliament's Army drawn up and quartered in the town'.[45]

Symonds records in his diary that:

> About two of the clock all the King's army was drawn down by the castle over the river and pitched in Battalia in the plain on the last ground we had before, a body of horse and a body of foot ranged together. About 4 the enemy drew of Newbury two bodies of horse and lined a hedge with musketeers, played upon our horse with their cannon as they marched up to them. And because the Queen's Regiment of Horse was drawn within danger of some musketeers which they drew down below Mr [Dolman's] House … and a body of the enemy's horse drew boldly out, the Prince Rupert commanded the Queen's Regiment of Horse and Prince Maurice his regiment of horse to charge them, who no sooner drew up to them but the Rebels wheeled off behind behind their own cannon and musketeers, which galled that body of ours … A musket bullet … shot the king's horse in the foot as he stood before his own regimen in his arms.[46]

Sir Edward Walker gives some additional information to this day:

> About three in the afternoon we advanced [to] within the reach of their cannon, which they discharged amongst us without doing any hurt. Then a body of our horse, charged another of theirs in the lower field, and routed them, [and] pursued them almost to their breastwork, when the Rebels musketeers place in the lane between the two fields gave fire on our horse and caused them to retreat, (though without disorder). In the interim we could discover a great body of their horse on the hill, on the south side of Newbury, almost at a stand [unsure] whether to come down or retire.[47]

The Parliamentarian generals held a Council of War to decide what to do. In a letter written by the Parliamentarian commanders they confirm the hesitancy of the combined armies:

> between 10 and 11 o'clock they [the Royalists] drew up to Donnington Castle, and from thence both horse and foot drew off into a plain field between Newbury and the castle. It was not considered safe for us to draw out in regard of the castle

---

45   BL: Add MS 16,370 f.60.
46   Symonds, p.148.
47   Walker, p.118.

ordnance, therefore we resolved to make good the town. The enemy came on upon us, but received such a repulse that he was fain to retreat.[48]

However, there is no mention of an argument which took place during the Council of War between the senior officers of the army on whether to fight or not. It was only later during an enquiry into the matter that Waller recalled:

A proposition was made to fight, saying that the King had hopes of a foreign aid, and particularly out of France. The Earl of Manchester then declared his opinion against engaging, saying to his knowledge there were no forces coming out of France and that if we beat the King never so often yet he will be king still, but if we are once beaten we shall be hanged, and our posterity will be slaves.[49]

Whereas Sir Arthur Heselrige also claimed that after hearing that French or any other foreign forces were being sent to England to assist the King, Manchester replied; 'Upon my credit you need not fear the coming in of the French, I know there is no such thing.' The Earl afterwards said 'That if we beat the King 99 times yet he is King still, and so will his posterity be after him, but if the King beat us once we shall be all hanged, and our posterity be made slaves'. To which Cromwell is said to have replied 'My Lord, if this be so, why did we take up arms at first? This is against fighting ever hereafter, if so, let us make peace, be it never so base.'[50] Cromwell admitted that he could not remember exactly what Manchester had said, stating 'that if we should beat the King never so often yet he would be King still and his posterity, but if he should beat us but once we must be hanged and our posterity undone', or words to that effect; to which this examinant [Cromwell] replied 'that if this principle was true it condemned all our former fighting as foolish, and was an argument against fighting for the future, and a ground for making a peace how dishonourable soever'.[51]

Charles did not know of the divisions in the Parliamentarian armies and his council of war advised him of the precarious situation he was in and so having already achieved his aim of retrieving his artillery from Donnington Castle he decided to withdraw. However, unlike the 27 October's battle when the Royalists had to march off under cover of darkness, Symonds recalls 'It growing night, the whole army marched off in full bodies, drums beating and colours flying, trumpets prattling their marches, all in the face of the enemy'.[52] Among those watching the Royalist army draw off was Colonel Ludlow, who recalled 'the King, in the face of our army, twice as numerous as his, had time to send his artillery from Donnington Castle towards Oxford. Without any opposition … by this time it was clearly manifest that the nobility had no further quarrel with the King'.[53]

---

48   CSPD 1644–45, p.108.
49   Ibid.
50   Ibid., p.151.
51   Ibid.
52   Symonds, p.148.
53   Ludlow, p.105.

Was Ludlow correct in his assessment that the Parliamentarians outnumbered the Royalists by two to one? Many of the soldiers had been sleeping in field despite the cold weather which must have resulted in sickness within the armies and many had deserted. On 15 November the senior Parliamentarian officers reported:

> The horse are so tired out with hard duty in such extremity of weather as hath seldom been seen, that of much more service be required of them you will quickly see your cavalry ruined without fighting. The foot are not in [a] better case, besides the lessening of their numbers through cold and hard duty; sickness also is much on the increase, which we dare not conceal from you, daily regarding their extreme sufferings with not a little sorrow. The places we are in do not afford firing, food or coverings for them, [the soldiers] nor is the condition of the people less to be pitied, who both within our horse and foot quarters are so exhausted that we may justly fear a famine will fall upon them.[54]

According to Skippon's letter to the Earl of Essex 'Sir William Balfour says, all your Excellency's Horse are not about 800 and Colonel Barclay (who calculated their numbers in the field this day) said, that the Foot (I mean your Excellency's) were not above 1,200.'[55] As to the army of the Eastern Association, on 22 November Manchester wrote to the Committee of Both Kingdoms:

> That for the preservation of Abingdon there are already two regiments and four companies in the pay of the Eastern Association, but, for the rest of the foot with me, they are so weakened and wasted that I may truly say they are not sufficient either with honour or safety to guard the train of artillery here with me … It is my duty to let you understand that it is expected from me that I should act as a protection to those counties which both raised these forces and still pay them with this intent.[56]

On 17 November Manchester finally left Newbury having received orders to quell a mutiny at Windsor Castle, whose governor John Venn held it for Parliament.

Meanwhile the rumours of Royalist movements that had worried the Committee of the Eastern Association, causing them to write to Manchester in September demanding his return, had proved correct and early in October they had seized Crowland once more; but instead of recalling Manchester, the Committee of Both Kingdoms ordered 300 foot from the garrison of Cambridge to retake the town and abbey. They were to be assisted by the trained bands of Cambridgeshire and Huntingdonshire, along with all able bodied men between the ages of 18 and 60. Plus any recruits intended for Manchester's army were to be diverted to the Isle of Ely, where Henry Ireton, the Lieutenant Governor, or in his absence Colonel Valentine Walton would

---

54   CSPD, 1644–45 p.125.
55   Rushworth, *Historical Collections*.
56   CSPD 1644–45, p.139.

take charge of them. They were to be joined by two troops of horse from Suffolk as well as Colonel Fleetwood's regiment of horse. Also any available forces from Nottinghamshire, Derbyshire and Lord Fairfax's army were also to assist in retaking Crowland. The siege was commanded by Lord Fairfax and Colonel Rossiter. On 13 October Sir Samuel Luke wrote to Cromwell informing him that 'all your Lincolnshire forces are now before Crowland'.[57]

However, the wet weather which had plagued the summer campaigns continued into the autumn and on 15 October Luke again wrote to Cromwell 'I am sorry for you have no better weather for your march, nor they for their siege at Crowland, that if this weather should hold it would be impossible to unnestle those bloody rascals that got in'.[58] A week letter nothing had changed when Thomas Bristow wrote to Sir Samuel Luke 'since the enemy's surprise of Crowland we have been perplexed in this county. We had hopes of gaining it by a sudden storming, but are prevented by the wetness of the weather. We are now forced to block it up and endeavour the storming of it'.[59]

The wet weather continued into November, when on 7 November Parliament informed the Associated Counties and the Committee of Northampton, 'by reason of the unseasonableness of the weather the approaches to the said garrison are become so unaccessable, that though forces were drawn down to reduce the same, it cannot now possibly be done without much charge and difficulty'. It added, that to prevent 'any inroads plunderings and other outrages', they should erect three 'forts or sconces … near a place called Brother House, in the county of Lincolnshire, another upon Dowsdale bank in the said county, and a third upon Barrow Bank in the county of Northampton'. The cost of these sconces was about £600 and each was to be garrisoned by about 50 men. Boats were also to be used to prevent any incursions by the Royalists.[60]

On 19 November Luke wrote to the Committee of the Eastern Association informing them that a letter had been found in the collar of a Royalist messenger's doublet, to the effect that the garrison of Crowland could expect a relief force within 14 days; it ordered that they should implement countermeasures, by ordering Colonel Rossiter's and Vermuyden's regiments of horse, who were then at Grantham, to intercept the relieving force.[61] By 29 November Colonel Rainsborough's regiment of foot and Lieutenant Colonel John Lilburne's regiment of dragoons had joined the siege.

However, with the drawing away of forces from other areas, this encouraged the garrison of Newark to launch raids into the counties of the Eastern Association. On 6 December Henry Mildmay, who was then at Cambridge wrote to Manchester:

---

57 H.G. Tibbutt, *The Letter Book of Sir Samuel Luke, 1644–1645* (Society of Bedfordshire, 1958), Letters no. 30, 861.

58 Ibid., letter 34.

59 Ibid., letter 954.

60 *Journal of the House of Lords* vol.7, pp.50–51.

61 Tibbutt, *The Letter Book*, letter 861.

the Newarkers be assurance of Prince Rupert is in Leicestershire and expected at Newark with 2,000 horse, if so your Lordship's men before Crowland will be in danger. I would your Lordship spend some time at Cambridge it would much advantage your Lordship's affairs … It extremely troubles me to consider the miserable condition this town of Cambridge will be in if but 500 horse should come against it in the condition it is now in. I beseech your Lordship to acquaint the Committee of Both Kingdoms what they must expect from this place unless they dismiss your Lordship from the engagement of your army so far west that you may be able fitly to keep those your friends in safety that that maintain your Lordship's army.[62]

The Royalist garrison of Crowland would finally surrender later in December, but not before they had pillaged the soldiers of Captain West's company of their clothes so that on 11 February 1645 £7 4s 10d had to be paid out to reclothe them.[63]

---

62   PA: Wil/2/37. According to the HMC Report this letter is probably dated 1643, but it is clear from the content that it is 1644.
63   CSPD 1644–1645, pp.20, 21, 166; SP: 28/244 part 4, unfoliated.

9

The Winter of Discontent

According to Bulstrode Whitelocke after the battle of Newbury, Cromwell 'seemed (but cautiously enough) to lay more blame on the officers of the Lord General's [Essex's] Army, than upon any other'.[1] Usually the events at Newbury during November are seen as the final break between Manchester and Cromwell, but on 16 September Robert Baillie had written:

> Our labour to reconcile them was [in] vain: Cromwell was pre-emptor, notwithstanding the Kingdom's evident hazard, and the evident displeasure of our Nation; yet if Crawford were not cashiered, his colonels would lay down their commissions. All of us, by my Lord Manchester's own testimony and the testimony of the Ministers in the army, finds Crawford a very honest and valorous man … only persecuted to make way to their designs on that army.[2]

The London merchant Thomas Juxon also heard rumours of tensions within the Eastern Association recording in his diary for 1 October, that there was plan to replace Manchester with Cromwell since he would not march into the west as ordered.[3] Now after the Council of War at Newbury the matter came to a head. On 25 November Cromwell spoke in the House of Commons, charging Manchester with:

> 1. His continued backwardness to all action, averseness to engagement, his neglecting opportunities, and declining to take or pursue advantages upon the enemy, contrary to advice given him and commands received, and when there was no impediment or other employment for his army.
> 2. That he had expressed much contempt and scorn of commands from the Parliament or the Committee of both kingdoms, requiring his advancing with his army, especially those for advancing westwards; and endeavoured to have his army drawn back into his Association to lie idle there, while the business of

---

1   Bulstrode Whitelocke, p.111.
2   Baillie, vol. 2, pp.230–231.
3   Thomas Juxon, *The Journal of Thomas Juxon, 1644–1647*, ed. Keith Lindley and David Scott (Cambridge: Cambridge University Press, 1999), p.59.

the kingdom needed it, and the aforesaid commands required it to be employed elsewhere.

3. That his Lordship used shuffling pretences and evasions sometimes to delay till 'twas too late, sometimes to avoid things propounded to him tending to action, of which the advantage and security were clearly urged upon him, in which he had seemed studiously to decline to gain such advantages, and sometimes to design the drawing of the army off from the advantages it had into a posture of less advantage.

4. That he uttered speeches and expressions concurrent with his said carriages, whereby he declared his dislike to the present war, or the prosecution thereof, his unwillingness to have it prosecuted to a victory or ended by the sword, and his desire to make up the same with some such peace as himself best fancied.[4]

The following day Manchester asked to defend his reputation in the House of Lords, and on 28 November he addressed the Lords in which he wished 'to clear myself from that ignominious brand of unfaithfulness towards the Parliament, who have thought me worthy of their favour and their trust'. He continued, 'from the time I came to join with my Lord General's Army, I never did anything without the joint consent of those that were the best experienced and chiefest commanders in all the armies'. He then referred to the council of war:

> Many arguments were given. Sir Arthur Heselrigge used some expressions to this effect, 'That we run a greater hazard than the king did, for if we beat him, his Army would not be ruined, but he being King still, and retreating to his garrisons, he would recruit his Army, it now being the winter season, but if he had the better of us, our whole forces would be ruined and the kingdom in extreme hazard, having no considerable reserve on this side [of] Newcastle, so that the enemy might without opposition march up to the very walls of London.' And after some others had delivered their opinions against fighting this opinion … was seconded by me, and there was not one present that delivered his opinion for fighting with the King at that time.[5]

In other words Manchester was accusing Heselrigge of saying the words he had been accused of. On 2 December Manchester presented his statement in writing, which the Lords sent to the Commons. The matter was to be divided into two: firstly 'the business of Donnington Castle', which included Manchester conduct during the second battle of Newbury, and secondly the conduct of Cromwell. Seven members of the House of Lords and seven from the Commons were to form a committee to look into the matter, although since Cromwell was an MP it was to be left to the Commons to investigate his conduct.[6]

---

4   CSPD 1644–45, pp.143–144.
5   Rushworth, *Historical Collections* Part III vol. 2, pp.733–735.
6   *Journal of the House of Lords*, vol. 7, p.80.

THE WINTER OF DISCONTENT

The Scottish commissioners were confident that Manchester would be able to clear himself and 'prevent all designs and plots of his enemies'.[7] In another letter the Commissioners in Edinburgh believed that Cromwell was:

> so destructive to the very ends of our mutual League and Covenant as we cannot but in high measure resent the same. His contempt of the [missing] of England, whose just privileges we are sworn to maintain, his h[atred] [a]gainst this nation he avows to be as great against any in his Majesty's Army, his design to see such as are of the Independent judgement in the Earl of Manchester's Army, that they might be able to prevent the [conclusion] of such a peace as might not stand with their ends and the only [missing], the heavy scandal he lays upon the learned and reverend Assembly of Divines of persecutors of honest men then themselves, are in all such testimonies of his seditious intentions that we conceive the honour of both nations is concerned in the exemplary punishment thereof, and particularly this, against whom he professeth he would as soon draw his sword as against these who are declared enemies to both kingdoms.[8]

The dispute even found its way into print, *The Sum of the Charge Given in by Lieutenant General Cromwell against the Earl of Manchester*, in which it charged Manchester of:

> always been indisposed and backward to engagements and against ending the War by the sword; and for such a peace to which a victory would be a disadvantage; and this declared by principles expressed to that purpose … Since the taking of York … he hath declined whatever tended to further advantage upon the enemy, neglected and studiously shifted off all opportunities to that purpose, as if he though the King to low and Parliament to high, especially at Donnington Castle. He hath drawn the Army too, and detained them in such a posture as to give the enemy fresh advantages.

In his *Englishmen's Birthright* printed in 1645 John Lilburne also referred to Manchester's 'treachery and baseness at Donnington Castle, and other places'.

However, the debate in Parliament and the press asked the question that no one wanted to answer. Since the beginning of the war, Parliamentarian propaganda had said they were fighting for 'King and Parliament' in order to protect Charles from his evil counsellors, but no one had decided on the end game. True there had always been a Peace Party in Parliament, but at this stage even the War Party did not want to depose King Charles I from the throne and even less wanted to execute him. Therefore a decision had to be made: do they demand a conditional or an unconditional surrender of the King?

What is clear is that despite Manchester's protests, under a strong leader the combined armies at Newbury might have proved decisive, but although he was loved by many of his men, Manchester was no such leader. Furthermore,

---

7   Henry W. Meikle, *Correspondence of the Scots Commissioners in London, 1644–1646* (Edinburgh: The Roxburghe Club, 1917), pp.49–50.

8   Meikle, *Correspondence*, pp.51–52. The square brackets are Meikle's.

the Committee of Both Kingdoms had shackled the army's hierarchy by imposing restrictions on them so they had to rely on a Council of War to make decisions, overseen by two observers, Sir Archibald Johnstone and John Crew, whose job it was to report to the Committee.

It was also becoming clear that something had to be done to settle this argument before the 1645 campaigning season began, so between 25 November and 6 January 1645 witnesses to these charges were heard by a Committee with Zouch Tate being in the chair. Tate was the MP for Northampton in both the Short and Long Parliaments and saw the dispute more as the result of 'pride and covetousness'. While it is seen as a quarrel between the factions of Manchester and Cromwell, Sir William Waller also appears to have played a leading role as the following entry in the *Journal of the House of Commons* clearly shows for 25 November:

> Ordered. That all the particulars of the narrative this day made upon the order and injunction of this House, by Sir William Waller and Lieutenant General Cromwell concerning divers passages and proceedings of the armies, be referred to the examination of the committee formerly appointed for my Lord General's Army, where Mr Tate has the chair: with power to send for parties, witnesses, papers, records, and to examine Sir William Waller, Lieutenant General Cromwell and Sir Arthur Haselrigge in this business if occasion shall be; and with power to send to the Committee of Both Kingdoms for copies of such letters as have been written upon occasion of this business: and they bring in a report with all convenient speed.[9]

The statements of 18 witnesses have survived, nine coming from Manchester's own army, and five from Waller's, including Waller and Heselrige. Sir James Harrington, the commander of the London brigade also gave evidence. Only Captain Thomas Rawlins can be identified as having a connection to Essex's army, although according to his statement he appears to have been with Manchester during of the second battle of Newbury. A Captain John Hooper also gave evidence but it is unknown which regiment he served with.[10]

No witnesses were called on Manchester's behalf by the Committee of Both Kingdoms, but one of Manchester's officers, William Dodson, claimed:

> The sinister ends of Cromwell … by the putting out of all brave gentlemen in the army by false suggestions to my Lord and bringing in of others in their places, who afterwards proved traitors and cowards, and still fomenting further mischief in the army, notably seconded by Pickering. Before York, our horse being absent from my Lord of Manchester in pretence of doing good service to the public,

---

9 *Journal of the House of Commons*, vol. III, p.704.
10 Lieutenant Generals Cromwell and Hammond, Colonels John Pickering and Edward Montagu, Lieutenant Colonels Nathaniel Rich, John Lilburne, Quarter Master General Henry Ireton and Major John Disbrowe or Disborough; Scout Master General Leon Watson came from Manchester's army; while from Waller's army was Waller himself, Sir Arthur Heselrige, Colonels Richard Norton, and Samuel Jones and Scout Master General James Pitson. Also Sir James Harrington, John Weaver the Judge Advocate. Captains Thomas Rawlin and John Hooper.

THE WINTER OF DISCONTENT

> Cromwell and his creatures did nothing but foment sedition and dissension in my Lord's army of horse.[11]

On 4 December 1644 after getting no satisfaction from the Committee of Both Kingdoms, Manchester wrote to the House of Lords:

> I cannot but wonder at so high a slander, and if this relate to those of my own army, wherein I hope there are many honest men, though differing in judgement to what I profess, yet I shall appeal to them whether I have at any time been failing in my respects unto them; and I can say that upon some of them I have looked with that value and esteem, as that the choice and approbation of most of the commanders in the army have been in their power. Lieutenant General Cromwell shall be my compurgator in this particular. He knows that I always placed him in chiefest esteem and credit with me. But it is true that of late I have not given so free and full a power unto him as formerly I did.[12]

Manchester went on to say that it was not just himself that Cromwell and the 'war party' were after, but also that they wanted to be rid of the entire nobility and that he showed nothing but 'contempt of the Assembly of Divines … animosity against the Scottish nation … [and that] he could as soon draw his sword against them as against any in the king's army'.[13]

Although the quarrel had begun between Manchester and Cromwell it soon turned towards the Earl of Essex, as Bulstrode Whitelocke states that he 'was set on by that party who contrived the outing of the Lord General and to bring in their own on their own designs'.[14] As early as the summer of 1643 efforts had been made to deprive Essex of his position as Lord General and appoint Waller in his place, since Essex had done very little since the surrender of Reading in April of that year. On the other hand Waller with his Western Association army had achieved a string of victories, but the battle of Roundway Down in July changed all that, since Waller's luck finally ran out and his army was routed; whereas Essex had finally stirred himself and had successfully relieved Gloucester, before winning the first battle of Newbury.

Meanwhile a Parliamentary delegation of the Peace Party had entered Oxford at the end of November and had been met with derision from their Royalist hosts, until Charles, who had just returned from collecting his artillery pieces from Donnington Castle, showed a willingness to open negotiations. On 3 December both Houses voted that a Royalist delegation should be allowed to come to Westminster to negotiate. That evening Essex held a meeting at his house in London to further the efforts of the Peace Party. At the meeting were several Scottish Commissioners who discussed what action they should take against Cromwell. One of these commissioners argued that:

---

11   Bruce and Masson, p.60.
12   BodLib: Tanner, MS. vol. 61. fol. 205.
13   Ibid.
14   Whitelocke, p.113.

Cromwell is no friend of ours and since the advance of our Army into England, he hath used all underhand and cunning means to take off from our honour and merit towards this Kingdom; an evil requital of all our hazards and services … for not only is [he] no friend to us, and to the government of our church, but he is also no well willer to his excellency [Essex] … and if he be permitted to go on in his ways, it may, I fear, endanger the whole business'.[15]

The Scottish commissioner went on to describe Cromwell as an 'incendiary, who kindleth coals of contention' who would divide Scotland and England, so that 'we will [have to] clip his wings from soaring to the prejudice of our Cause'.[16] Among those present was Bulstrode Whitelocke and John Maynard, who argued that Cromwell was in a too secure a position to be challenged and more evidence was needed to prove his guilt. Therefore the meeting agreed to obtain further proof before they could move against Cromwell.

However, according to Rushworth, at this meeting there were some 'false brethren' who informed Cromwell of the moves being made against him. Knowing this when Cromwell stood up to speak in the House of Commons on 9 December, he called for not just the aristocracy in the army to be removed but also the 'casting off [of] all lingering proceedings like soldiers of fortune [from] beyond sea'. He continued those:

members of both Houses have got great places and commands … in the army, will perpetually continue themselves in grandeur, and not permit the war speedily to end, lest their own power should [be] determine with it … I do conceive if the army be not put into another method, and the war more vigorously prosecuted, the people can bear the war no longer, and will enforce you to a dishonourable peace … [Therefore] let us apply ourselves to the remedy which is most necessary: And I hope, we have such true English hearts and zealous affections towards the general weal of our mother country, as no members of this House will scruple to deny themselves and their own private interests for the public good, nor account it be a dishonour done to them whatever the Parliament shall resolve upon in this weighty matter.[17]

Another MP declared that the victories obtained by the Parliamentarian armies had been 'put into a bag of holes, what we won one time, we lost another. The treasury is exhausted, the countries wasted. A summer's victory has proved a winter's story'.[18] To many it was clear that more was needed than just replacing Manchester and Essex. As early as the 2 July 1644 Waller had written to the Committee of Both Kingdoms for the need to reform the armies, but this was more about the London brigade under his command rather than foreign officers, 'My Lords, I write these particularities to let you know that an army compounded of these men will never go through with their service, and till you have an army merely [of] your own that you may

---

15   Rushworth, *Historical* Collections, part IV, vol.1.
16   Ibid.
17   Ibid, pp.1–2.
18   Ibid.

command, it is in a manner impossible to do anything of importance'.[19] A petition of the senior officers in Essex's army, dated 8 January 1645, records the 'additional forces sent forth for our supply out of the Trained Bands and Auxiliaries of London are found to be more destructive then supporting to us for their great pay in hiring soldiers they entreat ours to runaway and do but give us old soldiers put under new commanders'.[20] Unfortunately for the armies of Waller and Essex they were not strong enough to take the field without the support of the London trained bands, because their armies were a mere shadow of their former size and Manchester's was not much better. Therefore if Parliament was to win the war then it needed restructuring: not just the senior commanders but also the officers and men.

After some debate on 9 December, Zouch Tate proposed 'that no member of either House of Parliament shall during the war enjoy or execute any office or command military or civil and that an ordinance be brought in to that purpose'. This proposal was seconded by Sir Henry Vane.[21] This would later be known as the Self-denying Ordinance, since acts of Parliament needed the royal ascent. On 18 December it was proposed that Essex should be exempt from the Ordinance, which was rejected by 100 votes to 93, or just seven votes, as also was the proposal that all officers should take the Covenant. The following day the Bill was passed to the House of Lords for debate.[22]

On 24 December the Ordinance was heard in the Lords, and after much debate was finally thrown out on 13 January 1645. On 25 February a committee was appointed to compose a new ordinance, which appears to have been chaired by John Lisle. Meanwhile a committee was also set up to look into the 'new modelling' of the army chaired by Zouch Tate.[23] On 21 January Sir Thomas Fairfax was appointed to command this new army and a list of colonels were also presented to Parliament, which included Crawford, Pickering, Montagu, Ayloffe, Sydney, Rich, Vermuyden and Fleetwood, all of whom came from Manchester's army. The Commons went through the list 'one by one and one by one voted, all [were] approved', except Colonel Ayloffe. The proposed company commanders were also voted upon and Major Harrison and Captain Le Hunt were referred back to Sir Thomas Fairfax. What the MPs objections were towards these three is not recorded, but the problem with the major and captain was quickly resolved and their names were added to the list once more. However, the regiment which was to be commanded by Ayloffe, passed to Colonel Thomas Rainsborough.

On 10 March the list was sent to the Lords for approval, but they proposed a drastic alternation of the officers: Fairfax's, Skippon's, Holborne's and Crawford's were 'wholly approved of', but Rainsborough was to be replaced by a Colonel Ogleby and Colonel William Herbert was to replace Montagu. Unlike the company commanders to Rainsborough's regiment, a large number of officers of Montagu's regiment were also to be purged. The Lords

---

19 CSPD 1644, pp.300–301.
20 BL: Harl MS 166, f.174.
21 Rushworth, *Historical Collections*.
22 *Journal of the House of Commons* vol. III, p.726.
23 *Journal of the House of Commons* vol. IV, pp.25, 26.

also wanted Lord Robartes' regiment to replace Pickering's in the new army and be commanded by William Hunter, who had been Robartes' lieutenant colonel in Essex's army. The cavalry was not exempt either. Although no colonels were to lose their commands, several English officers in Middleton's regiment were to lose their positions in favour of Scottish ones, while four troop commanders of Sidney's regiment, three from Fleetwood's and just one from Vermuyden's, were to be replaced. As to Cromwell's old regiment, only two from Whalley's regiment were to be replaced.[24] On 13 March a conference was held between members of the both Houses to discuss the Lords' changes to the list of officers, which after much discussion decided that they were only 'recommendations' rather suggestions and so two days later the Lords decided to agree to the Commons' list of officers so the more radical officers remained.[25]

However, there would be further changes: Colonel Edward Aldrich, who had served with Essex's army wrote to Fairfax about the officers within his new regiment being 'of weak resolution so I conceive it to be both dishonourable for me to engage with them', and so was replaced. Colonel Algernon Sidney resigned his commission claiming that his old wound, which he had received at Marston Moor, made him unfit for military service, but not before he had been offered the governorship of Chichester in Sussex and Colonel of the city's garrison. Therefore Sidney and Aldrich's places were taken by their Lieutenant Colonels, Nathaniel Rich and Walter Lloyd, respectively. Sidney was not the only officer to be appointed to the new model army who was unfit for service: Captain John Gorges who was appointed captain to Sir Hardress Waller's regiment, but did not join the regiment until 8 July 1645 due to a 'sore wound … in his leg whereby he was disabled to serve'.[26]

At this stage the list still included the Scottish officers, Crawford, Middleton and Holborne, who were approved of by the Lords and it appeared that the commander of each regiment was now settled. However, Edmund Ludlow recalls, Parliament 'agreed upon the colonels, some whereof were Scots, as Middleton, Holborne and others, who disliking the design, refused to accept … [their] employments'. Unfortunately, Ludlow does not elaborate on what their objections were; it has been suggested that they resigned their commissions because there were no Scottish regiments included in the new model army, since Parliament wanted a purely English army. But there had not been any Scottish regiments in Manchester's, Essex's or Waller's armies either, just Scottish officers who had commanded regiments and companies raised in England. In fact five of the 24 regiments within the new model army were either to be commanded by Scottish or Dutch colonels, compared to two in Manchester's field army of 10 regiments or six in Essex's army which was composed of 18 regiments during the Summer of 1644. Moreover, there were more English officers who lost their commands on the formation of the new model army that Scottish ones. According to Richard Baxter, this meant

24   PA:, HL/PO/JO/10/1/182.
25   *Journal of the House of Lords*, vol. VII, pp.272, 274.
26   TNA: SP 28/31 f.158.

that some of 'the best of the old officers [were] put into rest [i.e. retired]', and unsuitable officers put in their place.[27]

Another reason given is that the Earl of Montrose, who was fighting for the King in Scotland, was gaining the upper hand so they wanted to protect their homeland, while another theory is one of religious differences in that being Presbyterians they did not wish to serve with the Independents who made up a large part of the new model army. This may be to a certain extent true, but there may have been a much simpler explanation. If they stayed in the new model army then they would be demoted to rank of colonel, whereas by transferring to the Scottish army they would retain their rank and status as major generals, or in Middleton's case, Lieutenant General of horse. True, this theory does not explain Colonel Harry Barclay, lately of Essex's army, but if he had stayed then he would have been the only Scottish officer serving in the army. Middleton in particular would probably have felt particularly snubbed by the remodelling of the army since he had commanded the cavalry in Waller's army and it was obvious that the position of lieutenant general of horse was being left open for Cromwell, even though he was disqualified from serving in the army since he was an MP.[28]

On 8 June 1645 the Dutchman Colonel Vermuyden, announced to Fairfax that he needed to resign his commission due to urgent business overseas, although according to Thomas Juxon he was blamed for the loss of Leicester, 'who had a great party of horse and did not interrupt the king as he might'.[29] With his departure it ended any 'foreign' involvement with the new model army, so that if it had been Cromwell's and the War Party's intention to have an English army they got it by default rather than design. However, even before Vermuyden's resignation he is also known to have been in contact with the Scottish Commissioner, because on 15 May they wrote to the Earl of Leven, 'to entertain kindly Colonel Vermuyden'. Middleton was already commanding a regiment in the Scottish army and on 20 May the commissioners recommended that Crawford should also be a major general in their army.[30]

Although he had been appointed commander of the army on 21 January, it was not until 11 March that Fairfax had the power to choose:

> all such lieutenants, sergeants and other under officers and soldiers, as he shall think fit … now or late in the several armies under the immediate command of the Lord General the Earl of Essex, the Earl of Manchester and Sir William Waller, and likewise all gunners, gentlemen of the ordnance and other officers and soldiers belonging to the several trains of artillery in the said several armies.[31]

27 Richard Baxter, *Reliquiae Baxterianae or Mr Richard Baxter's narrative of the most memorable passages of his life and times* (1696), p.48.
28 *Journal of the House of Commons* vol. III, p26; *Journal of the House of Lords*, vol. VII, pp.266, 278–279.
29 Juxon, p.79.
30 Meikle, p.75.
31 *Journal of the House of Lords*, vol. VII, pp.269, 293–296.

Therefore, he could not appoint the regimental commanders, nor the lieutenant colonels, majors and captains.

On 24 March the Self-Denying Ordinance was finally passed in the Commons and then on 3 April by the Lords, although by this time Manchester, Essex and Waller had already resigned their commissions along with others from the House of Lords and Commons who were serving in the army, which should have included Cromwell.

While the debates were going on in Parliament over the future of the army and its commanders, many officers and soldiers within these armies were loyal to their commanders and so did not want to see them replaced. On 6 January Adjutant General Richard Sterling (or Starling), the governor of Henley-on-Thames, held a meeting of his fellow officers to prevent Manchester from being dismissed:

> that his Lordship might command his army as he did formerly whereupon I replied in this manner, gentlemen let us take heed what we do for it is a very dangerous consequence to petition against the proceedings of the Houses of Parliament for I have heard that they have voted that no members neither Lords or Commons should command in the army and said again gentlemen let us therefore take heed what we do for I know by experience the danger of petitioning against the votes of Parliament.[32]

There was then a debate whether the matter had been voted on or not, while others argued that only the Commons had voted on it and not the Lords. Sterling then said that both the Earls of Essex and Warwick had already been voted in again, but not Manchester and he assured those present that the petition would not be sent without the approval of members of the council of lawyers, and said if they did not approve it then the petition would not be delivered. If it was approved the commander of each regiment would present it to the House. The petition appears to have been instigated by Captain Moses O'Neale of Manchester's regiment of foot. Captain Dennis Taylor of Montagu's regiment, who Montagu had cashiered as a trouble maker supported the petition, while Captain Richard Harby of Colonel Hobart's regiment did sign it, but later wrote to the Committee of Both Kingdoms apologising because 'contrary to [Sterling's] promise it was sent away privately by Captain O'Neale and no member asked to go along with it'.[33] While Captain William Wilkes refused to subscribe to the petition, and so was called an 'enemy unto my Lord'.[34]

On 10 January the matter was referred to the House of Commons who in turn referred it to the Committee for Regulating the Army. It seems that Captain O'Neale was seen as the main conspirator since he was to be brought to the House in 'safe custody … and all such papers and petitions as are about him to be seized; and that until he be examined no man be permitted to

---

32 SP: 16/106 f.29, Captain William Disney's account.
33 Ibid, f.28, Captain Richard Harby's account.
34 Ibid, f.27, Captain William Wilkes' account.

speak with him'.[35] Whereas Adjutant General Sterling was just 'summoned'. True this might have been due to his rank rather than lack of guilt, but on 28 February when the Committee reported back to the Committee of Both Kingdoms, that Sterling had not known who had drawn up the petition but Captain O'Neale was the one who showed it to him. He did admit that he had called the meeting of all the officers of the garrison of Henley to ask them their opinion of the petition. All but two objected to signing it, and those that did, did so under the condition that 'it should not be presented to the House if it were found unlawful or any way against the privileges of the House'. He further denied preventing any of the officers going to London and that he did not sign the petition nor knew of its whereabouts.[36] However, on the same day Sterling was summoned to London, Colonel Edward Montagu was appointed governor of Henley-on-Thames in his place. This petition was not the only disorder within the town's garrison, because a mutiny broke out within Montagu's regiment as we will see in the next chapter.

When Cromwell's regiment heard that Cromwell was to be replaced by a Scottish officer, it also mutinied until they were assured that this was not the case.[37] The regiment appears to have mutinied again in March, although the newspaper *The Moderate Intelligencer* disguises the fact by saying that 'there being many of Lieutenant General Cromwell's regiment who were gone into the country to visit their friends, and could not have timely notice of his going into the West'.[38] It was not just the regiments of the Eastern Association who mutinied, but also the soldiers of the Earl of Essex's army. On 31 March the House of Commons informed the Lords that 'the army is in mutiny and disorder, and they know not who to obey; And until this [Self-denying] Ordinance be passed Sir Thomas Fairfax has no power to do anything'.[39] Only Waller's army does not seem to have mutinied since it was too dispersed in the garrisons in the west to be of any sizeable threat. In May 1645 Edward Massey succeeded Waller as the commander of the regiments in the west.

On 1 May 1645 a Royalist newspaper recorded that Sir Thomas Fairfax had advanced with his army, 'with Major General Skippon marched in the van of the foot and leadeth the General's own Regiment, Sir Thomas Fairfax's colours are blue; the men are red coats all, the whole army, only are distinguished by their several facing colours of their coats, the firelock (only) some of them are tawny coats'.[40] This was the new model army which would go on to win the war for the Parliamentary cause. However, the transition from the old armies to the new was not as smooth as history has led us to believe. Although London and Kent supported the move, others did not, including those of the Eastern Association who feared for their security. On 30 January 1645 a conference was held at Bury St Edmunds, the chair being appointed from one of the members of Suffolk who set out why the Eastern Association

---

35 *Journal of the House of Commons*, vol. IV, pp.15–16.
36 CSPD 1644–45, pp.325–326.
37 Whitelocke, p.126.
38 BL: TT E 274/9, *The Moderate Intelligencer*, 13–20 March 1645.
39 *Journal of the House of Lords*, vol. VII, p.293.
40 TT E 260/32 *Perfect Passages of each days proceedings in Parliament*, 30 April–7 May 1645, p.218.

had raised regiments 'to aid and assist one another … for the mutual defence of the said counties', and that it was now 'in danger of disturbance'.[41]

The meeting then discussed that the new model army would be 'for the safety of the kingdom', but it was pointed out that 'this was not our work being then met as Committees for the Association'. This meeting then discussed what the new model army meant which resulted in Colonel Henry Mildmay reciting what he had heard in London and what he had read in the various newspapers.[42] The meeting then discussed another question: 'How far the incorporating of our associated army in the New Model doth impair the Association? Affirmed by the most that the consistence thereof was taken away and by all that the ends and purpose thereof are abrogate'.[43]

The chairman then went on to 'whether it be not necessary to endeavour the repair and preservation of the Association'? To which the minutes record, 'The affirmative passed … till it came to the gentleman of Hertfordshire who insisted that the contrary thereto might be beneficial for the Kingdom and the counties'.[44] The meeting then set out:

the fears of the people;
1. The danger of dissolving the bond of the association.
2. The withdrawing of their army from this their mutual assistance by incorporating it with the other forces employed for the good of the Kingdom.
3. Their disability of subsistence and consistence.
4. Their complaints of extreme charge not only in maintaining their army but of the other forces employed for the Kingdom and not relating to the mutual subsistence of the Associated counties and their surcharges in raising the trained bands and other auxiliaries in case of alarms in the absence of the associated counties.[45]

They also feared that the Association would not have a say about the regiments which they had already raised once they entered the new model army. Therefore it was proposed that a letter with instructions rather than as a petition be sent to Parliament and after some consultation the chairman presented a draught to the meeting that afternoon;

We hold it our duty to render an account to your lordships of a general meeting of deputy lieutenants and committee selected and deputed from the seven associated eastern counties assembled at Bury St Edmund to advise for the mutual and future assistance of each other for the composing of the fears of the people and for answer of your Lordships letter concerning recruits of our army and according to the result of the said conference we humbly exhibit to

41 PA: MAN/32. Unfortunately the minutes do not record who the chairman was. Maurice Barrow, the High Sherriff of the Suffolk, Sir William Spring, Sir John Wentworth, Henry North senior, Francis Bacon, Thomas Terrell, Thomas Bacon, Gibson Lucas, Thomas Chaplin, Thomas Gibbs, Brampton Gurdon junior and Nathaniel Bacon represented the county at this meeting.
42 Ibid.
43 Ibid.
44 Ibid.
45 Ibid.

your Lordships consideration the sad apprehension had by the people of these counties of the alteration of the army now in agitation in the Parliament as that which will take away from them not only the head and body of their strength, designed, promised and by ordinance settled for their mutual assistance, but also deprive them of [the] means of future subsistence and consistence and so render their solemn promise of Association ineffectual which God almighty hitherto hath graciously honoured, by witness of His concurrence with success of victory to the army and general peace of the most part even to their borders to the wonderment of all observers and envy of the enemy. We may not conceal from your Lordships [any] other [of] their complaints of being left naked to the secret Malignants at home and to the watchful enraged enemy abroad, not to be withstood without hindrance of their callings and spending of their stocks upon alarms, as hitherto they have been, and yet deeply charged also in maintenance of our army and other forces in service elsewhere. By all which your Lordships may conjecture how hardly recruits will arise especially to unknown captains and commanders. Nevertheless, for our own parts none of their discouragements or any private regard shall withdraw our zeal from the service of your honours, the Parliament and kingdom not only in [the] recruiting of our army, but by giving all encouragement we are able to the forces to go to the west or whither soever they shall be ordered, according to our proportion in defence to the other armies. Yet for the facilitating of the said recruits we humbly offer to your Lordships that one ordinance or more may be passed to enable us to impress men and to deduct money for the coat and conduct of the soldiers out of the weekly assessments which shall be laid upon us without which the work can never be effected; and that for the encouragement of the soldiers each county may have power to pay their own men and that some provision may be made for [the] relief of sick and maimed and by this means we hope the work may prove successful and seasonable; which being done, if we may not have their continuing assistance for our mutual defence, which we cannot but desire in consistence with the public we make this our humble and most earnest request that our brethren of the Scots Army in the North parts may forthwith be speeded down to Newark and besiege that place which hath been a sore to the Association from the beginning of these wars hitherto and is like to prove an issue to waste the poor remainder of the means thereof and more especially of our associated friends of Lincolnshire if some speedy proceedings be not made against that place. This together with the peoples expectation of your Lordships' care of them in relation to this our humble proposal will we hope settle the disturbed motions of their minds and keep them ready at your service. To which also we humbly offer ourselves.[46]

The instructions were:

1. That no military power be exercised in the Association but by Ordinance of Parliament.

---

46   Ibid.

2. That all the forts and magazines in each county of the Association be committed to the care and disposal of such persons as the Deputy Lieutenants and committee of each county shall confide in.

3. That every committee may be enjoined to pay their forces monthly and that in case they should fail of treasure sufficient, they may be enabled to advance money upon interest to be repaid out of the next moneys. This will both prevent mutinies and usual recruits in a great measure.

4. That the Deputy Lieutenants and committees of each county may put in execution all former and future ordinances.

5. That the seven associated counties and the two cities of Norwich and Lincoln may have their several and certain proportion of men, money and horses set by Parliament.

6. That in case any alarm come from a considerable body of the enemy to any county of the Association which shall be and continue above three days necessitating the raising of the trained bands or auxiliaries that then the charge shall be born by every county in the Association according to proportion.

7. That in case these forces now intended to be raised by authority of Parliament shall not be thought sufficient for accomplishment of a desired period to this destructive civil war, that then this Association will use their best diligence and endeavour to raise their uttermost power and strength to join with proportionable forces of other parts with the counties for the speedy furnishing and eradicating of this unnatural war.[47]

It was the decided that two men from each county should present the letter and instructions and at midnight the meeting or diet broke up.[48] Although 33 men are recorded as attending the meeting, 35 signed the letter of which 16 presented it to the House of Lords on 5 February 1645. The Lords recorded the letter in their journal, but appear to have done little else to appease the fears of the Committee of the Eastern Association.

---

47   Ibid.
48   Ibid, *Journal of the House of Lords*, vol. VII, p.178. In part 7 of the instructions in the *Journal of the House of Lords* reads slightly differently: 'proportionable forces of other parts and counties'.

10

Last Campaigns

The Royalists knew of the infighting in Parliament and the reorganisation of its main armies, which they dubbed 'The New Noddle Army', and so they had a great opportunity to recruit and organise their armies, but unfortunately for Charles, the grandees and faction fighting within his army meant that little was done and the time was wasted.[1] Although one unexpected opportunity arose in November, when Roger Le Strange and other gentlemen of Suffolk and Norfolk sent a letter confirming their loyalty to Charles I. On 28 November, Roger Le Strange received a letter of thanks from George Digby, who commissioned him to seize King's Lynn with the loyal inhabitants being rewarded with service or money. Once the town had been secured he would be made governor and Charles would send a 'considerable power' to garrison it. Unfortunately for Le Strange, despite the letter he had little support and when he tried to bribe a sea captain by the name of Leaman with £1,000, the captain informed Colonel Valentine Walton, who promptly had him arrested and at a court martial he was condemned to death. However, his sentence was commuted to imprisonment, where he remained until 1648 when he managed to escape and flee abroad. It was not until 1653 that he returned to England, having made his peace with the Commonwealth government.

In January 1645 Manchester's infantry mustered the following:[2]

Regiment	Strength
Manchester's	984
Crawford's	267
Pickering's	243
Hobart's	(254)
Montagu's	(285)
Russell's	422
Hoogan's (formerly Palgrave's)	526
	2,981

---

1   Clarendon, p.255.
2   Holmes, *The Eastern Association*, p.238. No muster rolls survive for Hobart's or Montagu's regiments so the figures in brackets Clive Holmes based on treasury returns.

As well as these regiments there were another three forming garrisons which brought his infantry up to about 4,200 men. In addition there was the regiment of dragoons mustering 263 men and five regiments of cavalry forming about 3,744 troopers, or a total of 8,207 men.[3] On 16 January the counties of the Eastern Association were ordered to recruit another 3,000 men, with Hobart's and Montagu's regiments each receiving 500 of these men. These two regiments were to receive batches of 100 to 200 recruits once they became available rather than wait until the full 500 men had been recruited. The Committee of Both Kingdoms added that, 'we recommend it unto you to have them levied in those places from whence those regiments have been levied'.[4]

With the beginning of the campaigning season it was decided to split Manchester's army into two: Cromwell was ordered to assist Waller in the west, while Crawford was ordered to Cheshire to assist Sir William Brereton.

Cromwell

During the winter some of Manchester's cavalry appear to have been quartered around Swallowfield and Stratfield Saye in Hampshire, because complaints were made to the Commons that 'my Lord of Manchester's forces had lain there so long … there was not subsistence for horse'. The petitioner must have belonged to the army because he does not mention the sufferings of the local residents, who had to feed and quarter not only the horses but the troopers too.[5] Fearing a Royalist invasion through Hampshire and Surrey on 13 January, the Committee of Both Kingdoms ordered detachments of Essex's and Manchester's armies to march to Farnham to await further orders. The plan was that they would be joined by Lieutenant General John Middleton with a detachment of horse that was quartered at Guildford in Surrey.[6] However, the threat of invasion soon passed and after approaching Farnham, the Royalists withdrew again to Andover and then into the west. On 2 February Waller wrote to the Committee of Both Kingdoms:

> I have had conference with Colonel John Greaves and the foot officers, from whom I have this information, that the Lord General's horse are about 600, his and Manchester's foot 2,000, and Manchester's horse near 700. I cannot yet give a particular account of my own forces, both in regard they are quartered more remote from me, and I know not to what proportion they are recruited. To-morrow morning I propose to take a view of the foot, and in the afternoon of the Lord General's and Manchester's horse.[7]

3   Ibid., p.237.
4   CSPD 1644–1645, p.258.
5   *Journal of the House of Commons*, vol. IV, p.16.
6   CSPD 1644–1645, p.249.
7   Ibid., p.282.

Having examined the cavalry Waller returned to his base at Farnham, from where on 7 February he again wrote to the Committee, informing them:

> I have sent you enclosed an account of Manchester's horse, by which you will see how far short they fall of your reckoning, and you will perceive by the Commissioners that the Lord General's troops hold out no better. It was your resolution that these troops in all should make up 1,500 horse, besides seven troops which were appointed of the remainder of Lieutenant General Cromwell's Regiment to join with me by way of [an] addition to my forces. If they should only amount to a little over the half, I desire to know how far you will think fit I should engage, and beg to have some instructions to direct me.[8]

Unfortunately Waller's account of the condition of the Eastern Association has not survived. Two troops of Cromwell's regiment of horse which had reinforced the garrison of Henley-on-Thames were ordered to march into the west on 1 March, their place being filled by Captains Tomlinson and Neville's troops of Manchester's regiment of horse. Two days later Cromwell was ordered to join Waller to relieve Melcombe Regis with 'all possible expedition'.[9]

On 8 March Waller and Cromwell beat up the Royalists' quarters at Andover. Among the prisoners of Lord Percy's regiment Cromwell noticed:

> A youth of so fair countenance, that he doubted of his condition; and to confirm himself willed him to sing; which he died with such daintiness that Cromwell scrupled not to say to Lord Percy, that being a warrior, he did wisely to be accompanied by *Amazons*: on which that Lord in some confusion, did acknowledge that she was a damsel; this afterwards gave cause for scoff at the King's party, as that they were loose and wanton, and minded their pleasure, more than either their country's service or their master's good.[10]

This young woman was Lord Percy's mistress rather than a trooper. The action at Andover was followed four days later by the two generals destroying a Royalist regiment of horse, under the command of Sir James Long, in a series of skirmishes between Westbury and Steeple Ashton.[11] After these skirmishes Waller seems to have sent Cromwell to join elements of his army already in the west, where he would again meet his old adversary Lord George Goring. On 27 March Waller wrote from Downton:

> Our duty and marches have been extreme, so that we are here a tired company and necessitated to make some stay for our refreshing. Lieutenant General Cromwell I presume, is this day joined with Major General Holborne for he was

8   Ibid., pp.291–292.
9   Ibid., pp. 331, 334.
10 Sir William Waller, *Recollections*, in *The Poetry of Anna Matilda* (1788), pp.125–126.
11 BL: T E274/14, Waller Sir William, *A Copie of Sir William Waller's letter of the great victory obtained by Sir William Waller and Lieutenant General Cromwell against Colonel James Long (High Sheriff of Wiltshire) who was driven from Devices and his whole regiment taken* (London: Robert Austin, 1645).

last night at Bridport. I hope General Goring's drawing down after me towards Mere and leaving [Sir Richard] Grenville with his and Berkeley's forces at and about Chard, may afford our forces some good opportunity. I have sent an express with all speed after Lieutenant General Cromwell to know where and how I may join him, and I shall apprehend the first opportunity to do it. I cannot but advise you that since my coming thither I have observed a great smoke of discontent rising among the officers. I pray God no flame break out. The ground of all is the extremity of want that is among them, indeed in an insupportable measure.[12]

The following day he proceeded to Calne, while the forces of Cromwell and Holborne had joined at Bridport, together their forces were about 4,500 strong. On 29 March *Mercurius Aulicus* records:

Cromwell lying at Dorchester with all his own horse and the united forces from Taunton, Poole and Weymouth, 4,000 in all. Goring had notice of it and advanced towards them with 1,500 horse the rest of the Royal cannon and army being ordered to follow for securing the retreat. 800 of the Parliament horse disputed a pass up on a little river; but some of Goring's horse facing them there whilst others got in behind them, they presently quitted the pass and fled. Whereupon Goring chased them four miles; took many, with two colours of horse and great store of carbines and pistols and slew more. Their forces were so beaten and scattered that, of 4,000 at first they durst not next morning draw out of the town against 1,500 of Goring's horse; although his horse, foot and cannon were full 6 miles behind.

Later that day the forces of Cromwell and Holborne were reported to have joined Waller at Cerne Abbas, bringing their combined strength to about 8,000 horse and foot.[13] However, the campaign was taking its toll on the Parliamentarian force. In a letter to his father Sir Samuel Luke records:

If I should tell of Waller and Cromwell losing 800 or 900 horse and foot you will hardly believe it, and though I heard of it about seven nights ago yet I perceive it is not yet come to London, though bonfires were made at Oxford on Friday last and bells rung for it also ... I fear the cavaliers have had good success which makes your Diurnals so silent in London.[14]

Waller and Cromwell decided to retire to Salisbury in a series of night marches to conceal their movements from Goring. A short time later Waller and Cromwell parted, Waller heading for Reading while Cromwell marched into Oxfordshire. On 24 April Symonds recalls in his diary:

Cromwell's horse and dragoons ruined some of our horse quartered about Islip of the Lord of Northampton's command. 21 buried in Islip, 18 buried in [blank] over against Kidlington; and this day they demanded up Bletchingdon, a house

---

12   BL: Tanner MS 60/15, Sir William Waller to the Speaker of the House of commons, William Lenthall, 27 March 1645.
13   TT E 278/8, *The Weekly Intelligencer*, 8–15 April 1645.
14   Luke, *The Letter Books of Sir Samuel Luke*, no. 540.

belonging to Sir Thomas Coghill, where in Colonel Windebank had 200 foot, sans works, and provisions only for two or three days … About two or three of the clock, Friday [25 April] the colonel valiantly gave up the house and all his armed, besides 50 horse that came thither for shelter; and this without a shot.[15]

On 3 May Richard Symonds recorded in his diary 'Cromwell's forces removed to Faringdon, else if they had stayed Prince Rupert and General Goring had fallen upon them. They were twice repulsed by Farringdon men with great loss to them.'[16]

Crawford

After the three armies had dispersed from Newbury, Crawford went to Reading and was still there on 22 December, before proceeding to Aylesbury, to replace 600 men of Lieutenant Colonel Martin's regiment, who on 13 January had been ordered to march to Henley-on-Thames. However, on 16 January this order was changed and Martin was ordered to march to Farnham. On 5 February the Committee of Both Kingdoms changed their minds again and ordered him to return to Aylesbury.[17] Upon Martin's return Crawford was to march to Henley, but he was still at Aylesbury on 13 February, since his force had mutinied over their arrears of pay, which prompted the Committee of Both Kingdoms to write:

> [We] are sorry to hear that your officers and soldiers are not in so good a temper as we could wish. The Earl of Manchester has taken care for sending down money, which will be on its way down tomorrow. You may for the present forbear your preparation to march to Henley, and by the time you have distributed the money you shall receive further order from us whither you are to march with your forces.[18]

However, Crawford's men do not appear to have received their arrears because on 25 February the Committee informed him that they had ordered a fortnight's pay be delivered to him. Therefore his officers and soldiers decided to imposed their own taxes on the population of Buckinghamshire, which was a 'very great oppressions upon the people'. Crawford was ordered 'to give express charge to all the officers of your forces that in future no such taxes or assessments are to be imposed, and that no levies be made of any already set. You are to give speedy order in this matter that we not be further troubled with any such complaints.'[19]

By 16 January the regiments of Sir Miles Hobart and Colonel Montagu, were at Henley-on-Thames. It was here that during the third week of February

15   Symonds, p.163.
16   Symonds, p.164.
17   CSPD 1644–45, pp.250, 256, 287.
18   Ibid., pp.287–288, 304.
19   Ibid., p.318, 321.

From *Le Mareschal de Bataille, Contenant Le Maniment Des Armes*, Paris 1647.
From a contemporary drill book these musketeers were engraved in 1645-6 and are near identical in appearance, albeit much more detailed, to those shown in a 1642 work published in London. Whilst there are a number of 'eccentric' uniforms shown in Le

Mareschal… these two are in fairly typical clothing of the period, the added ribbons are the sort of decoration that some soldiers personally enhanced their appearance with and which many others disapproved of. Note that both men still carry rests, which many musketeers did at least as late as 1645.

Montagu's regiment also mutinied. At first it was only one company but soon spread to the major's and Captains Taylor's and Weekes' companies, who refused to muster when called upon to do so and gathered on the side of a hill about a quarter of a mile from the town. The other companies of the regiment did obey the command, but seeing their comrades' actions they also mutinied. Finally the regiment was only coaxed back to obedience with the promise of their pay, but as Lieutenant Colonel Grimes admitted 'I can do is little enough to appease and prevent combustion especially seeing their pay is so little, and private incendiaries many.' Montagu blamed Captain Taylor and Lieutenant Rowse as ringleaders of the discontent within the regiment, despite them being cashiered and imprisoned 'some months since'. However, Manchester released them and restored them to their commands. In his report Captain Denis Taylor claimed that although he was at Henley at the time he had nothing to do with the mutiny and that it was the soldiers themselves who demanded six weeks' pay.[20] Fortunately, the mutinous conduct of Montagu's regiment does not appear to have spread to Hobart's regiment, nor the rest of Henley's garrison.

On 28 February Crawford was still at Aylesbury, when he received orders to march to Huntingdon with all his infantry which were at Aylesbury, plus 200 horse from Northampton because a large body of Royalist cavalry was prowling on the borders of the Eastern Association and he was to prevent any incursions, 'and preserve the country from the spoil which it might otherwise suffer by them'.[21] On 6 March the Committee of Both Kingdoms wrote to Manchester to ask him to order Crawford to march with 400 horse along with:

> two companies of dragoons under Major Ewer and Capt. Abbott now about Newport Pagnell, and as many of Captains. Mercer's, Beaumont's, and Lilburne's dragoons as he can speedily draw together, do march towards Coventry, where he shall receive into his charge such of the Lord General's horse as shall come thither under the command of Col. Sheffield; as also such as shall come unto him from county of Worcester, and from Colonel Fox, all which are to march under Crawford's command to the assistance of Sir William Brereton.[22]

The Committee of Worcester were ordered to send 250 horse to march to Coventry where they were to await orders from Crawford.

All this time Prince Rupert was marching towards Sir William Brereton, who was then besieging Chester. Brereton fell back to Middlewich and Nantwich, but instead of pursuing Brereton, Rupert was eager to recruit his army and it was feared that he might join Sir Marmaduke Langdale, who had defeated a Parliamentary force at Melton Mowbray on 25 February 1645 and relieved Pontefract on 1 March.

As well as ordering Crawford to march to Brereton's assistance, on 8 March the Committee of Both Kingdoms appealed to the Scottish army, which was

---

20   Ibid., pp.314–315, 318–319, 325.
21   Ibid., p.326.
22   Ibid., p.337.

then at Newcastle, to also assist him. The Committee also allocated Crawford's own regiment of foot along with Manchester's regiment to join him, but on 21 March they told Crawford not to wait for these two regiments, since they wanted their pay which had still not been forthcoming, although Crawford was asked to try and 'persuade the foot, if you can, to march along with you, and the money will be sent after them'. The soldiers expected to receive their money at Northampton, unfortunately the pay receipts for this time have not survived for these two regiments, apart from Major Holmes' and Captain Johnson both of Manchester's regiment which are dated 31 March 1645.[23]

Coventry was to be the rendezvous for the forces gathering to assist Brereton, but Crawford made slow headway in his advance. On 20 March while he was still at Bedford he wrote to Brereton:

> I am making what haste I can. I have been about Bedford three days to receive such forces as have been ordered to march under my command, but they are not yet come. This day I received a new order from the Committee of Both Kingdoms to take along with me two regiments of foot consisting of 1,400 men ... If you send me word from time to time to Coventry what I shall do, I will obey. If your necessity be so great, it will be of advantage to bring the foot with me: if not I will leave them at Coventry, and so hasten my march to you ... The forces intended for your relief being once joined will make a brave army.[24]

Crawford had also appealed to the Committee of the Eastern Association for dragoon horses, which were not forthcoming, and also the detachment of Essex's cavalry had still not joined him, although there seems to have been a lot of jealousy on the Earl of Essex's part since he ends a letter that had as much effort been taken towards his army the previous year as that being now shown to Brereton's then 'the war in all probability, had been ended'.[25]

Two days later Crawford was still at Bedford. On 23 March Brereton had written to him appraising him of the movements of the Royalists believing that the combined strength of Rupert and Langdale's forces were between 7,000 and 9,000 horse and foot, having withdrawn various detachments from garrisons. Brereton went on to advise him to 'dispose yourself in some convenient place about Leicester or between Leicester and Coventry where your forces may join with such other of the Parliament's forces for the annoying and interrupting of the enemy'. However, such was the fluidity of the situation that the following day Brereton again wrote to Crawford 'to make all possible speed', to join him, adding that 'if God give a blessing to the forces, Parliament have assigned for these parts it will much conduce to shorten the war'.[26]

On 26 March Crawford was at Northampton when he wrote to Brereton, apologising for the delay in marching towards him, adding, 'This day I did

23 Ibid., pp.356, 362.
24 R. N. Dore, *The Letter Books of Sir William Brereton* (Record Society of Lancashire and Cheshire, 1984), vol. I, pp.98–99.
25 PA: Man/34, Earl of Essex to Manchester, 23 March 1645.
26 Dore, vol. I, pp.114.

expect all my party to come together at Northampton, but as yet they are not, so I am resolved if they come not tomorrow to set forward with what I can, which will be 1,000 horse and 1,200 foot', but he hoped to be at Coventry on Saturday. On 29 March Crawford was at Kingsthorpe and planned to proceed to Rugby to await further orders.[27] The Parliamentarians still did not know which way Rupert would go, and the Committee of Both Kingdoms feared that he might slip past Crawford and march towards the Eastern Association if Crawford continued to march towards Brereton. Therefore, Crawford was ordered to march towards Aylesbury once more, where he could not only protect the Eastern Association from Rupert's advance, but it was also intended that his forces were to be reorganised into the New Model Army.[28]

In April Waller had returned to Parliament to resign his commission due to the Self-Denying Ordinance, Cromwell, however still retained his, and was sent into Oxfordshire. This brought criticism from his opponents who saw it as a political manoeuvre to keep him away from Parliament so that he could not resign his commission. According to John Lilburne's *England's Birth Right*, Cromwell 'was posted away Uriah like, by special command, with his own regiment of horse to lie betwixt Oxford and Worcester … and after he was posted place to place and never suffered to come to the Parliament since'.[29] Since Cromwell had the support of the War Party it was decided that he should keep his current position within the New Model Army on a temporary basis. Therefore on 10 May 1645, his appointment to serve for 40 days as lieutenant general of horse was granted: this was extended on 18 June for a further three months, then for a further four months, until finally his position became permanent.[30]

It was estimated that Manchester's army had 3,578 infantry at this point, while Essex's had 3,048 and Waller just 600, which could be reduced into the New Model Army leaving 7,174 men to be recruited for the infantry.[31] On 9 April the companies of Captains William Disney, Richard Harvey and William Puckle of Sir Miles Hobart's regiment were mustered at Windsor, where they were reduced into Major General Lawrence Crawford's new regiment, some of the corporals and sergeants or 'lesser officers' re-enlisting as private soldiers, while those officers who were dismissed from the regiment received £148 14s 4d.[32] On the same day Colonel Hoogan's regiment, which had originally been commanded by Sir John Palsgrave, also mustered at Windsor and was disbanded, none of its company commanders appear to have served in the new army. On 16 and 17 April Colonel Francis Russell's regiment mustered for the final time at Maidenhead, where the major, three captains, seven lieutenants and nine ensigns were not selected

27   Ibid., pp.119, 136.
28   CSPD 1644–1645, pp.370–371, 378. 384, 387, 390, 391.
29   John Lilburne, *England's Birth Right Justified against all Arbitrary Usurpation, whether regal or Parliamentary or under what vizor soever* (London: October 1645), pp.2–337.
30   *Journal of the House of Lords*, vol. VII, p.532.
31   HMC 13th Report Appendix, Part 1, *The Manuscripts of his Grace the Duke of Portland preserved at Welbeck Abbey* vol. 1 (London: HMSO, 1891), p.215.
32   TNA: SP 28/29 ff.15, 348–349.

to serve in Rainsborough's new regiment.[33] On 17 April Colonel Crawford's old regiment mustered at Beaconsfield and was reduced into his new regiment, although when he resigned his commission the regiment passed to Robert Hammond. Montagu's and Pickering's regiments were transferred to the new model almost unchanged.[34] Although many regiments were disbanded, others continued to serve under new colonels, such as Colonel Thomas Rainsborough's which passed to Colonel Henry Grey and which was not incorporated into the New Model Army. The majority of captains, and probably soldiers of Sir Thomas Fairfax's regiment came from Manchester's regiment of foot.

On 25 April Manchester's regiment of horse mustered at Amersham Heath to the reduced into the New Model with its former lieutenant colonel, Nathaniel Rich, taking command.[35] Cromwell's regiment was divided into two, half being commanded by Sir Thomas Fairfax and the rest by Edward Whalley, who had served as its lieutenant colonel for most of the war. However, Captain Ralph Margery, Cromwell's 'plain russet coated captain', was transferred to Sir Robert Pye's regiment of horse. Colonel's Vermuyden and Fleetwood's regiments of horse also entered the new army. Part of the Association's train of artillery had been left at Cambridge from where on 28 March, Lieutenant General Hammond was ordered to retrieve it and incorporate it into the train of the New Model Army.[36]

On 15 March the Commons ordered that all those soldiers entering the new army should receive a fortnight's pay and clothing,[37] whereas of those being dismissed, the officers were to receive 14 days' pay and the soldiers two months of their salary. However there was not enough money to pay all the troopers and some, like Richard Kizby and Edward Tynggey, had to wait until 20 May 1648 before they received their payment.[38]

---

33   Ibid., ff.383–385, 415, 459.
34   Ibid., ff.287–288, 476.
35   Ibid., f.285.
36   Ibid., f.172.
37   *Journal of the House of Commons*, vol. IV, p.76.
38   TNA: SP 28/29 f.6; SP 28/223 part I, unfoliated.

Conclusion

Officially the Army of the Eastern Association would continue until the 23 May 1646 when it was ordered that the troops in the garrisons of King's Lynn, Boston, and the Isle of Ely plus all the garrisons in Cambridge, Huntingdon, and Bedfordshire should be disbanded.[1] However, the Committee could still rely on the county's trained bands for their defence. Neither did the military careers of those not selected for the New Model Army end: Colonel Francis Russell became the governor of the Isle of Ely, and even Manchester continued to sit on the Committee of Both Kingdoms.

Cromwell's star would continue to rise, succeeding Fairfax as lord general on 28 June 1650. The following year he retired from army life, but not before he had defeated the Royalist–Scottish army at the battle of Worcester on 3 September. On 16 December 1653 he was appointed Lord Protector. On 23 February 1657 a remonstrance was presented to Parliament asking Cromwell to become King Oliver I, followed on 24 March by the Bill, *The Humble Petition and Advice* which was passed by 123 votes to 62 in favour. On 9 April 1657 a select committee met to negotiate with Cromwell to accept the Crown, but he was indecisive about accepting it. This brought him ridicule from many, as a Royalist spy, Alan Brodrick, informed Sir Edward Hyde on 7 May, Cromwell could not accept the Crown:

> but with extreme disadvantage, which renders him an ill judge of opportunity in the mildest sense of his most partial friends, a wild and wanton lavisher of his good fortune in the opinion of the impartial, the Aldermen [the Major Generals] and townsmen [the officers of the army] laugh at his hopes and despise him for his fears, [being] the effects of a feeble inconstant mind. The Exchange [Parliament], at least all that were engaged for him, which were complete two thirds, tremble at the apprehension of his proving bankrupt.[2]

Finally Cromwell, fearing a split in the army, who reminded him that he should remain loyal to 'The Good Old Cause', rejected the Bill on 8 May although other clauses were accepted by him including the establishment of Upper House, and both the Lords and Commons were to meet every three years. When Cromwell was re-elected Lord Protector it was with all the pomp and circumstance of a coronation and he would be addressed as 'your

---

1   *Journal of the House of Lords*, vol. VIII, p.351.
2   SHC: 1248/1 f.25.

highness', and his wife was known as 'her highness' or Princess Elizabeth and later Lady Elizabeth Dowager Princess. They not only lived at the royal palace of Whitehall, a residence they had occupied since he retired from the army, but also at Hampton Court.

On hearing of the execution of the King, the Reverend Ralph Josselin wrote in his diary, 'I was much troubled with the black providence of putting the King to death; my tears were not restrained at the passages about his death; the Lord in mercy lay it not as [a] sin to the charge of the kingdom, but in mercy do us good by the same', but on 3 September 1658 on hearing the news of Cromwell's death Josselin wrote, 'Cromwell died, people not much minding it'.[3]

At the Restoration Cromwell's body was dug up and unceremoniously 'executed' and his head put on a spike at Tyburn, the traditional place of execution in London. A different fate awaited Manchester: he had opposed the trial and execution of the King, and retired from public life. In 1657 he was offered a seat in Cromwell's new Upper House, but refused. He was reappointed as Speaker of the House of Lords just before the Restoration, and so welcomed Charles II when he returned to England. He carried the Sword of State at the King's coronation and Charles bestowed many honours on him including Commissioner of the Great Seal and the Lord Lieutenancy of Northampton and Huntingdonshire. He was also appointed Knight of the Garter, an honour reserved for a select few. During the Second Dutch War (1665–1667) he was again appointed a general and given the command of a regiment. He died in 1671.[4]

After his arrest in 1643 William Lord Grey of Warke would become the speaker of the House of Lords and so mediated in the dispute between Manchester and Cromwell. For his part in the war he was pardoned at the Restoration and lived until 1674.

One of the greatest supporters of Cromwell was Charles Fleetwood, who would rise to the rank of lieutenant general under the Protectorate, although no doubt becoming Cromwell's son-in-law in 1652 helped his career prospects. Despite him being described as 'weak of character', on 7 June 1659 he was appointed commander of the army. He was stripped of his command in December of that year and at the Restoration appears to have lived a quiet life and died in October 1692.[5] The Major of his regiment in the Eastern Association, Thomas Harrison, would also rise to the heights of power in the army and became MP for Wendover in 1646. He escorted Charles I from the Isle of Wight to London for his trial, and when Cromwell imposed his Major Generals in 1655 Harrison was responsible for Wales. He was opposed to the Lord Protectorate, and Cromwell had him imprisoned on several occasions.

---

3 Josselin, pp.63, 125.
4 Ian Gentles, 'Montagu, Edward, second Earl of Manchester' in *Dictionary of National Biography* (accessed 31 March 2020).
5 Maurice Ashley, *Cromwell's Generals* (London: Jonathan Cape, 1954), pp.181–198.

Following the Restoration he was arrested again as a regicide and hung, drawn and quartered on 13 October 1660.[6]

Other regicides who had served in the Eastern Association were Edmund Whalley, Henry Ireton and Valentine Walton. Ireton had been the Deputy Governor of Ely during the First Civil War and had been a captain in Cromwell's regiment, before being appointed a colonel in the New Model Army, commanding the regiment of horse previously commanded by Sir Michael Livesey. He would die in Ireland in 1651 having reached the rank of major general. At the Restoration his remains suffered the same fate as Cromwell's. Whalley was at Cromwell's deathbed and supported his son Richard as the new Lord Protector, but at the Restoration he fled to America. He died in 1675 and was buried in an unmarked grave, fearing that it might be desecrated as Cromwell's and Ireton's had been. Walton joined Cromwell's Council of State, but being a Republican he fell out with Cromwell when he became Lord Protector and fled to Hanau at the Restoration. Fearing that he might be assassinated or kidnapped by agents of Charles II he went into hiding, so we cannot be certain when he died, although it is believed to have been shortly after.

Others would not live to see the end of the war: Major General Crawford would be killed at the siege of Hereford on 3 August 1645 serving with the Scottish army and Lieutenant Colonel John Clifton of Manchester's regiment would die in 1646. Clifton had made out his will in 17 August 1644, in which he bequeathed £23, his black stone horse, saddle and bridle and a case of 'little snaphaunce pistols' to his father at Hashingbrooke in Stamford Le Hope in Essex. His remaining estate was to go to Edward Atkinson the surgeon 'to my Lord's Regiment', and he wished to be buried by Henry Field, who was the regiment's preacher although by the time of his death the regiment had been disbanded.[7]

Colonel John Pickering died on 24 November 1645 of plague while at Ottery St Mary. His lieutenant colonel, John Hewson, took command of his regiment and commanded it until the Restoration. In 1660 having signed the King's death warrant, Hewson fled to Europe where he is believed to have died in 1662. Thomas Rainsborough would side with the Levellers, a radical political group, and took part in the Putney debates in 1647. During the Second Civil War he was tasked with capturing Pontefract Castle where on 29 October 1648 he was surprised in his quarters at Doncaster and killed. Some Levellers claimed that it was Cromwell who had ordered his assassination to rid himself of such a troublesome officer. An investigation found that he was killed by a party of Royalists wanting to capture him and exchange him for Sir Marmaduke Langdale. Another Leveller was John Lilburne, who at first supported Cromwell but later became his opponent. He died in 1657.

In September Colonel Edward Montagu brought the news to Parliament of the surrender of Bristol, and he was voted to be a Knight of the Shire of Huntingdon and on 13 October he took his seat in the Parliament. Due

---

6   Ian Gentles, 'Thomas Harrison', in *Dictionary of National Biography*; Maurice Ashley, *Cromwell's Generals* (London: Jonathan Cape, 1954), pp.83–99.
7   TNA: PROB11/198/363, Will of Lieutenant Colonel John Clifton.

to the Self-Denying Ordinance this disabled him from serving in the army, although he was appointed to the Committee of the Army. His regiment passed to John Lambert. Montagu supported the Protectorate, being a member of the Council of State, but on Cromwell's death changed sides and supported the Restoration. Charles II ennobled him with the title of Earl of Sandwich and he became the ambassador to Portugal, and then to Spain. During the Second Dutch War he commanded a squadron of ships and was killed at the battle of Solebay in 1672 and was buried in Westminster Abbey.

One senior officer of the Eastern Association who did not support the Restoration was Algernon Sydney. He became MP for Cardiff until 1653 when Cromwell dissolved Parliament. He was a commissioner during the trial of Charles I; although at first he did not support the execution of Charles I, he later changed his mind and later defended it. When Parliament was recalled after Cromwell's death he retook his seat, but at the Restoration went into exile. He returned to England in 1677 on the death of his father, but continued to support the Republican party. In June 1683 he was implicated in the Rye House Plot, which was said to have planned the assassination of Charles II and the Prince of Wales (later James II), so he was beheaded on 7 December 1683.

Sydney's lieutenant colonel, Nathaniel Rich, became colonel of Sydney's regiment in the New Model Army. In 1649 he became MP for Cirencester and the following year put down a Royalist rising in Norfolk. He was a supporter of the Republic, although became opposed to Cromwell when he was made Lord Protector, being imprisoned several times. He was cashiered from the army and arrested in 1659, and again during the reign of Charles II. He died in 1702. Cromwell would employ Colonel Francis Russell during the Protectorate since his daughter had married Cromwell's son, Henry. In 1654 he became MP for Cambridgeshire, and again in 1656.

How many lesser officers and soldiers of the Eastern Association who did not return home is unknown, but in his *Going to the Wars*, Charles Carlton estimates that during the Civil Wars 3.7 percent of England's population died, along with 6 percent of Scotland's and 4.1 percent of Ireland's, because of the fighting or disease. This is a larger percentage of the population than the First World War, when 2.61 percent are estimated to have died, including those victims of the 'Spanish flu', or 0.6 percent during the Second World War.[8] However, Carlton states that 'it must be stressed that the figures … are very rough estimates, and should be taken with a pinch of caution, and [a] pound of scepticism.'[9] Despite this caveat he repeats this claim in his book *This Seat of Mars*, but he revises the figures down for the Civil Wars to 8.6, and for the First World War to 2.61 and 0.94 percent of the population for the Second World War.[10] True, civil wars are bloodier to a nation than

---

8   Charles Carlton, *Going to the Wars: the Experience of the British Civil Wars, 1638–1651* (London and New York: Routledge, 1994), pp.202–203, 214.

9   Ibid., pp.202–203, 214.; Geoffrey Parker, *The Military Revolution, military innovation and the rise of the West, 1500–1800* (Cambridge: Cambridge University Press, 1988), pp.53, 177.

10 Charles Carlton, *This Seat of Mars: War and the British Isles, 1485–1746* (Yale University Press, 2011), pp.150–151. He estimates the death toll as 4.6 per cent for England, 9.2 per cent for Scotland, and for Ireland 20.6 percent.

fighting a foreign war since by their very nature one countryman is killing another countryman, rather than a foreign enemy, but no detailed statistical figures were kept during the first half of the seventeenth century either of the population itself or the number of casualties. In fact both sides exaggerated their enemy's losses while playing down their own. Also diseases like the plague appeared even in peacetime. When there was an outbreak of disease, people such as Captain Robert Cobbett of Sir Thomas Barrington's regiment saw it as an act of God. On 22 July 1643 he wrote about his newly raised company: 'it hath pleased God to visit many of my men with sickness'.[11] What disease Cobbett's company was inflicted by is not recorded, but typhus was a common disease that soldiers suffered from due to insanitary conditions and was often called 'camp fever'.

When it comes to the wounded it is even harder to estimate their number, since they could vary in their degree of severity. After the battle of Roundway Down, Captain Edward Harley, of Sir William Waller's regiment of horse wrote to his father, 'I lost ten horses and two men in the fight last week and last time I have lost five or six more so that my troop is now very weak.' At the battle of Lansdown on 5 July his troop mustered 54 troopers, but by 3 August 1643 13 troopers were no longer with the troop, nine of whom were reported as missing after Roundway Down, and a further nine were wounded, at least one trooper being wounded both at Lansdown and Roundway Down.[12]

On 24 October 1642 Parliament passed an ordinance for the widows and orphans of soldiers who had been killed as well as 'maimed soldiers', which, in theory, would grant a 'competent maintenance and allowance for such of them as shall be maimed and thereby disabled from their labour … and in case any such person shall be slain, that they will make provision for the livelihood of their wives or children'. This was one of many ordinances passed during the war and the Commonwealth. On 14 November 1642 'the Committee of Sick and Maimed Soldiers' was established to oversee their care, but due to the influx of claims on 6 March 1643 Parliament put the emphasis of maintenance on the parish where the soldier or his family had last settled. To prevent abuse they also had to bring a certificate from their colonel, officer or clerk of his regiment. Then in July 1645 a separate committee was formed for wives and widows, which was known as the Committee of the Military Garden. Unfortunately, for the wives and widows of the soldiers this committee appears to have been overwhelmed by the demand so the number of claimants were limited to two women a day. In August 1646 they demonstrated outside Parliament for relief which resulted in £10,000 being released for their pensions. However, Parliament disbanded the committee in the September of the following year. The Committee of Sick and Maimed Soldiers would continue until April 1653 when it was replaced by the Hospital Committee and by 1659 Ely House and Savoy Hospitals in London were handling over 4,000 widows' pensions. In December 1660 the Hospital Committee was disbanded.

---

11   BL: Egerton, MS 2647 f.49.
12   HMC: Portland Manuscripts p.113, Edward Harley to Sir Robert Harley at Westminster, 15/25 July 1643.; BL: Add MS 70004 ff123, 124.

Unfortunately the pension records for these committees have not survived, moreover since these committees were based in London, to claim a pension a person would have to journey to London, which ruled out many due to the expense involved. Instead they had to rely on their parish's poor relief or claim a pension from their county's Quarter Session, although the survival of these records is at best patchy. For the county of Essex only the order book between 1652 and 1661 survives, the one covering the Civil War period has been lost and so has the one from 1662. Nevertheless this book records the pensions for 83 soldiers and 40 widows, including an entry for Anne Larke of Great Coggeshall in Essex, who on 20 April 1658 petitioned that she 'hath been the wife of two men who served the Parliament in the late wars and were so wounded as petitions were granted unto them. And that her last husband lately deceased, his pension is ended and praying the continuance of the same for herself and the children left her by them'.

She was paid 40s 'for this time only; and she is to trouble the court no further for relief'. She is probably the husband of Thomas Larke of the same parish as Anne who applied to the Essex Quarter Sessions on 10 July 1655 being 'a long time a soldier in the service of Parliament and thereby become very impotent, and having a wife and five small children destitute of relief'. He was granted a yearly pension of 40s.[13] Unfortunately, Anne's and her second husband's petitions have not survived but other petitions vary in detail, some recording that they had served Parliament in many engagements before being maimed, while others go into a great deal of detail like Martha Emming of Coggeshall in Essex, who in 1653 petitioned for a pension since her husband, who was a soldier in Captain Boyce's company, and had been killed at Heslington during the siege of York and one of her sons killed in Ireland. She described herself as 'being very aged and past her labour, and not long before this time come to the charge of the parish had not her son helped to provide for her'. She received 40s gratuity. In Essex widows made up just 34 percent of petitioners, but they received 38 percent of the pensions.[14]

Sometimes a widow might petition for her husband's arrears of pay, such as Anne Alliston of Sunbury in Suffolk who in April or early May 1644 petitioned that her husband, Roger Alliston, was a soldier under Captain William Ayers of Cromwell's regiment who 'ventured his life in the cause of Christ … but so it hath pleased God in the service he hath lost his life'. Anne did not know where he had died but at one point he had been a prisoner at Newark. His death left her 'a poor distressed widow with three very small fatherless infants, the eldest of five years of age and not any estate to the value of five shillings'. She asked that she might have her husband's arrears of £20 since 'I am credibly informed you have lately received monies to pay the arrears of your soldiers'. The petition was passed to the Committee of Suffolk who agreed that she could have his arrears.[15]

13 Allen, *Essex Quarter Sessions*, pp.xxvii, 128.
14 ERO: Q/BSa2/82.; David Appleby, 'Unnecessary Persons? Maimed Soldiers and War Widows in Essex, 1642–1662', in *Essex Archaeology and History* (2001), p.212.
15 TNA: SP 28/243 f.142, undated petition.

On 16 July 1650 Richard Spurrell of Thurgarton in Norfolk who had served in Captain George Burrell's company of Hobart's regiment had become 'blind by reason of colds and distempers he got in that service'. Due to his sufferings he received a pension of £3 per year, plus 10s 'towards his charges to London … where he, we hope to get some ease and recovery of his blindness'.[16] No doubt they believed he would get better treatment in one of the London hospitals than he would in his home parish. It was not just soldiers who applied for pensions: in 1646 Thomas Higharne of Coggeshall was an Ensign to Captain Jermin, 'who has been long in the Parliament's service under the Lord Grey of Wark, before Reading and afterwards in other good services, in which services your poor petitioner has lost his limbs and is no[t] able to subsist of himself, but is like to come to great poverty'.[17]

However, with the Restoration many of these pensions were cancelled and awarded to maimed soldiers and widows whose husbands had fought for the Royalist cause. In January 1661 at the Essex Quarter Sessions four pensioners were to be paid between £1 and £2 1s as compensation for losing their pensions, although for some unspecified reason they decided that the £4 per year pension of one Thomas Butcher should continue. Butcher had been awarded a pension on 9 January 1655 after 'it appearing that he received wounds in the service of Parliament under the Earl of Manchester whereby he is much disabled in the body'. At this point he received a pension of £3, which was increased by £1 at the session held on 6 October 1657.[18]

At the April 1661 session another 31 ex-Parliamentarian soldiers were given a gratuity of between 20s and 30s in compensation for losing their pensions. They were followed in the October 1661 Session by a further 14 who were each paid £1 as compensation, except Matthew Woodward who received £4. There was also one widow, Mary Bromfield, who received just 10s. Mary had received a pension of £3 at the Session held on the 11 January 1653. In their place the order book begins to award pensions to former Royalist soldiers, mainly to those who had been at the siege of Colchester in 1648 during the Second Civil War, although it would not be until June 1662 when a new act of Parliament superseded those passed during the Civil War and Commonwealth, which awarded pensions to soldiers, or their widows, who had fought for the King, and disqualified those who had had fought for Parliament or had changed sides during the war. Unfortunately, since the order book covering the period from 1662 has not survived, we do not know how many others lost their pensions.[19] This was probably typical of the Quarter Sessions for other counties and they would probably have to throw themselves on the mercy of their friends and family once more.

---

16   Norfolk Record Office (NRO): Quarter Session records.
17   ERO: Q/SBa2/61.
18   Allen, *Essex Quarter Session*, pp.55, 112, 176.
19   Allen, *Essex Quarter Sessions*, pp.20, 181–182, 203.

Notes and Observations of the Eastern Association Cornets

By Stephen Ede-Borrett

Cornets of Horse

Each troop of horse carried a cornet, although the term 'standard' was coming into use the more commonly found name for them in 1644 was still cornet. These were approximately, and surviving examples vary from 22 inches to 27 inches, 24 inches square with a fringing along the three 'flying' sides around two inches deep. Usually this fringe was alternately metal (white/silver or yellow/gold) and colour (everything else) in two inch pieces – the colour plates illustrate this. There is a single example of an all gold fringe (although this may be a trumpet banner) and another of a three-colour fringe – red/white/blue/white/etc. but neither relates to the Army of the Eastern Association. The cornet was traditionally carried on a lance-type staff[1], rather than a plain pole, with a large 'staple' near the hand grip which could be attached by a spring clip to a baldric worn by the bearer, the cornet, who ranked third in the troop's four officers. At the top of the staff just below the lance-head a pair of short gold bullion tassels were fixed, these were, as far as we can tell, customarily gold and about two feet long – they do not seem to have extended below the cloth of the cornet itself.

In the Eastern Association Army, as in the other Armies of Parliament before the creation of the New Model Army in 1645, the design, motto, device, etc of a troop's cornet was the choice of the troop captain. Some may have been influenced by earlier, similar flags created for tournaments which had a 'characteristic combination of motto and picture designed to express the personal intentions, aspirations, or state of mind of their bearers ...'[2], and this certainly explains many, perhaps most, cornets with devices. Other cornets, particularly those which have no more than a motto, are simply the

---

1   Cornets were carried on a staff NOT on a pole!
2   *The English Emblem Tradition 3: Emblematic Flag Devices of The English Civil Wars, 1642–1660*: Alan R. Young. University of Toronto Press, Toronto 1995, p.xxiii.

'sound bite' of their day, although they do tell us something of the thoughts of the captain who commissioned them.

It is often stated that colonels of horse, echoing the colonels of foot, carried plain cornets. In the regiments of horse of the Eastern Association this does not appear to have been the case. Although generally plainer in design than many (although certainly far from all) of their captains' cornets, the recorded colonels' cornets all carry a simple motto; there are no recorded 'plain cornets' for the Eastern Association. Whilst this might be explained as the cornet predating the officer's promotion to colonel and continuing in use, this is certainly not so here since Manchester, Norwich and Sidney had not served as troop captains before their commissioning as colonels (for Sidney, however, see the main text).

One thing that is noticeable with the cornets of the Army of the Eastern Association is that none are recorded with mottos in French. Whilst French mottos only amount to around six percent of all of the recorded Parliamentarian mottos, if they were not used in the Army of the Eastern Association then this percentage increases dramatically for the other armies. There is certainly work to be done to look at this bias.

It is worth noting that, unlike later, there appears to have been no effort to enforce any sort of uniformity of field colour within the regiments of horse of the Eastern Association. This is common across Parliament's armies and whilst often said to be due to the regimenting of previously independent troops this cannot be so. A prime example of this are the cornets of the Earl of Manchester's Regiment. Commissioned as a regiment in autumn 1643, the known troop cornets include fields of light blue-green, red and blue. Some regiments may indeed have had uniform fields to their cornets, as the Royalist armies usually did, but this is definitely not customarily the case.

All cornets here have been taken from British Library Add MS (latterly Sloane MS) 5247 which is certainly amongst the earliest of the dozen or more manuscripts illustrating Civil War cornets, and must have been started in the first months of 1643, although not 'finished' until perhaps 1647. The folio number of the original illustration is given after the notes for each cornet. The disproportionate number of cornets recorded that can be attributed to only a small number of Manchester's Regiments of Horse is probably a reflection of that perhaps they were made by specific tailors and 'herald painters' and that the work of others in those professions avoided the notice of the manuscript painter.

Note: Whilst we can translate the Latin mottos easily enough, their meaning to the bearer who commissioned them is often going to be a matter of pure conjecture.

Colour Plate Commentaries

By Stephen Ede-Borrett

A.1 Captain James Berry
Lieutenant-General Oliver Cromwell's Regiment of Horse
1644–1645

Pro Rege et Lege Parati (Ready For the King and the Law)

The cornet must date to the autumn of 1644, when Berry was promoted to captain in succession to William Ayres in Cromwell's Regiment of Horse. The choice of red as a field is suggestive that the regiment, at least by that time, had red, perhaps fringed red and yellow, cornets. (see the notes to Captain Ireton's and Captain Sparrow's cornets, which are both fringed red and white). Note this is 'suggestive' only, there are certainly indications that the Eastern Association regiments of horse never completely standardised the fields of their troop cornets, and may not even have tried to do so.

Note: When Berry entered Sir Thomas Fairfax's Regiment of Horse in the New Model Army in 1645 he used a different motto on his new cornet. However a manuscript in the library of the Society of Antiquaries of London states that the motto on Berry's cornet in Cromwell's Regiment was the same as that used on his cornet in Fairfax's Regiment – *perhaps* this cornet is that used by Ayres and continued by Berry until he had a new cornet made?

British Library Add 5257, f.30r.

A.2 Captain William Dingley
The Earl of Manchester's Regiment of Horse
1643–1645

We Are Released to Fight for the Gospel Laws and Liberty

This cornet device is, to say the least, obscure in its meaning. Prestwich[3]

---

3 *Prestwich's Respublica*: John Prestwich. London 1787. Prestwich's list of cornets is simply a text
   description of British Library Add MS 5247)

comments that this shows the doors of Newgate prison but that begs the question as to why would any captain celebrate or suggest that his army was composed of felons? Unless maybe it is intended to suggest that those held in Newgate were there unlawfully held. In truth I think that the intention behind this device and motto will probably always be contentious and obscure.

Dingley was in the regiment from its raising until it was disbanded into the New Model Army in 1645, he then appears to have retired to civilian life.

British Library Add 5257, f.65r.

B.1 Captain John Disbrowe
Lieutenant-General Oliver Cromwell's Regiment of Horse
1643–1645

An unusual cornet in having a device without a motto, the reverse is often true but a device without a motto is recorded on only one other cornet in the whole of the manuscript, and that one is itself contentious.

Given in the manuscript as 'Captain' John Disbrowe[4], this cornet must have been made in April 1643 and in use before Disbrowe was promoted to major of the regiment in October of that year. Undoubtedly the cornet continued in use after Disbrowe's promotion. In April 1645 Disbrowe entered the New Model as major of Sir Thomas Fairfax's Horse, and it is possible that this cornet continued in use in Fairfax's Regiment.

British Library Add 5257, f.100r.

B.2 Captain John Grove
Lieutenant-General Oliver Cromwell's Regiment of Horse
1644–1645

For Truth and Peace

Similar to perhaps the majority of the cornets of the war, Grove has no device, only a motto.[5] 'Truth' is a fairly common motto, as is 'Peace' and there are three cornets that are known that carry the simple motto 'Truth and Peace' (including the Earl of Manchester's cornet).

Grove entered the New Model in 1645 and it is not impossible that this cornet dates to that period.

British Library Add 5257, f.97r.

---

4   The rank given to the bearer in Add MS 5247 must be that at the point of the cornet being made or ordered.

5   Such cornets were, of course, simpler and cheaper to make and did not require the expense *and time* of involving a herald painter.

C.1 Captain Thomas Hammond
The Earl of Manchester's Regiment of Horse
1644–1645

Nescit Virtus Stare Loco (Virtue Cannot Stand in Place)

The motto implies that 'action' is required for virtue to continue.

Hammond had been captain in Urry's Regiment and then in Meldrum's Regiment, both of the Earl of Essex's Army, before transferring to Manchester's command in early 1644. Hammond was also lieutenant-general of the ordnance and is thus unlikely to have commanded the troop in person.

The cornet was almost certainly that used by Hammond's troop in both of his earlier regiments.

British Library Add 5257, f.33r.

C.2 Captain Ralph Knight
The Earl of Manchester's Regiment of Horse
1644–1645

Pro Reformatione Pugnandum (To Fight for the Reformation)

The depiction of an orange scarf on the horseman is noteworthy, but the depiction of the horseman as a cuirassier follows convention and not indicative of the appearance of Knight's own troop.

Knight was in Manchester's Regiment by April 1644 and his troop is often referred to as 'Manchester's Lifeguard'. Knight entered the New Model in April 1645 as captain in Pye's Horse and this cornet may have continued in use.

British Library Add 5257, f.96r.

D.1 Colonel Algernon Sidney
Earl of Manchester's Regiment of Horse
1644–1645

Sanctus Amor Patriae dat Animus (Sacred Love of Country Gives Courage)

Sidney was commissioned colonel commander of Manchester's Horse in April 1644, and in April 1645 he entered the New Model as colonel of horse and may have continued the use of this cornet, assuming that the cornet was not made specifically for that commission, which seems unlikely.

British Library Add 5257, f.92r.

D.2 Captain Henry Ireton
Francis Thornhagh's Regiment of Horse, then Oliver
Cromwell's Regiment of Horse
1643–1645

Pro Divinis Qui Admittit Servat Pro Humanis Vim Vi (He Who Surrenders to God Saves [prevents] Human Violence)

A somewhat obscure motto, which I have been unable to trace to a classical or biblical reference despite it sounding as if it should be. Ireton had, like many others, trained at the Inns of Court and it may have been something he had come across there.

This was Ireton's cornet as captain, and probably as major, in Thornhagh's Regiment. When he transferred into Cromwell's he would have continued to carry the same cornet – there is no evidence for officers having a new cornet made under such circumstances. It suggests, but no more than that, that Thorhagh's Regiment *may* have had cornets with red fields.

Ireton Entered the New Model in 1645 as Commissary General and Colonel of Horse.

British Library Add 5257, f.25v.

E.1 General the Earl of Manchester
Colonel, own Regiment of Horse
1643–1645

Truth And Peace

The cornet of the colonel's troop of his own regiment of horse. The field of this cornet is often shown in modern illustrations as dark green but the original manuscript source definitely shows this light blue-green hue. The other known cornets of the regiment are a mixture of red fields and blue fields. As with many colonels' troop cornets in the Eastern Association Army this carries a simple motto, and is not the oft-stated 'plain'.

'Truth' is a fairly common motto, as is 'Peace' and there are three cornets that are known that carry the simple motto 'Truth and Peace' (Captain John Grove's cornet of Cromwell's Horse carries the same motto), thus there is no secret meaning to be inferred in the use of this motto by Manchester.

The cornet is almost certainly the one referred to in an undated warrant in the National Archives.[6]

British Library Add 5257, f.75r.

---

6   TNA SP 28/299.

E.2 Captain Zachary Walker
Lieutenant General Oliver Cromwell's Regiment of Horse
1643–1644

For These Distracted Times

Walker's motto appears to be a plaintive cry about the hurt being done to his heart by the wars.

Walker may be the man who had served as Quartermaster-General to Waller's Army in 1643 and the blue field of his cornet, which he would have brought with him into Manchester's Army, perhaps dates from that service. He was cashiered in March 1644 and discharged as a malignant; his troop was disbanded, although I would suggest it unlikely that the troopers were discharged. Interestingly Firth in his panegyric on Cromwell's Regiment, 'The Raising of the Ironsides', does not mention this troop, perhaps because it does not suit his narrative.

British Library Add 5257, f.51v.

F.1, F.2 Captain Anthony Markham
Edward Rossiter's Regiment of Horse
1644–1645

1.   For the Cause of the Lord I Draw my Sword
2.   Si Pereo Pereo (If I Perish, I Perish)

The illustration of two separate cornets for the same 'Captain Markeham [*sic*] of Lincolnshire' has been suggested to show the two sides of the same cornet. However, the design is so different that it would seem certain that they are actually two different cornets and that 2 is a replacement for 1, especially given its somewhat fatalistic motto of the latter. There is no record of the loss by Markham of his cornet but that is not unusual, most such losses are not specifically noted.

In 1645 Rossiter's entered the New Model and Markham continued in place. There seems no reason why Markham, or any of the other officers of Rossiter's, would have had new cornets made and it seems certain that they continued the use of their existing cornets, especially as the regiment was absorbed complete.

1.   British Library Add 5257, f.77v.
2.   British Library Add 5,257, f.101v.

G.1 Captain Thomas Moulson
Sir John Norwich's Regiment of Horse
1643–1644

Pro Patria Lacerata Pugna (I Fight for my Torn [Wounded] Country)

Moulson served with the regiment only briefly from October 1643 to around August 1644. Whether he was killed, wounded or simply resigned is not known. Other recorded cornets of Norwich's have orange or red fields, although a *possible* identification also has one with a green field. Despite the many known exceptions, a great many cornets had a motto without a device, which would have made them considerably cheaper to make, as well as faster to produce.

British Library Add 5257, f.48v.

G.2 Colonel Sir John Norwich's Regiment of Horse
1663–1647

Pro Christo et Ecclesia (For Christ and the Church)

Alan Young suggests that this should be read as 'his Church' but that is not what the motto actually says, and it may be an allusion simply to the reformed Church. Noticeable in this respect is that is says 'Christo' (Christ) not 'Deo' (God).

Norwich's Regiment was reduced in April 1645 when Norwich himself became governor of Rockingham Castle in Northamptonshire, where he is recorded as having a troop of horse as a part of the garrison. It is probable that Norwich continued the use of this cornet into his new garrison.

British Library Add 5257, f.18r.

H.1 Captain William Packer
Lieutenant General Oliver Cromwell's Regiment of
Horse
1644–1645

Sapienta et Fortitudine (Wisdom and Bravery)

A simple motto but an unusual, and rarely recorded, style of scroll – the gold edging being necessary to avoid breaking the heraldic rule of not putting a colour on a colour (albeit that this was widely ignored).

Packer had been Valentine Walton's lieutenant and took over the troop after Walton's death from wounds received at Marston Moor (2 July 1644). He continued in command of the troop when it became a part of Fairfax's Horse in the New Model. This cornet may have been taken into Fairfax's Regiment although the motto scroll/colour is unlike the rest of those in use in that regiment.

British Library Add 5257, f.102v.

H.2 Captain Robert Sparrow
Lieutenant General Oliver Cromwell's Regiment of Horse
1644 (–1646?)

Si Leges Rerum (if the Laws of Things)

Alan Young suggests the motto should be Si Leges Regum (if the Laws of Kings) but all manuscripts that record this cornet show the word 'Rerum'. However it is highly likely that a number of these manuscripts were simply copied from one original[7] so the error would simply have been repeated. Whatever the motto said it does not appear to make sense to the modern mind.

Interestingly National Army Museum (NAM) manuscript 6208-1 shows the same design, including 'sparrow' and rose, but with the motto Res Nomines (Business Names), which also seems gibberish but is confirmed by Bodleian Library Manuscript D942. It is possible that the cornet illustrated here is a replacement for the earlier one shown in the NAM and Bodleian manuscripts and which had been lost.

The bird is obviously a pun on his name and intended as a sparrow. Sparrow's coat of arms included three red roses and the rose on his cornet is an allusion to that.

Sparrow did not enter the New Model and in July 1644 had taken over an Essex troop in the garrison of Abingdon, which he commanded until 1646. The troop was not the same one that he had commanded in Cromwell's Regiment but he may have taken his cornet with him.

British Library Add 5257, f.61r.

Guidons of Dragoons

The Eastern Association's Army had only a single regiment of dragoons that operated with the main army, that of the Earl of Manchester (later of Robert Lilburne). Aside from the fact that the regiment would have carried swallow-tailed guidons absolutely nothing is known of their precise appearance and we can only guess generalities.

Guidons were, as said, swallow-tailed, about two feet on the staff and three feet flying. Like cornets of horse they were carried on a lance-like staff, were fringed on all flying edges, and had the, usually, gold cords.

In the Civil War, two completely different designs of cornet were displayed. One essentially copied the 'Venn system' of the infantry colours described below; the other mimicked that of the cornets of horse. Which of these two Manchester's Dragoons followed is impossible to say.

---

7   Probably British Library Add MS 5247, which appears to be the earliest.

Colours of Foot

As every troop of horse carried a cornet so every company of foot carried a colour. These were approximately six and a half feet square (again surviving examples vary but six and a half feet is both around the average, and also the intended, size). Unlike cornets, they were NEVER fringed.

The following repeats what many readers will already know, but it is the most concise description. The system known today as 'Venn' was described thus:

> The Colonels Colours in the first place is of a pure and clean colour, without any mixture. The Lieutenants Colonels only with Saint Georges Armes in the upper comer next the staff: the Major's the same; but in the lower and outermost comer with a little stream Blazant, And every Captain with Saint George Armes alone, but with so many spots or several Devices as partain to the dignity of their respective places.[8]

This has become known as 'Venn A' with a known variant of 'Venn B' having one device for the major, two for the first captain, etc.

Whilst other 'differencing systems' are known from the wars there are no known examples of the use by any Parliamentarian regiments of any design other than the Venn system. Thus the Venn systems were undoubtedly that in use by the armies of the Eastern Association.

Having said that we have reference to only one stand of colours of the Eastern Association's Army:

> Ffor 10 silk Ensigns of rich watchet [a mid sky-blue hue] taffeta with distinctions of white crosses furnished with staves and tassels[9]

These were sent to Lord Willoughby of Parham in 1643 and were probably for his own regiment of foot.

Colours, as indicated by this warrant, were carried on simple staves/poles and had a pair of cords, again round two feet long,[10] attached just below the lance point. Attachment to the pole was by a series of nails along the length of the sleeve.

Apart from the reference above there are no records of the appearance of any of the colours of the army. It is likely that differencing devices were simple geometric shapes, rather than anything heraldic but this is inference and likelihood and cannot be evidenced. When the Eastern Association supplied regiments into the New Model Army in 1645 all received a new

---

8   *Military Observations or the Tackticks put Into Practice*: Captain Thomas Venn, London 1672, p. 181. Although Venn's work was not published until 1672, as with most such works it echoes back to an earlier age, and this section on colours describes the system in use before the Restoration in1660 and the deliberate alteration of the appearance of English military colours by Charles II.
9   TNA SP28 /300. The warrant suggests a Venn system.
10   Some modern illustrations show them longer, all contemporary illustrations show them short.

stand of colours, which were probably of a different hue than those they had previously carried.[11]

_____

11   See *The Army of the Eastern Association*: Laurence Spring. The Pike and Shot Society, London 2016.

Appendix I

Organisation

Types of Soldiers

Like all armies of the early seventeenth century, the Eastern Association was divided into cavalry, dragoons, infantry and artillery. When Manchester raised his regiment of foot, the colonel's company was to have 200 men, the lieutenant colonel's 160 men and the major's 140 men. The other regiments were to have 160, 140, and 130 men respectively, while the captains' companies of all regiments were to be 120 strong. A warrant dated 1643 records that in Essex, at least, each regiment was to have two captain adjutants; 'to assist the captains in the exercise of their soldiers and unless there be captains found well experienced in each regiment these adjutants are likewise to be assistants to your field officers'.[1]

There was also to be a troop of horse or dragoons 'annexed to each regiment to make discoveries on all occasions and to fetch provisions, also at least two surgeons and that carts or wagons be allowed for the officers and provisions'. How far these measures were implemented is unknown, certainly no dragoons or troopers appear to have been attached to the regiments of foot in late 1642 or early 1643, so they probably failed to materialise for lack of horses. A later letter also proposed that the independent dragoon companies be formed into a single regiment.

In theory a company of foot had a company commander (colonel, lieutenant colonel, major or captain), a lieutenant, an ensign, three sergeants, three corporals and two drummers, whereas a troop of horse had its troop commander, a lieutenant, a cornet and two or three corporals, plus two trumpeters. The colonel's company and troop usually had a captain lieutenant since the colonel had other duties and no matter how strong or weak the company or troop was, it always had the full complement of officers and 'lesser officers'.

---

1   BL: Egerton, 2651.

According to the military manuals of the time the cavalry were divided into cuirassiers and arquebusiers. Cuirassiers were armoured from head to knee and were armed with a sword and two pistols. However, only one regiment, Sir Arthur Heselrige's, composed of eight troops of horse which formed part of Waller's Western Association, appear to have been entirely cuirassiers, but after the battle of Roundway Down in July 1643 when his regiment of 'lobsters' were routed the regiment dispensed with its cuirassier armour. More common were troops of cuirassiers within a regiment which usually belonged to the colonel, such as several regiments that served in Ireland and during the Bishops' Wars, plus those of the Earl of Essex and Sir William Balfour, who also served in Essex's army. However, by the summer of 1644 they also appear to have dispensed with their cuirassier armour. This was usually down to the cost of the armour itself, and the time taken to make a set of full armour as compared to pikeman or arquebusier armour. Moreover, when writing his *Observations Upon Military and Political Affairs* George Monck dismissed the cuirassier 'because there are not many countries that do afford horses fit for the service of cuirassiers'.[2]

In one of the first biographies of Cromwell, James Heath in his *Flagellum* describes his regiment as being cuirassiers, which is repeated by Fuller's *England's Worthies*, while Fletcher in his biography of Cromwell refers to them as armed 'cap a pe, after the manner of the German crabats'.[3] Even Colonel Ross who wrote the first history of the regiment referred to them as cuirassiers until they were absorbed into the New Model Army. However, all these references are wrong. Rather than being armoured from head to foot, the Crabats or Croats were light cavalry who did not wear armour, and Heath and Fuller were writing after the Restoration when cuirassiers were known just to have worn a 'back and breast' plates with a helmet. Cromwell's regiment is also referred to as 'Ironsides', but this is also a later nickname for it, coming from a dubious reference of Prince Rupert referring to Cromwell, not his regiment, as 'Old Ironsides' just before the battle of Marston Moor.

Cromwell's regiment were arquebusiers, which were the most common type of cavalry. In theory they were equipped with a back and breast plate, a helmet and an elbow gauntlet to protect the left arm, and a buffcoat. They were armed with a sword, two pistols and a carbine. But by the time of the Civil War this description also appears to be wrong: from the surviving accounts, an arquebusier either wore a back and breast plate with a helmet, or a buffcoat and a hat, and not both. When John Barriffe published his treatise on cavalry in 1661 he recalled that the arquebusier was armed 'only with a breast, back and casque (or pott) for defence, a case of pistols short, and a carbine hanging by a belt with [a] swivel on his right side, of 2 or 3 and a half foot in length of the barrel and a good sword'.

On 27 July 1642 a Mr Vaughan purchased 53 buffcoats for a troop of cavalry raised at Watford with sleeves for 38s each, although the warrant did

---

2   George Monck, *Observations upon Military and Political Affairs written by the most honourable George, Duke of Albemarle* (London: 1671), p.25.

3   Heath, p.29.; Henry Fletcher, *The Perfect Politician, or, A Full View of the Life and Action (Military and Civil) of O Cromwell*, p.4.

not state whether they had leather or cloth sleeves, both of which are known to have been attached to buffcoats.[4] On the other hand in July 1643 a trooper of Sir Thomas Martin's 'trained troop' of Cambridgeshire included a buffcoat which cost £7, while two other troopers' buffcoats cost £2 each. Each of the troopers also were issued with a scarf of an unspecified colour for 10s. At least one trooper was also issued with a cloak bag for 3s.[5] A contract between Colonel Valentine Walton, the governor of King's Lynn, and Nicholas Marshall, Thomas Stephens and Peter Newton, dated 14 January 1644, was for the delivery of 800 'breastplates, (high pistol proof) a back [plate] and a pot head piece with three bars'. The cost was 33 shillings per trooper, or £1 13s which was cheaper than a buffcoat.[6]

The 'pot' or helmet worn during the Civil Wars usually had a three-bar visor to protect the face, although other variants such as the *zischagge* only had a single bar to protect the face. This type of helmet was usually imported from Europe and both these helmets had a neck and ear guards.

It was not just the troopers' armaments that were needed, as the cavalry also needed horses. On 8 April 1644 a Lieutenant Russell was paid £500 to buy an unspecified number of horses and another payment of £300 was made to him for buying horses in Bedfordshire on 16 April. One of the horses Russell bought at Northampton for £6 15s 00d 'died at Stamford'. The prices of horses varied greatly from £4 to £14, although sometimes a horse was just taken, with a ticket being given to the owner which in theory could be redeemed at a later date. The horses for the train of artillery were much cheaper: one payment of £10 00s 00d was made for eight horses or roughly £1 10s per horse.[7] Another source of horses was the capture of them from the Royalists: John Hole was paid £4 by Lieutenant Colonel Rich for 'a bay nag which he took from the enemy at Marston Moor and now rideth on him as a soldier in the troop'. Corporal Thomas Hurdman also of Rich's troop was paid £6 for a bay horse that he also captured at Marston Moor, along with a saddle and a pair of pistols.[8] There does not appear to have been any colour coordination of horses within a troop or regiment. These horses also needed saddlery: among the accounts of the Committee of the Eastern Association is a payment of £12 16s 00d for 16 saddles for Major Alfold of Manchester's own regiment of horse and Captain Knight was paid £12 00s 00d for 30 saddles. Both these payments were made on 13 April, but why Alfold's saddles were more expensive is not specified. Another account dated 20 August 1644 records that £390 was paid for 300 'cantle padded saddles and furniture', at £1 6s per saddle and £220 for 200 'plain padded saddles' at £2 2s per saddle. This account also lists the cost of bridles as 3s 6d each.[9]

As for the infantry or foot they were also divided into two types, musketeers and pikemen. The pikeman, or as he was sometimes referred

4   TNA: SP 28/17, ff.262–263.
5   TNA: SP 28/222, ff.437–441.
6   HMC: Appendix to 8th Report, p.60.
7   TNA: SP28/139; SP28/155.
8   TNA: SP 28/23, ff.61.
9   TNA: SP28/139; TNA: SP 28/23, f.14.

to in contemporary accounts a 'corselet', was armed with a pike, which was between 15 and 18 feet long and made of ash about 1¾ inches thick. It had a steel head with two metal strips about two feet long running down the shaft of the pike. The pikeman was also armed with a sword and to protect himself he (in theory) had a back and breast plate, tassets, which protected the thighs, a gorget which protected the neck, and a helmet. The average armour with tassets weighted about 11 kg and some back plates were also fitted with a hook, where the pikeman could hang his helmet on and so, according to Markham, 'will be a great ease to the soldiers and nimble carriage in the time of long marches'. These hooks do not usually survive on sets of armour. As to helmets, in 1622 Francis Markham recommended that the pikeman's 'morions [be] well lined within which a quilted cap of strong housewives linen; for Buckram which is the usual lining is too course and galleth the soldier's head, as also is too stiff and unplyable by which means it will not guilt like the other. The ear plates shall be lined also.'

The account of John Wedell for Captain Balloon's troop includes £1 16s 'for lining and quilting of 24 head piece's and there are several surviving examples of helmets having cotton lining, including two at the Wallace Collection in London. One is a red woollen and linen cap stuffed with raw cotton wadding designed for a burgonet helmet. The other is made of canvas and linen padded with bast. Armour could also be lined with leather, but this added to the cost of the back and breast plates and most surviving examples do not appear to have been lined. As the war dragged on the armour appears to have been discarded.[10]

The musketeer 'must be armed with a good musket (the barrel of four feet long, the bore of 12 bullets in the pound), a rest, bandoleer, headpiece, a good sword, girdle and hangers'.[11] However, as muskets became lighter the rest was discarded. The flasks or 'boxes' of the 'pair' or 'collar' of bandoliers, was where the musketeer kept his gunpowder to pour down the barrel of his musket. These flasks were often made of wood, but tin was also used in their production and either painted or covered with leather. Archaeological discoveries, including at Marston Moor, show that sometimes they were capped with lead. The bandoliers often had a larger flask where they kept powder to charge the musket's pan. Twisted thread was used to attach the flasks to a belt because it was considered better than leather strips which were likely to rot, but thread could be easily broken, hence the discovery of the lead caps at Marston Moor. The amount of gunpowder each flask held is not specified, but had to be half the weight of the musket ball, so a ball weighing 40 grams had to have 20 grams of powder to propel it towards the target.[12]

The gunpowder in the pan was ignited with a lighted piece of match, from where the matchlock musket gets its name. The match was carried between

10   Francis Markham, *Five Decades of Epistles of War* (London: 1622), p.39; SP 28/233; A. V. B. Wallace Norman, *Wallace Collection Catalogue, European arms and armour supplement*.

11   Anon., *Directions for Musters, wherein is shewed the order for drilling for the musket and the pike* (Cambridge: Thomas Buck and Roger Daniel, 1638).

12   TNA: WO 49/79.

the fingers of the left hand and burnt at both ends, in case one went out. In 1614 Sir Horace Vere commanded that 'the musketeers are always to have [a] good store of match hung at their bandoliers', but in bad weather the match was likely to get wet if carried like this. It was estimated that a musketeer could use two fathoms of match every 24 hours, so even on the march, or on sentry duty, musketeers would still be burning match even before they came within sight of the enemy. To save match, musketeers could extinguish it leaving every eighth man's (probably the file leader) still alight, but this could lead to a desperate scramble for the other musketeers to light theirs if the enemy was spotted.[13] Another disadvantage with match was that at night its glowing ends could be seen in the darkness and so give away a musketeer's position, although this could be turned to advantage when musketeers wanted to withdraw unnoticed, such as at the battle of Lansdown in June 1643 when Waller's musketeers left their lit match on a wall to disguise their retreat. A Dutch invention, said to have been the idea of the Prince of Orange himself, was a tin pipe about a foot long in which the match was placed.

The musketeers also carried a sword, although there are various accounts of them using the butt of their musket as a club and Johan Wallhausen, who wrote *Kriegkunst zu Fuss* early in the seventeenth century, also suggests that the musketeers used their bandoliers, musket rests, helmets and fists to fight the enemy if necessary.

The dragoon was a hybrid of a musketeer and a cavalryman, although mounted on an inferior horse, and he was, where possible, armed with a flintlock musket, with a hook and swivel on which to attach it to a belt. He would ride to an engagement and then dismount to fight. However, horses were in short supply and in January 1644 of the 38 men in Captain Miller's company of dragoons only 18 had horses. This was not unique because Captain Holcroft's company of dragoons mustered 41 men, 31 wanting horses.[14] They could be also be issued with bandoliers, but 500 'cartouches' or cartridge boxes 'for dragoons muskets', were purchased for Colonel Okey's regiment in the New Model Army at a cost of 10d a piece.[15]

The accounts of John Cory, who was the treasurer of the Norfolk's committee, record that between 29 April and 10 June 1643 John Wyn, Thomas Armstrong, Christopher Ludlam, Peter Dale, David Cherry, Thomas Brown supplied swords. The entry for 1 June records that Christopher Ludlam, was paid £9 02s for 17 swords at 7s and 24 belts at 22d a piece and 12 belts at 19d. The entry for 29 April 1643 also records that David Cherry also supplied musket rests and on 26 May William Weston was paid £11 10s 00d for 10 muskets, rests and bandoliers for 23s each, while on 22 June John Dussing was paid £90 in part for 100 muskets. On 3 June William Wilson was paid for 100 'Swedish feathers' at 14s a piece: these were short pikes designed to protect the musketeers, and so sometimes fitted with a rest-type attachment

---

13   TNA: SP 16/88, f.82, WO 49/57, SP 9/202/1.; BL: TT E 39/8.

14   TNA: SP 28/25, ff.212, 305.

15   TNA: SP 28/29. The cost would suggest that they were boxes rather than cartridges which were used to load the muskets.

so that they could also act as a musket rest.[16] The suppliers of these arms often came from London, so we also find payments for their transportation, for example Alderman Moody presented his bill to the Committee of Suffolk for £126 3s 14d, for carriage of arms from London, between December 1643 and January 1644, which included 110 pairs of pistols, 412 muskets and 1,124 swords as well as several sets of armour and saddles.[17]

Among those who supplied the forces from Essex was John Watson, a gunmaker of London who charged 50 shillings for a flintlock or 'snaphaunce' pistol and 17s 6d for a 'full bore' matchlock musket and rest and between 1s 2d to 1s 10d for a 'pair of bandoliers'. A warrant dated 8 December 1642 recorded '3,000 fire stones' or flints for 5s per 100 weight, while another 2,500 fire stones for 4s per hundredweight. Another warrant, this time dated 5 October 1642, listed 1,000 fire stones at 10s per 100 weight, with 116 pistols, which may be pyrites or fool's gold which was used to ignite wheellock pistols.[18] Watson also supplied muskets 'with ring nails and swivels', which were to be issued to the dragoons. Bandoliers for the dragoons were supplied by Thomas Jupe for 20d a pair. Among those who supplied swords for the Essex soldiers was Captain Lawrence Bromfield, who received £105 on 21 September 1643 for 300 swords.[19]

Unfortunately, when it comes to swords, the accounts during the Civil War only refer to them as swords rather than specifying their type. However, during the 1650s there are references to ammunition swords and hangers, each costing 4s and cavalry swords, which cost 5s. The difference between the ammunition sword and a hanger is not recorded, but hanger was the name later given to swords with curved blades.[20] The 1635 instructions to the trained bands ordered that the cuirassiers should be armed with a sword 'three foot and an a half in length at least, hilt and all, which is to be stiff, sharp, pointed and cutting'. Presumably the arquebusier were also to carry a similar length sword. On the other hand the pikemen (and musketeers) were to have 'a good sword of three foot long, cutting stiff, pointed'.[21]

On 18 October 1643 John Watson, a gunmaker of London, received £193 6s 8d for '200 muskets and rests at 17s 6d, plus 200 pairs of bandoliers at 1s 10d per pair', which were to be delivered to Sir Thomas Barrington for the use of the forces of the county of Essex.[22] However, the following account dated the 6 April 1644, for arms 'bought and provided for the right Honourable the Earl of Manchester by me Samuel Moody', does not mention musket rests:[23]

16   BodLib: Tanner, MS 66 ff.3–7.
17   TNA: SP 28/243, unfoliated.
18   TNA: SP 28/262, ff.202, 205, f.327.
19   TNA: SP 28/227.
20   During the early part of the seventeenth century, the term 'hanger' also referred to a piece of leather which attached the sword to a waistbelt, but this does not appear to be what the accounts meant in this instance.
21   TNA: SP 18/167, *State Papers relating to musters, beacons, ship money etc in Norfolk*.
22   TNA: SP 28/227, unfoliated.
23   TNA: SP 28/24 part II f.191.

1,000 muskets at 14s 6d the piece	£725 00s 00d
1,000 swords and belts at 6s	£300 00s 00d
1,000 bandoliers at 17d a the piece	£70 16s 08d
400 pikes at 4s 2d the piece	£83 16s 08d
50 pikes at 5s the piece	£12 10s 00d
255 cases of pistols at 38s the case	£484 10s 00d
55 pairs of holsters at 3s 4d the piece	£9 03s 04d
170 saddles and furniture at 20s the piece	£170 00s 00d
20 back, breast and head pieces for Captain John Moody lined	£34 00s 00d
with leather at 34s the piece	£10 00s 00d
8 drums at [blank]	£6 10s 00d
2 colours for Col. Russell and for mending the rest	£12 00s 00d
2 trumpets, banners and strings for Captain John Moody	
Total	£1917 16s 8d

When it came to raising a regiment of foot the following account, dated 2 June 1644, for Colonel Rainsborough's regiment was probably typical:

Swords 300 at 6s 6d per sword	£97	10	00
Swords 300 at £6 6s 8d per score	£95	00	00
Halberds 22 at 6s per halberd	£06	12	00
Drums 22 at 25s per drum	£27	10	00
Partizans 10 at 12s per partizan	£6	00	00
Snapsacks 600 at 9d per snapsack	£22	10	00
Ensigns 10 at £4 per ensign	£40	00	00
Drum heads & snares 40 pairs	£10	00	00
For carriage of arms from London ...	£15	00	00
For mending arms			
	£6	00	00
Total	£363	12	00

Partizans and halberds were usually carried by the company commanders and their sergeants, as a badge of their positions. These were both polearms usually with a large spear-shaped head for the partizans and a large axe shaped head for the halberds.

When Manchester returned to the counties of the Eastern Association after his victory at Marston Moor, among the arms sent to Cambridge to re-equip his army were 448 new muskets, 553 fixed muskets, 700 new bandoliers, 320 old bandoliers, 210 new snaphaunce muskets, 250 pairs of pistols without holsters, 73 holsters and 63 spanners. The warrant continues:

I have about 60 more of them in the magazine, the reason why I did not send them is because there must be longer holsters made purposely for them for our ordinary holsters will not serve. I shall God willing send to London to have some made for them with what speed I can ... The workmen are fixing more muskets with all the speed they can.[24]

---

24 PA: Wil/2/48.

Artillery

No army would be complete without its artillery train, although less is known about the artillery of the Eastern Association than its other branches. On 20 September 1643 two culverin, three sakers and six 3-pounders (sakeret or minion) were ordered to be delivered to Manchester for his artillery. These were described as being brass ordnance mounted on a gun carriage with shod wheels, plus a mortar. Wagons would also be needed to carry the 120 round-shot for the culverins, 180 for the sakers and 360 for the 3-pounders and 40 grenades for the mortar, plus the 200 barrels of powder and the equipment to go with them.[25] The artillery carriages and wagons are usually described as being painted with a 'fair lead' colour, but unfortunately what shade this colour was is unknown. It has been suggested that it might be a grey colour (that is, the colour of lead) while others say red, which was the colour of artillery carriages later in the century.

As well as the wagons for the artillery train, each regiment would also have its own carriages for carrying their ammunition and supplies. These might have 'flags of distinction', which would identify a regiment's own wagons and possibly those carrying gunpowder.[26]

When Manchester commanded the Association, the artillery was placed under the responsibility of Lieutenant General Thomas Hammond, and by 12 September 1643 Manchester's wagonmaster general was Thomas Richardson, while the master gunner was John Stilgoe, who had 10 gunners under his command.[27]

Regimental Colours

Without its colours a company, troop or regiment was considered to be incomplete, no manner how understrength it was, likewise if a company or troop was cashiered then its colour would be torn from its staff in disgrace. It was the responsibility of each county within the Eastern Association to purchase the colours for its regiments. In theory an ensign measured six feet square, but the few surviving examples attributed to the English Civil War period show that they were larger, 6 feet high by 6 feet 6 inches wide in the case of Sir John Gell's colour, or 6 feet by 6 feet 8 inches wide for another unknown colour. A third colour is 6 feet 6 inches by 7 feet wide. According to Thomas Venn:

> The colonel's colour in the first place is of a pure and clean colour, without any mixture. The lieutenant colonel's only with the Saint George arms in the upper corner next [to] the staff; The majors the same, but in the lower and out most corner with a little stream blazant, and every captain with Saint George's Arms

25   BL: Add MS 34, 315.
26   TNA: WO 49/79.
27   TNA: SP 28/264, ff.139, 146.

alone, but with so many spots or several devices as pertains to the dignity of their respective places.[28]

The St George's cross on the surviving ensigns also varies in size. 'Metal' colours (yellow and white) and proper colours, that is, blue, red etc. were not to be mixed, so a yellow colour should not have white devices or a blue colour have red devices. A blue colour with white devices was acceptable, although having a black spot, or spots, was considered a dishonour. The red cross of St George was usually made out of material, whereas the devices were painted on, probably using a stencil.

Unfortunately, the purchases of regimental colours are recorded in various accounts, for example on 12 April 1643 John Cory paid 'to Mr Richard Kett by warrant to buy ensigns for Colonel Hobart's Regiment, £30 00s 00d'.[29] Also as described above when Rainsborough's regiment was raised £40 was paid for 10 ensigns or £4 each. Rarely do we find payments which describe the colours, such as a warrant addressed to Lord Willoughby of Parham, 'For 10 silk ensigns of rich watchet [sky blue] taffeta with distinctions of white crosses furnished with staves and tassels at £4 a piece. Total £40'. On 18 March 1652 'eight ensigns of yellow Florence sarsnet with crimson cross crosslets ... with gilt heads and tassels', were delivered to the Isle of Ely's regiment of trained bands. Unfortunately, it is not known whether the regiment carried similar colours during the First Civil War.[30]

Sometimes when new colours were in short supply, old ones might be reissued. In early October 1643 Sir Thomas Barrington records:

> The Earl of Manchester writes for drums, colours and other necessaries which we hope Major Sparrow by your direction hath already supplied, we have sent some colours and drums that belong to the associated forces formally sent out under my Lord Grey, but for the colours we conceive in respect of the differences they will not serve in a regimental way as for the arms if it be thought fit to make use of them.[31]

This was not the only time old colours were reissued. In October 1644 when the Earl of Essex's army was issued with new colours there were not enough for all the regiments, therefore the Board of the Ordnance records 'Old ensigns taken out of the office 5s which were repaired and 20 made into fair at 5s a piece. For three ells and a half of white Florence sarsnet for the making of the distinctions of the same aforementioned ensigns at 9s per ell, 31s 6d'.[32]

Likewise in July 1645 when Colonel Willoughby took command of John Barker's Warwickshire regiment, since the regiment had only been issued colours that January a Mrs Pott was paid 13s 'for setting in 36 mullets' in

28 Captain Thomas Venn, *Military Observations*, p.181.
29 BodLib: Tanner MS 66.
30 TNA: SP 28/223 part 3, unfoliated.
31 BL: Egerton, MS 2647.
32 TNA: WO 49/82, f.60. The other colours were orange with white mullets, crimson with yellow annulets, green with yellow bullets, crimson with white balls, green with yellow half-moons, green with white diamonds.

these colours. What the devices were beforehand is not recorded, but rather than paint over the old devices '1¾ ells of sarsnet was needed for these new devices made into fair at 5s a piece'.[33] Florence sarsnet was cheaper than silk or damask which was also used for making colours.

During the summer of 1643 Hertfordshire raised three auxiliary regiments: a green, an orange and a black regiment, one being commanded by Colonel Alban Coxe and another by Sir John Wittrough. The major and Captain Ewer's companies of the Earl of Warwick's regiment of the Essex Trained Bands were issued with two new colours in August 1643, with three spots on, presumably the major's colour had one spot and Ewer's two so he must have been the senior captain. Therefore this regiment, like the regiments of the London Trained Bands, strayed from the system described by Venn, by having the first device for the major's company. The three Essex trained band regiments are known to have been issued with blue, white and yellow ensigns.

On 24 March 1644 Sir Samuel Luke records that on the previous Sunday, 17 March, 'the Newark forces had taken the blue regiment and slain all the red regiment which lay before it'. These colours probably belonged to either Colonel Hobart's, Palgrave's, King's, Russell's and Lord Willoughby's regiments of foot, all of whom are known to have been at the siege.[34]

One is tempted to look at the regiments of Manchester's old army which served in the New Model Army for clues as to their colours, but a summary of warrants among the State Papers held by The National Archives clearly shows that the Eastern Association's regiments were issued with new colours, whereas Essex's old regiments seem to have retained their old ones and just bought new colours for their newly raised companies:[35]

> Colonel Montagu 10 blue colours
> Colonel Crawford 10 colours
> Major General Skippon two colours
> Colonel Fortescue two colours
> Lt Gen. Hammond two colours
> Colonel Rainsborough 10 colours
> Colonel Aldrich two colours
> Colonel Pickering 10 blue colours
> Colonel Sir Hardress Waller 10 black colours

Fairfax's, Crawford's, Rainsborough's, Skippon's, Aldrich's and Hammond's ensigns cost £2 3s each, whereas those for Pickering's cost £2 3s ½d. Crawford's regiment was also to be furnished with 20 drums at £1 4s each, whereas Montagu's regiment was to have 22 drums, although it is interesting to note that when Hammond took over Crawford's regiment as Colonel a further two ensigns were purchased for the regiment. Several of these colours were observed at the storming of Basing House in October 1645, which stated that

---

33   TNA: SP 28/137 ff.23, 303.
34   I. G. Phillips, *The Journal of Sir Samuel Luke*, p.269.
35   TNA: SP 28/29, ff.170, 176, 180, 209, 247, 248, 259, 270; TNA: SP 28/30, f.339.

Pickering's and Montagu's regiments carried blue ensigns and Sir Hardress Waller's had black ones.[36]

Cavalry cornets were about two feet square with a fringe, usually in two different colours around three sides. These could either be of a plain design, or have a motto within or without a scroll or have an elaborate design. Although he did not serve with the Eastern Association, Hugh Croxton's bill to Lionel Copley is an excellent example of the cost of a cavalry cornet. On 22 March 1643 it gives the following details:[37]

For ¾ Damask	£0 07s 06d
For 1½ ells of taffeta	£0 19s 06d
For 4 ord of fringe	£0 10s 00d
For a pair of cornet strings	£0 03s 06d
For 2 pair of cordwell strings	£2 12s 00d
For 8 pairs of ribbon	£0 02s 00d
For painting the banners and cornet with a horseman & horse & a motto	£2 00s 00d
For making the cornet and banners	£0 10s 00d
Total	£12 04s 06d

On 18 December 1644 Croxton was again called upon to supply a cornet to Copley's troop:

For ¾ of orange damask	£0 11s 00d
For 1½ ord of silk and silver fringe	£0 08s 06d
For a pair of silk and silver cornet strings	£0 16s 00d
For painting the cornet	£0 15s 00d
For the cornet staff and case with belt, boot and swivel	£1 08s 00d
For making the cornet	£0 03s 00d
Total	£4 02s 00d
The embroidering of your cornet cost	£1 09s 00d

There is no mention of the banners for the troop's trumpets, but these were usually the troop commander's coat of arms, or if he did not have one, then it was identical to the cornet.

Some cornets carried by the troops of the Eastern Association are known. Manchester's own cornet was green with the motto 'Truth and Peace' in yellow running diagonally from the canton to the bottom corner, with a green and white fringe. Colonel George Fleetwood's cornet was blue with blue and yellow fringe. His devices was a hand holding a sword emerging from a cloud with the motto 'God is my Strength' in a yellow scroll. These two cornets are unusual because the motto is in English rather than Latin, like Sir John Norwich's cornet, which was orange with an orange and white fringe,

---

36 TT E 304/24.
37 TNA: SP 28/42.

with the Latin motto 'Pro, Christo, et Ecclesia' which also ran diagonally from the canton in a white and yellow scroll.

As for troop commanders, Manchester's regiment of horse included the following cornets:

> Captain Sparrow had a red cornet with a red and white fringe and the motto, 'Si Leges Rerum', in a white scroll, and a sparrow on one of the tails of the scroll and a rose on the other. His coat of arms was three red roses on a while field with a thick red border at the top.
>
> Captain Dingley's cornet was red with red and white fringe, its device being a group of dismounted knights sallying forth from a castle, with the motto, 'We are released to fight for the Gospel, laws and liberty', in a white and yellow scroll

Unfortunately the details of Cromwell's own cornet is not known, but those of several of his troop commanders are:

> Captain Samuel Porter's cornet was yellow field with yellow and white fringe and a white cloud, with a flesh coloured arm holding a sword with a white blade and yellow hilt, scroll white with the motto, 'Pro vide semei tradita'
>
> Captain James Berry's was red with the motto 'Pro Rege et Lege Parat' in white and with a red and yellow fringe
>
> Captain Henry Ireton's cornet was also red with a red and white fringe with the motto 'Pro Divinis qui admittit Servat Humanis vim vi' in a yellow and white scroll

A Captain Walton's troop also carried a red cornet with a red and white fringe, and the motto 'Gavdet Tertamine, Virtus' in a white and yellow scroll, but it is not known whether this was Colonel Valentine Walton's cornet, whose troop served in Manchester's regiment, or that of his son who was killed at Marston Moor and was part of Cromwell's regiment.[38]

Dragoons carried guidons which were similar in size to the cavalry cornets, except they had a 'swallow tail'. The design of which were similar to the infantry colours, sometimes with a St George's Cross in the canton and with devices or mottos, but unfortunately as with the infantry colours little is known about those carried by the dragoons in the Eastern Association. On 16 August 1643 the dragoon companies of Captains Halcroft, Harbottle and Miller received £9 for three colours and six drums, but unfortunately there is no description of them.[39]

---

38   BL: Sloane, MS 5247. Usually when it comes to scroll, the motto is on the white part of the scroll and the yellow part is joining two pieces of white scroll together.
39   TNA: SP 28/227.

Clothing

Unlike the Earl of Essex's army, whose regiments of foot appear to have changed the colour of their coats with every issue of new clothing, the regiments which made up Manchester's infantry seem to have been predominantly red, although Manchester's own regiment of foot appear to have partly issued with green coats faced red, with the other part of his regiment in red coats faced green.[40]

Manchester's lifeguard are known to have worn scarlet coats, some of which were made by John Burton a tailor from Cambridge who charged £5 10s for making 10 coats at 11s per coat.[41] In March 1644 a Mr Weaver also presented his bill for making coats for the lifeguard which is more detailed:[42]

Item 32 yards ½ ells of fine scarlet broad cloth at 12s per yard	£20 07s 10d
Item 33¾ yards of fine green London bayses at 2s 4d [a] yard	£6 05s 05d
Item 5 ordinary of grass green and crimson silk	£00 10s 00d
Item 14 dozen, 7 yards of grass green and galloon at 3s per dozen	£02 03s 09d
Item 15 dozen of grass green bobbing loop lace at 3s the dozen	£02 05s 00d
Item 10 grass green neck buttons	£00 06s 08d
Item half a yard of canvas	£00 00s 07d
Item 15 gross, 3 dozen of grass green and strawberry buttons at 4s gross	£03 01s 00d
Item 15 dozen of large cloak buttons at 9d [per] dozen	£00 11s 03d
	£35 11s 05d

Thomas Buckley also made coats for the Eastern Association, and on 27 March 1645 charged the Association for the coats he had supplied the previous year:[43]

---

40 These were for Lieutenant Colonel Clifton (141 coats), Captains Johnson (109), O'Neale (110), Tolley (40) Waldon (60), Southcoat (104) and Meredith (10) plus 100 other coats that were ready but not yet allocated to a company or soldier. TNA: SP 28/25, f.345.
41 TNA: SP 28/24 part III, f.254.
42 TNA: SP 28/24 part III, f.334.
43 TNA: SP 28/28, f.136.

Delivered to Major Holmes by order 20 green coats [faced] with red and on red coats faced with green to Captain Southcote.	[missing]
For Colonel Montagu's regiment in red coats faced with white, 416	[missing]
Delivered to Major Holmes in green coats faced with red, April 24 1644, 50	£25 [missing]
The 13 May 1644 green coats faced with red and red faced with green, 220	[missing]
Delivered in red coats faced with blue 828/400 at 11s and 428 at 10s	£43 [missing]
Sent more in red coats faced with blue, 38	£19 [missing]
Delivered to Captain Taylor May the 9 1644, 43 coats	£21 10s
[Delivered] May the 26 1644, 100 lockrum shirts 3s 8d,	£17 6s
For 54 fine broad cloth coats with bayes buttons and loop lace and making 43–6	£117 [missing]
Item 13 pairs of broad cloth beeches with linings and making at 16s 6d a pair	£10 14
Item in red coats faced with blue, 71	£35 10s
Item in green coats faced with red, 500	£250 00 00
Item 28 long coats with bayes buttons and silk and 28 pair of breeches with lining and making	£84 00 00
Item in red coats faced with blue according to order, 128	£64

Unfortunately, part of the right side of the document with the total amount is missing, but the total cost of this clothing was £1,407 00s 2d.[44] The green coats faced red and the red coats faced green cost 10s, but it is unclear why the red coats faced blue had two prices, 10s and 11s. It does not appear to have been because they were two sizes because no other of the entries have two prices. It is possible that they were faced differently going to two different regiments, but if so how? Perhaps the coats with loop lace are for drummers and the long coats are for cavalry. Not all the infantry of the Eastern Association were clothed in red or green coats.

One regiment whose coat colour is not known is that of Major General Crawford's, but Mr Ogden's account of the battle of Marston Moor refers to 'Manchester's blew coats', which possibly refers to his regiment.[45] An

---

44   TNA: SP 28/26, f.186.
45   Young, *Marston Moor*, p.217.

undated warrant by Thomas Barnes records 180 blue coats being supplied to an unidentified Hertfordshire regiment, although Crawford's regiment was not raised in this county. There is a shipment of 985 grey coats being sent to Wisbech and later a further 608 coats of an unspecified colour was also sent to the same place. These coats may have been for the regiments of Sir Miles Hobart or Colonel Palgrave, both were known to have been at Wisbech and both came from Norfolk, although in March 1644 Hobart's regiment is probably the one described as 'the Norfolk redcoats' at the siege of Newark.[46] It is also possible that these coats were being shipped elsewhere.

In April 1644 a Mr Moody of Bury St Edmunds received £998 for clothing 1,273 Suffolk men belonging to Colonel Francis Russell. In another warrant Russell's regiment are described as red coats. Moody seems to be a major supplier of coats since he was paid a further £2,488 for 5,240 coats which were to be distributed between the regiments of Colonels Russell, Hobart, Palgrave, Walton and Pickering.[47] He is probably Samuel Moody who on 17 October 1644 was ordered to make 1,000 coats 'at the usual rate for the garrison of [King's] Lynn', for 9s 6d each. It was not until 13 December 1644 that he received £475 payment for this order.[48]

According to a letter describing the garrison of Abingdon in April or May 1645 Colonel Thomas Rainsborough's regiment mustered about 550 redcoats. However Rainsborough's regiment was at Grantham at this time, so it may be that Royalist spy mistook Colonel Ayloffe's regiment, which is known to have formed part of Abingdon's garrison at this time, and was then reduced into Colonel Rainsborough's regiment in the New Model Army.[49]

The soldiers were not just issued with coats: on 21 December 1643 the Committee of the Eastern Association received coats, breeches, boots and stockings and shirts for the soldiers to the value of £380 plus £60 for 'buying clothes, boots etc., for his Lordship's Regiment'.[50] On 13 April 1644 1,000 shirts were delivered to Captain Daniel Axtell for Pickering's regiment and on 8 June Thomas Buckley was paid £15 6s for 'clothes for poor soldiers which were received into [Lieutenant] Colonel Warner's and Colonel Pickering's companies'.[51] Another warrant for an unidentified regiment gives the price for each item at 3s 10 for a waistcoat, stockings 2s 4d per pair, shirts 3s, a pair of shoes cost 6d and a pair of breeches 10s. Breeches do not appear to have been regularly issued, but just for modesty's sake when a soldier was recruited or if he had lost his for some reason.

Officers also appear to have received cloth to be made into coats of their own design, so on 22 April 1644 Captain Harbottle, who commanded a company of dragoons, was paid £5 8s 7d for 'cloth and manner of linings' for

46   TNA: SP 28/299.
47   TNA: SP 28/128 part 8, ff.9, 10; SP 28/25 ff.426, 427, 428; SP 28/24 part III, f.388.
48   TNA: SP 28/19, f.257.
49   BL: Add MS 18,982, f.409. Also gives Major General Browne's regiment as grey coats and Colonel George Paine's as blue coats. Paine's regiment was formed of three London auxiliary regiments which had been reduced to one.
50   TNA: SP 28/26.
51   TNA: SP 28/128 part 8, ff.10, 118.

Lieutenant Watson, although the treasurer refused to pay a further 20s for the clothing of another officer who was not present at a muster.[52]

Shoes and stockings are the most common items mentioned in the accounts. These included for 13 August 1644, Richard Crofts who was paid £130 14s 4d for 1,012 pairs of shoes 'for the use of the State', and on 18 September Edward Poole was paid £125 for 1,000 pairs of shoes for the use of Manchester's army. Sometimes the regiments bought their own shoes, such as on 28 November Lieutenant Colonel Hewson was paid £28 6s 8d for 200 pairs of shoes he had purchased for Pickering's regiment at 2s 10d a pair.[53]

Presumably some of the clothing mentioned above was also for dragoons, but sometimes they have their own entries, such as on 22 March 1644 John Crofts, a shoemaker of Bedford, was paid £12 and John Symes was paid £13 for boots and shoes to Captain Holcroft's company of dragoons, while John Symes received a further £10 8s 7d for shirts and stockings for this company. References to hats or caps being issued are rare, but on 22 March 1644 William Fenn was paid £10 10s for hats for Captain Ewer's company of dragoons of an unspecified design.[54]

Less information is available for the clothing for the cavalry, apart from the buffcoats mentioned above. The largest collection of buffcoats, 37 in total, have leather sleeves and are collectively known as the Littlecote Collection, after the Popham family's stately home where they were stored for many years until purchased by the Royal Armouries. These are yellow ochre in colour, but underneath their lining is natural coloured leather, which is the same colour as other surviving examples, which would suggest that they were stained sometime after they were made, probably as late as Victorian times when they were mounted on the walls of Littlecote House.[55]

As well as making shoes for the dragoons John Crofts also made boots for the cavalry: on 9 October 1644 he was paid £77 00s 4d for stockings, boots and spurs for Colonel Vermuyden's troop and a further £36 4s 2d for shirts and spurs for Captain John Jenkin's troop which also belonged to Vermuyden's regiment.[56] Boots could also be mended, several entries in the accounts for Captain Lawrence's troop record 1s for 'soling' a pair of boots and 2s for 'soling, lacquering and mending' another pair.[57]

Provisions

Each soldier was, in theory, issued with a pound of bread, and either a pound of cheese or meat per day and there are various warrants for deliveries of

52   TNA: SP 28/223, unfoliated.
53   TNA: SP 28/25, f.136, 144, 171–172.
54   TNA: SP 28/128 part 8, ff.51, 6.
55   It is clear from the catalogue of the Littlecote Collection that the owners did not respect the items which formed this collection, since holes have been drilled into the armour to make mounting easier and the leg armour from a set of cuirassier armour has been fitted to an arquebusier's breast plate.
56   TNA: SP 28/19, ff.271, 273.
57   TNA: SP 28/25, f.143, 144, 163, 167.; TNA: SP 28/233.

bullocks, cows, sheep being delivered to the various regiments, for example on 20 July 1644 a John Parry was paid 22s for eight sheep for Montagu's regiment. Parry along with a Swinen Keen was paid a further £7 on 20 October 1644 for 35 sheep, while a William Grove supplied 16 sheep to Pickering's regiment for which he received £5 6s 8d on 11 October. A further 27 sheep were delivered to Pickering's regiment for which Thomas Jenner was paid £9 on 24 October 1644.[58] The account book of Sir William Waller's commissary general, who was responsible for feeding his army, records that fresh meat was only issued to the officers and sick soldiers.[59] The ordinary rank and file were issued with salted meat to preserve it, which to make it edible had to be soaked to wash away the salt.

Likewise with no preservatives the bread would quickly go stale which would mean having to bake fresh bread every few days. Among those who supplied bread were Robert Tirrell, Peter Thorne, 'the widow Day', Thomas Frome, Humphrey Hewes, Robert Creed, Francis Brown and Edward Brown. In 1640 a recipe for bread for the soldiers was two parts rye and one part wheat or barley, while another recipe states two parts wheat and one part rye. Sometimes during the Civil War only wheat was delivered to a regiment, for them to make their own bread or biscuits, such as on 20 July 1644 when John Jackson was paid £2 6s for delivering 16 bushels of wheat to Montagu's regiment.[60]

Whatever the ingredients no doubt water was added to bind the ingredients together. Although one alternative was the issue of biscuits, which appears to have been similar to the hard tack biscuits issued in later centuries. Biscuits were measured by the bag rather than the dozen; On 22 April 1645 112 bags with 10,000 weight of biscuit were purchased for the New Model Army at 12d per bag for a total cost of £5 12s, while another contract was for 149 bags containing 13,300 weight of biscuits at 12s per 100.[61]

Officers would probably get better quality bread. However, the bread might be 'half baked' by an unscrupulous baker so that the water would not evaporate which would make it heavier. Coupled with the fact that the weight of the meat might also include bone, this would further undercut a soldier's ration. Cheshire and Suffolk cheese are often mentioned in account books as being supplied to the soldiers. On rare occasions tobacco is also recorded, smoking being a popular pastime with soldiers.

On campaign each soldier was issued with a snapsack (or 'knapsack'), in which they could keep their rations and belongings. A warrant paid £1 for 120 snapsacks which makes two pence per snapsack, whereas another warrant for 12 shillings for a dozen snapsacks or 1s per item. Why there was such a difference in price is not recorded, but they could be made either of leather or canvas.[62]

---

58   TNA: SP 28/25, ff.183, 271, 295.
59   TNA: SP 28/135.
60   TNA: SP 28/25, ff.272, 273.
61   TNA: SP 28/29, f.244.
62   TNA: SP 28/243, unfoliated.

In 1647 the soldiers in Ireland complained that such was the want of clothes that they had tear 'our snapsacks to patch a hole to hide our naked and staved flesh'. Bread seems to have been issued to the soldiers to last a few days at a time, whereas according to Robert Ward, in 'hot weather the sutlers belonging to every company may march with their wagons between companies whereby they may the sooner relieve [the soldiers] with meat and drink, which otherwise they cannot come unto but once a day'.[63]

This could account for Henry Foster's claim that on the march to relieve Gloucester in 1643, 'we could get no accommodation either for meat or drink, but what we brought with us in our snapsacks'. An English volunteer in the Bohemian army in 1620 records that:

> our General gave command to draw out part of every company to be of the forlorn hope … Doctor Burges our minister, did encourage us to fight valiantly, and did assure us we should find our reward in heaven; whereupon we feasted ourselves with such victuals we had and threw away our snapsacks, with all our provisions, both linen and woollen because it would be troublesome to us.[64]

Whether it was standard practice for soldiers to discard their snapsacks before a battle is not known.

Discipline

The Parliamentarian armies were guided by the *Laws of War* laid down by the Earl of Essex. On 12 October 1642 John Partridge was paid £100 for printing 8,000 copies of the *Ordinances of War* or 3d per copy. Each book was composed of four sheets and was delivered to the Earl of Essex while he was at Northampton.[65] The book was reprinted several times between 1642 and 1644, always with amendments. In addition to these laws the Committee at Cambridge also issued several warrants on discipline, one being published on 16 April 1643 which stated that the officers were to prevent soldiers getting drunk in 'taverns, inns, alehouses and other places of tippling, nor any court of guards be suffered to keep or suffer to be kept any soldier or soldiers tippling in their or any of their houses, or courts of guard to the waste of their pay and to the ill example of their fellow soldiers'. They were also to keep a 'strict eye' upon their soldiers not to 'shoot, pawn, sell, throw away or otherwise embezzle any powder, arms or ammunition whatsoever'. Those who broke these rules could expect 'severe punishment'. These laws were to be read out to the garrison of Cambridge and other regiments the day after their arrival and each week during their stay.[66] Unfortunately, no court martial papers are known to exist apart from those of Waller's army during 1644 and a few for the New Model Army, so we do not know how widely these

---

63 Robert Ward, *Aminadversions of Warre* (1638), book 2 p.23.
64 Anon., *A Relation of the passage of our English Companies from time to time* (London, 1621).
65 TNA: SP 28/261, f.390.
66 BL: Egerton, MS 2651, f.140.

laws and warrants were followed. However, the newspaper *Special Passages* for April 1643 records that Cromwell 'exercises strict discipline [amongst his regiment], for when two troopers would have escaped, he sent them back and caused them to be whipped at the marketplace in Huntingdon being before dismounted and disarmed, and turned off as renegadoes'.[67]

The following month the same newspaper recorded that 'no man swears but he pays his twelve pence; if he be drunk he is set in the stocks or worse; if one calls the other "Roundhead" he is cashiered'.[68] Punishment for calling fellow soldiers derogatory names is mentioned in the Articles of War for both sides and is sometimes used as an example of the strict discipline imposed on soldiers of the New Model Army.

However, not all the soldiers, as *Special Passages* implied, were well behaved; some of Manchester's soldiers and troopers plundered the Royalists' baggage train after the surrender of York, who had been given safe passage. Manchester ordered that those responsible were to return their plunder to their captains. If they failed to do so they were to 'expect no favour or mercy at all, but the uttermost severity, being death by the Articles of War, published by his Excellency the Earl of Essex', but at the Council of War that followed it showed that Cromwell was willing to be lenient on those of his own faction. Another example of this is when Lieutenant General Crawford wanted to cashier an officer for ill-discipline by disobeying him, but the case against the officer was dismissed since he was 'a Godly officer'

Casualties

Each regiment had its own surgeon and a surgeon's mate. Jonathan Crosse, the surgeon of Manchester's own regiment of horse, was paid £20 on 27 August 1644 to buy a 'chest of medicaments and instruments for surgery'. Crosse was also paid £30 for being the regimental surgeon between 25 March to 26 August 1644 or 4s a day as the regiment's surgeon, but he also supplemented his wages 'in respect of extraordinary pains sustained in dressing maimed men which were not of his Lordship's regiment', for which he received £20. Manchester's own regiment had two surgeon's mates who were paid 2s 6d per day.[69]

Although hospitals were known at the time of the Civil War, many soldiers were cared for by individuals, such as John Watson who looked after John Straight, 'a lame soldier under the command of Captain Mattersley' from 18 December 1644 to 10 February 1645, for which he received six pence a day or a total of £1 7s. In addition he received 4s for washing his linen and clothes. Watson looked after another sick soldier, Ralph Hawkins of Captain Masterson's company, from 8 January to 6 February 1645. This time his fee was 14s for food and lodging, 3s for a woman to look after Hawkins for a

---

67   Both quoted in C.H. Firth, 'Raising of the Ironsides'.
68   *Continuation of Certain Remarkable Passages from Both Houses of Parliament* (London: Coles and Leach, 11–18 May 1643).
69   TNA: SP 28/25, ff.299, 313.

week, plus 2s for washing.[70] On 19 June 1644 having recovered from his sickness, William Reed of Newton, who was a soldier in Colonel Russell's regiment, was given an unspecified amount of money for him to rejoin his regiment at York; unfortunately we have no way of knowing whether he arrived or became one of the many deserters that roamed the countryside.[71]

Unfortunately not all soldiers survived. In April 1644 a Mr May claimed for paying a woman 14s for watching Trooper Richard Barker for three weeks, plus 12s for her meals, and when Barker died, 7s was paid for a sheet to bury him in and 3s for 'church duties to bury him'. A payment of 3s was also paid 'for washing up my linen and all other things belonging to the bed. In all Mr May claimed £4 10s 6d, although he appears to have been paid just £3 6s 6d.[72] John Freeman was in Captain Stawton's company and was cared for by Daniel Jolly of Chesterton when he died on 30 June 1644. Among the payments made to Jolly was 4s for a sheet to bury him in and 1s 8d for 'burying him and carrying him to [his] grave'. Therefore it is clear that it was the responsibility of the person who was caring for the soldier to also have him buried.[73]

70   TNA: SP 28/23, ff.429, 430.
71   TNA: SP 28/243.
72   TNA: SP 28/223/ part 3, unfoliated.
73   TNA: SP 28/26, f.187.

Appendix II

Journal of Colonel Montagu's Regiment[1]

6 November 1643. Four companies of Colonel Montugu's Regiment newly raised lying near Cambridge, viz., Chesterton, Fenne Ditton, Darnwell and Waterbeech marched from thence the first day by water to Ely and from Ely to Wells the 9th day.

10th from Wells to Wisbech.

11th From Wisbech to Long Sutton and Gedny.

12th from Long Sutton and Gedny to Spalding.

13th From Spalding to Gosberton.

14th From Gosberton to Boston.

16th From Boston to Swinghead and Kirton.

24th From Swinghead and Kirton to Heckington and lay in the church all night.

25th From Heckington to Naneby.

26th From Naneby to Washingburgh, Heakington, Cammick and Bramston.

10 December, Where we received Captain Cunningham and his company from Lincoln who being come thither from Hull and marched from thence to Sleaford.

11th, From Sleaford to Burne.

13th From Burne to Peterborough.

17th From Peterborough to Stukeley, Brampton and Huntington.

20th from thence to Roxton.

21st From Roxton to Bedford, where we lay six weeks and received Major Popley and Captain Taylor and their companies and marched from thence 15 February to Newport Pagnell and lay there eleven weeks and received Captain Freeman and whilst we lay there we took Hilsdon House, Sir Alexander Daynton, Colonel Smith, 30 officers and 300 prisoners and then upon the 20th April 1644 being Easter Even we marched to Goldington in Bedfordshire.

---

1   BodLib: Carte, MS 74, ff.159–160. Journal of Colonel Edward Montagu's Regiment of Foot.

21st From Goldington to Budgen and Brampton where the next day being Easter Monday we met with my Lord of Manchester and his train of artillery and;

22nd March to Barnewell and the headquarters was that night at Ownedle.

23rd To Collyweston and Dunnington and the headquarters was at Stamford.

29th To Burkeminster and Sewston and the headquarters [was] at Coltsforth.

30th To Grantham in Lincolnshire where the headquarters was.

2nd May, To Wellmore and the headquarters [was] at Naneby.

3rd To Lincoln where we took the city the same day the enemy running up to the hill or Closse which we took also the 6th day 50 officers, and between 700 or 800 prisoners and about 60 slain with all their great gun carriages, arms and ammunition.

8th from thence to Torksey and left my Lord at Lincoln and Colonel Palgrave regiment to keep the city.

13th To Gainborough.

20th To Belton in the Isle of Axholme.

21st To Thorne in Yorkshire.

23rd To Doncaster.

25th To Thorne again.

27th To Wistow beyond Selby and the headquarters was then at Selby.

1st June, To Osbaldwick and the headquarters at Helslington near York.

3rd To York leaguer at Clifton.

16th We stormed the Manor House.

1st July We raised the siege.

2nd We met Prince Rupert on Marston Moor with the Earl of Newcastle and General King, we fought and routed their army, took 20 great pieces, 12,000 small arms all their carriages, 1,700 prisoners and slain 4,150.

3rd We kept the field.

6th To Heslington where we continued until the 15th day on which we had a parley.

16th The city was yielded unto us.

20th We advanced to Kirkby Wharfe and the headquarters was then at Tadcaster.

22nd To Sir John Rumsden's House near Ferrybridge where the headquarters was.

23rd To Wheatley Sandon and Barnebydon and the headquarters was at Doncaster and whilst we stayed there Tickhill Castle and Welbeck House were yielded unto us upon compassion.

1st August. Three regiments marched to Rotherham viz, Major General Crawford's, Colonel Montagu's and Colonel Pickering.

2nd To Sheffield [Castle] where we beleaguered the castle until the 10th day. In which time we made 468 great shot against the castle then we had a parley and it was presently yielded, about this time Colonel Fretzwell's House at Stalye being a strong garrison for the King was yielded unto us. Where we had 11 great pieces and drakes with arms and ammunition.

13th To Bolsover Castle in Derbyshire which after we had faced them yielded the 14th day.

17th To Little Normanton, Thorneton and Pilsby.

18th To Allferton.

[20th][2] 21st We faced Wingfield Manor with our regiments where Sir John Gell had beleaguered the same a month before and after some few great shot we had a parley.

[21st] 22nd It was yielded to us.

[22nd] 23rd To Mansfield in Nottinghamshire. [An upon the 22 day we matched to Mansfield and from thence to Redford]

[22nd] 24th To Redford.

23rd, and from thence to Littleburgh

[24th] 25th To Gainsborough in Lincolnshire.

2nd September to Nettleham.

3rd We met with our army and train of artillery against and then we advanced to Ashby and the headquarters [were] at Digby.

4th To Osburnby and the headquarters [were] at Sleeford.

5th To Burn where the headquarters was.

6th to Paston near Peterborough where the headquarters was.

7th To Fassett in Northamptonshire.

9th To Witton and Hootton in Huntingtonshire and the headquarters at Huntingdon.

10th To Gamlingay in Cambridgeshire.

11th To Baldock in Hertfordshire and the headquarters at Bigglesworth.

12th To Winly and the headquarters at Hitching.

13th To St Albans the headquarters.

14th To Conye.

21st To Bushy and the headquarters at Watford.

23rd To Denham and the headquarters at Uxbridge.

26th To White Walton and the headquarters at Maidenhead.

27th To Wargrave near Reading where the headquarters was.

29th To Ruscombe and Hurst.

---

2   Sometime after 14 August the person who kept the journal seems to have added a day, so the dates and words in square brackets thereafter come from *A Journal or true and exact relation of each days passage, of that party of the Right Honourable the Earl of Manchester's Army, under the command of the ever honoured Major General Crawford from the 1st August to the end of the same month* (London: Hugh Perry, 1644).

5th October To Willington in Hampshire our regiment and Colonel Hubbard's advanced.

6th To Newbury.

17th To West Sherborne.

19th To Basingstoke the same day to West Sherborne.

20th To Basingstoke again.

21st To Harkwood Park and lay there all night.

22nd Through Basingstoke again and there we met my Lord General's Army and the City Brigades and marched to Mortmore and lay in the field all night.

23rd To Reading.

24th To Buckleberry in Berkshire.

25th To Thatcham were we lay in the field all night.

26th To the field near Shaw by Newbury.

27th We fought with the King's Army lying in Shaw and Newbury and Donnington Castle and drove them out of the town's where we took 356 prisoners with the Earl of Cleveland and the Lady Ruthven, seven field pieces. The King flying towards Bath with 10 men only.

2nd November From Shaw to Compton.

3rd To East Harkborne in the Vale of the White Horse.

6th To Bucklebery.

7th To Speen and Marsh Benham where we had 12 great shot made against us from Donnington Castle they espying our Colours.

9th To Newbury at 12 o'clock in the night at which time the King's Army relieved Donnington Castle where we had some skirmishes with them took some prisoners and made their whole body to retreat towards Wallingford.

10th We marched into the field after them and the same day back to Newbury.

17th From Newbury to Aldermaston where we expected the King would have given us battle but they did no so much as face us with a party.

18th To Morlemore.

19th To Paternoster Hatch in Herkefield parish.

20th To Reading.

21st To Ruscombe and Wargrave.

26th To Maidenhead.

3rd December To Amersham in Buckinghamshire.

4th To Wendover.

5th To Aylesbury without the works in Waltham.

9th To Wendover again.

10th To Wickham.

11th To Henley upon Thames in Oxfordshire.

Appendix III

Captured Regimental Colours

Royalist Colours Captured at Marston Moor

A white cornet of dragoons [guidon], with a blue and white fringe in the midst whereof is painted a Roundhead's face and on its top the letter P (which is conceived to signify a Puritan) with a sword in a hand reached from a cloud, with the motto 'Fiat Justitia'.

A black cornet with a black and yellow fringe, and a sword reached from a cloud, with the motto, 'Terribilis ut acies ordinata'.

A blue [cornet] ad on it a crown toward the top, with a mitre beneath the crown with the Parliament painted on the side, and this motto 'Nolite tangere Christos meos', to wit, the crown and mitre.

A black [cornet] with a black fringe, and in the middle three crowns gilded, with this motto 'Quarta perennis erit'.

A blue [cornet] with a silver fringe.

A willow green [cornet] and in the middle the portraiture of a man holding in one hand a sword and in the other a knot with this motto 'This shall untie it'.

A yellow [cornet] and in the middle a stooping lion at whose breech lieth snatching a mastife dog, with this word as it were proceeding from his mouth 'Kimbolton' and at his feet little beagles, and before their mouths, 'Pym, Pym, Pym' with these words proceeding from his mouth 'Quousque tandem abutere patiendtia nostra?' That is, how long will you abuse our patience.

A blue [cornet] with the motto that cannot be read.

Another coloured [cornet] with a face and this motto 'aut mors, aut vita decora'.

A white [cornet] with a blue and white fringe and a red cross in the middle.

A red [cornet] with a white cross and this motto 'Pro Rege & Regno'.

A black [cornet] with a black and yellow fringe, and a red cross and white cross in the middle and a yellow streamer sloping down from the cross.

A red [cornet] with a red fringe.

A red [cornet] with a silver fringe.

A blue [cornet] with a blue fringe.

Another of the same.

A red [cornet] with a red and white fringe.

A red [cornet] with a black fringe.

A black [cornet] with a black and white fringe.

A flesh coloured cornet.

Some torn ensigns.

Prince Rupert's standard with the ensigns of the Palatinate, near five yards long and broad, with a red cross in the middle.

Three green ensigns whereof two with a red cross upon white and four or five little crosses sloping downward.

Six yellow ensigns with red crosses and one with a red cross, and three black roses. The rest only yellow.

Four white with red crosses, whereof one with five black streamers.

Eleven red [ensigns] with white crosses.

A blue [ensign] with a red and white cross

Bibliography

Primary Sources

The National Archives

SP 9/-	State Papers, Miscellaneous
SP 16/-	State Papers Domestic, Charles I
SP 28/-	Commonwealth Exchequer Papers
WO 47/-	War Office, Minutes
WO 54/-	War Office, Registers
WO 55/-	War Office, Miscellanea
PROB	Probate Records

Bodleian Library

Tanner MS 62–66	Collection of papers and correspondence of the Speaker of the House of Commons
Carte MS 74	Journal of Colonel Edward Montagu's Regiment of Foot

British Library

Add MS 16,370	Plans by Sir Bernard de Gomme
Add MS 18,982	Royalist correspondence addressed primarily to Prince Rupert, 1642–1643
Add MS 22,619	Letters and papers relating to the history of Norwich
Add MS 33,084	Correspondence of the Pelham family of Sussex, 154–1722
Add MS 34315	Register book of the Ordnance Office, 1634–1644
Add MS 37,491	The minute book for the Parliamentary Committee of southern Essex
Egerton MS 785	The letter book of Sir Samuel Luke
Egerton MS 2643	Barrington family correspondence
Egerton MS 2646–2651	Barrington family correspondence
Harl MS 166	The diary of Sir Symond D'Ewes
Harl MS 6851	Papers of Sir Edward Walker relating to the Civil War
Harl MS 6804	Correspondence relating to the affairs of the latter end of the reign of Charles I
Stowe MS 164	Minute book for the Parliamentary Committee for Essex
Thomason Tracts	(See footnotes for details)

Essex Record Office

Q/BSa2/82	Petition of Martha Emming, widow of Coggeshall, Essex
Q/SBa2/61	Petition of Richard Ellsing a weaver of Helions Bumpstead, 1646
D/Y/2/9	

Hampshire Record Office
Q1/4   Petition of Thomas White, 1662

Hertfordshire Record Office
70539   Letter from Captain Silas Titus to Colonel Coxe, nd [1644]

Parliamentary Archives
Man/-   Archives of the Earl of Manchester
Wil/-   Photographs of the Earl of Manchester's Archives not included in Man/-

Norfolk Record Office
NCR 13b/3   Colonel Vermuyden wrote to the Committee at Norwich, nd

Somerset Heritage Centre
Q/SPET/1/106   Petition of William Stoakes, 23 April 1661

Surrey History Centre
1248/1   Letterbook of the Brodrick family

West Yorkshire History Centre
QS1/13/4/6/5,   Petition of Christopher Wilson of Reedness, West Riding, 28 April 1674
QS1/38/3/6.   Petition of James Moore of Letwell in Yorkshire, 1699.

Printed sources

Anon., 'Map of York' *c.*1600

Anon., *A Relation of the passage of our English Companies from time to time* (London, 1621)

Anon., *Directions for Musters, wherein is shewed the order for drilling for the musket and the pike* (Cambridge: Thomas Buck and Roger Daniel, 1638)

Anon., *London's Love to her Neighbours in general and in particular to the Six Associated Counties, namely Norfolk, Suffolk, Essex, Cambridge, Hertford and Bedford* (London: John Hammond, 1643)

Anon., *His Highness Prince Rupert raising of the Siege of Newark upon Trent, 21 March 1643 written by an eyewitness to a person of honour* (1643)

Anon., *A Continuation of Certain Remarkable Passages from Both Houses of Parliament* (London: Coles and Leach, 1643)

Anon., *A Brief Relation of the Siege of Newark as it was delivered to the Council of State at Derby House by Lieutenant Colonel Bury* (London: Peter Cole, 26 March 1644)

Anon., *An Ordnance of the Lords and Commons assembled in Parliament for putting the Associated Counties of Suffolk, Norfolk, Essex ... in to a Posture of defence. By the better regulating of the trained bands and raising other forces of Horse and Foot ...* (London: Edward Husbands, 5 July 1644)

Anon., *A Sermon preached at Kingston upon Hull upon the day of Thanksgiving after the battle and that marvellous victory at Hessem Moore, near York* (London: Grays Inn, 1644)

Anon., *A Catalogue of Remarkable Mercies conferred upon the Seven Associated Counties* (April, 1644)

Anon., *A Journal or true and exact relation of each days passage, of that party of the Right Honourable the Earl of Manchester's Army, under the command of the ever honoured Major General Crawford from the 1st August to the end of the same month* (London: Hugh Perry, 1644)

Anon., *Journal of the House of Commons vol.II–IV* (London: HMSO, 1802)

Anon., *Journal of the House of Lords, vol.V–VIII* (London: HMSO, 1786–1800)

Anon., *Extracts from the Presbytery Book of Strathbogie 1631 to 1654* (Aberdeen: Spalding Club, 1893)

Adair, John, *They Saw it Happen, contemporary accounts of the Siege of Basing House* (Hampshire County Council, 1981)

Allen, D. H., *Essex Quarter Sessions Order Book, 1652–1661* (Chelmsford: Essex Record Office Publications, 1974)

Atkins, Richard and John Gwyn, ed. Brigadier Peter Young and Norman Tucker, *Military Memoirs, The Civil War, Richard Atkins and John Gwyn* (Longmans: Green and Co. Ltd, 1967)

Baillie, Robert, ed. D. Laing, *Letters and Journals of Robert Baillie* (Edinburgh: Bannatyne Club 1841)

Baxter, Richard, *Reliquiae Baxterianae or Mr Richard Baxter's narrative of the most memorable passages of his life and times* (1696)

Bruce, John and David Masson, *The Quarrel between the Earl of Manchester and Oliver Cromwell* (London: Camden Society, 1875)

Carlyle, Thomas, et al., *The Letters and Speeches of Oliver Cromwell*, vol.I (London, Methuen & Co, 1904)

Collier, I.P. et al., *Trevelyan Papers* vol. III, new series (London: Camden Society, 1872–1873)

Clarendon, Earl of, ed. Roger Lockyer, *The History of the Great Rebellion* (Oxford: Oxford University Press, 1967)

Cooper, Charles Henry, *Annals of Cambridge*, vol. III (Cambridge: Warwick and Co, 1845)

Crawford, Laurence, *Colonel Crawford his Remonstrance, declaring why he deserted his employment in Ireland* (London: H Elsing, 3 February 1644)

Dore, R. N., *The Letter Books of Sir William Brereton* (Record Society of Lancashire and Cheshire, 1984)

Douglas, Robert, 'Diary of Mr Robert Douglas when with the Scottish Army in England', in *Historical Fragments relative to Scottish Affairs from 1635 to 1664* (Edinburgh: Thomas Stevenage, 1833)

Dowsing, William, ed. Rev. C.H. Evelyn White, *The Journal of William Dowsing of Stratford, Parliamentary visitor appointed by the Earl of Manchester for demolishing the superstitious pictures and ornaments of church etc., within the county of Suffolk in the year 1643–1644* (Ipswich: Pawsey and Hayes, 1885)

Ede-Borrett, Stephen, *The Iter Carolinum of Charles I (1642–1649) and the Journal of Prince Rupert's Marches, (1642–1646)* (Oxford: The Pike and Shot Society, 2013)

Everitt, Alan, *Suffolk and the Great Rebellion, 1640–1660* (Suffolk Record Society 1960)

Fairfax, Sir Thomas, 'A Short Memorial of Northern Actions during the war there, from the year 1642 till 1644', in *Journal of the Society for Army Historical Research*, vol. V (1926)

Fairfax, Sir Thomas, 'A Short Memorial of the Northern Actions in which I was engaged, during the war there, from the year 1642 to the year 1644', in *Yorkshire Archaeological Journal* (vol. VIII, 1884)

Firth, C. H. and R.S. Rait, *Acts and Ordinances of the Interregnum 1642–1660*, 3 vols (London: 1911)

Firth, C. H., *Oliver Cromwell and the Rule of the Puritans in England* (London: and New York: G.P. Putnam's Sons, 1929)

Fletcher, Henry, *The Perfect Politician, or, A Full View of the Life and Action (Military and Civil) of O Cromwell*

Fuller, Thomas, ed. Richard Barber, *Fuller's Worthies, Selected from the Worthies of England* (London: The Folio Society, 1987)

Gent, S.T., *Flagellum: or the Life and Death, Birth and Burial of Oliver Cromwell* (London: 1663)

Green, Mary Anne Everett, *Calendar of the Committee for the Advance of Money* (London: HMSO, 1888)

Hamilton, William Douglas and Sophie Crawford Lomas (eds), *Calendar of State Papers Domestic, Charles I, 1641–1643* (London: HMSO, 1887)

Hamilton, William Douglas and Sophie Crawford Lomas (eds), *Calendar of State Papers Domestic, Charles I, 1644* (London: HMSO, 1888)

Hamilton, William Douglas and Sophie Crawford Lomas (eds) *Calendar of State Papers Domestic, Charles I, 1644–1645* (London: HMSO, 1890)

Hamilton, William Douglas and Sophie Crawford Lomas (eds), *Calendar of State Papers Domestic, Charles I, Addenda 1625–1649* (London: HMSO, 1897)

Heath, James *Flagellum* (London: 1665)

Hinds, Allen B., *Calendar of State papers relating to English Affairs in the Archives of Venice, 1642–1643* (London: HMSO, 1925)

Hinds, Allen B., *Calendar of State papers relating to English Affairs in the Archives of Venice, 1643–1647* (London: HMSO, 1926)

Historical Manuscripts Commission, 7th Report (London HMSO, 1879)

Historical Manuscripts Commission, Appendix to 8th Report (1907–1909)

Historical Manuscripts Commission, 11th Report Appendix 3, The Manuscripts of the Corporations of Southampton and King's Lynn (London: HMSO, 1887)

Historical Manuscripts Commission, 13th Report Appendix, Part 1, The Manuscripts of his Grace the Duke of Portland Preserved at Welbeck Abbey vol. I (London: HMSO, 1891)

Historical Manuscripts Commission, Report on the Manuscripts of the late Reginald Rawdon Hastings (London: HMSO, 1930)

Holles, Denzil, Memoirs of Denzil, Lord Holles (1699)

Holmes, Clive, The Suffolk Committees for Scandalous Ministers (The Suffolk Records Society, 1979)

Hope, Sir Thomas, A Diary of the Public Correspondence of Sir Thomas Hope of Craighall, Bart, 1633–1645 (Edinburgh: 1893)

Horsley, Benedict, The Ichnography or Ground Plot of ye City of York, 1694 (1697)

Hutchinson, Lucy, Memoirs of the Life of Colonel Hutchinson (London: Henry and Bohn, 1846)

Josselyn, Ralph, ed. E. Hockliffe, Diary of Rev. Ralph Josselyn (London: Camden Society, 1908)

Juxon, Thomas, ed. Keith Lindley and David Scott, The Journal of Thomas Juxon, 1644–1647 (Cambridge: Cambridge University Press, 1999)

The King's Cabinet Opened or certain packets of secret letters and papers written with the King's own hand, and taken in his cabinet at Naseby field, 14 June 1645 (London: 1645)

Lilburne, John, England's Birth Right Justified against all Arbitrary Usurpation, whether regal or Parliamentary or under what vizor soever (London: October 1645)

Lilly, William, William Lilly's History of his Life and Times (London: Charles Baldwin, 1822)

Ludlow, Edmund, ed. C.H. Firth, The Memoirs of Edmund Ludlow, Lieutenant General of the Horse in the Army of the Commonwealth of England, vol. I (Oxford: Clarendon Press, 1894)

Markham, Francis, Five Decades of Epistles of War (London, 1622)

Meikle, Henry W., Correspondence of the Scots Commissioners in London, 1644–1646 (Edinburgh: The Roxburghe Club, 1917)

Monck, George, Observations upon Military and Political Affairs written by the most honourable George, Duke of Albemarle (London: 1671)

Newcastle, Margaret, Duchess of Newcastle, ed. C.H. Firth, Life of William Cavendish, Duke of Newcastle (London: J. C. Nimmo, 1886)

Phillips, I.G., The Journal of Sir Samuel Luke, Scoutmaster General to the Earl of Essex, 1643–1644 (Oxfordshire Record Society, 1952–1953)

Rushworth, John, Historical Collections of Private Passages of State (London: D. Browne, 1721)

Thomson, Alan, The Impact of the First Civil War on Hertfordshire, 1642–1647 (Hertfordshire Record Society, 2007)

Slingsby, Sir Henry, ed. Rev. Daniel Parsons The Diary of Sir Henry Slingsby (London: 1836)

Stevenson, William, The Presbytrie Book of Kirkcaldie (Kirkcaldy: James Burt, 1900)

Symonds, Richard, ed. Charles E. Long, Diary of the Marches of the Royal Army during the Great Civil War kept by Richard Symonds (London: Camden Press, 1859)

Somerville, James, Memoire of the Somervilles, being a history of the baronial house of Somerville (Edinburgh: James Ballantyne and Co., 1815)

Sprigg, Joshua, Anglia Rediviva, England's Recovery being the history of the motions, actions and successes of the army under the immediate command of His Excellency Sir Thomas Fairfax (1647)

Stockdale, Thomas, 'Letter to John Rushworth, 5 July 1644', printed in C. H. Firth, Transactions of the Royal Historical Society New Series, vol. II (London: Longmans, Green and Co. 1898)

Thurloe, John, ed. Thomas Birch, A Collection of the State Papers of John Thurloe, vol. I (London: 1742)

Tibbutt, H.G., The Letterbooks of Sir Samuel Luke, 1644–1645 (Society of Bedfordshire, 1958)

Venn, Captain Thomas, Military and Maritine [sic] Discipline in Three Books (London: E. Tyler and R. Holt, 1672)

Vicars, John, God's Ark, Overtopping the World's Waves or the third part of the Parliamentary Chronicle (London: M. Simons and J. Macock, 1646)

Vicars, John, England's Worthies under whom all the Civil and Bloudy Warres since anno 1643 to anno 1647 are related (London: J. Rothwell, 1647)

Walker, Sir Edward, Historical Discourses, Upon Several Occasions, vol. I, The Happy Progress and Success of the Arms of King Charles I (London: Samuel Keble, 1705)

Waller, Sir William, Recollections in the Poetry of Anna Matilda (1788)

Ward, Robert, Animadversions of Warre: Or, A Militarie Magazine of the Truest Rules and Ablest Instructions for the Managing of Warre (London: 1639)

Warwick, Sir Philip, Memoirs of the Reign of King Charles the First (Edinburgh: John Ballantyne and Co., 1813)

Newsbooks

Certaine Informations from Several Parts of the Kingdom (London: Henry Overton, 1643–1644)
Mercurius Aulicus (Oxford: H. Hall, 1643–1646)
The Kingdomes Weekly Intelligencer (London: 1643–1649)
The Scottish Dove sent out and returning bringing intelligence from their army (London: Laurence Chapman, 1644–?)

Secondary Sources

Appleby, David, 'Unnecessary Persons? Maimed Soldiers and War Widows in Essex, 1642–1662' in *Essex Archaeology and History* (2001)
Appleby, David and Andrew Hopper (eds), *Battle-Scarred, Mortality, medical care and military welfare in The British Civil Wars* (Manchester: Manchester University Press, 2018)
Ashley, Maurice, *Cromwell's Generals* (London: Jonathan Cape, 1954)
Barres-Baker, M.C., *The Siege of Reading* (Ottowa: ebooksLib, 2004)
Carlton, Charles, *Going to the Wars the experience of the British Civil Wars, 1638–1651* (London: and New York: Routledge, 1994)
Carlton, Charles, *This Seat of Mars, War and the British Isles, 1485–1746* (Yale University Press, 2011)
Clarke, J.S., *The Life of James the Second, King of England etc.* (London: Payne and Foss, 1816)
Coates, Rev. Charles, *History and Antiquities of Reading* (J. Nichols and Son, 1802)
Cooke, David, *The Road to Marston Moor* (Barnsley: Pen and Sword, 2007)
Emberton, Wilfred, *The English Civil War Day by Day* (Stroud: Alan Sutton Publishing, 1995)
Firth, Charles H. and Davis, Godfrey, *The Regimental History of Cromwell's Army* (Oxford: Clarendon Press, 1940)
Firth, C. H., 'Marston Moor', in *Transactions of the Royal History Society*, new series vol. XII (London: Longmans, Green and Co., 1898)
Firth, C.H., 'Two accounts of the battle of Marston Moor', in *The English Historical Review*, ed. Rev. Mandell Creighton, vol. V (London: Longmans, Green and Co, 1890)
Gardiner, S.R., *The History of the Great Civil War* (Longmans: Green & Co., 1893)
Gaunt, Peter, *The Cromwellian Gazetteer, An illustrated guide to Britain in the Civil War and Commonwealth* (Stroud: Alan Sutton Publishing, 1994)
Gentles, Ian, *The New Model Army, in England, Ireland and Scotland, 1645–1653* (Oxford: Blackwell Publishers, 1992)
Hargrove, E., *The History of the Castle, Town and Forest of Knaresbrough …* (Knaresbrough: and Harrogate: Hargrove and Sons, 1809)
Holmes, Clive, *The Eastern Association in the English Civil War* (Cambridge: Cambridge University Press, 1974)
Hunter, Joseph, *The History and Topography of the parish of Sheffield in the county of York* (Lackington, Hughes, Harding, Mavor and Jones, 1819)
Hutton, Ronald, 'For King and County' in Lesley Smith (ed.), *The Making of Britain, the Age of Expansion* (Oxford: Macmillan, 1986)
Ketton-Cremer, R.W., *Norfolk in the Civil War* (London: Faber and Faber, 1969)
Keys, David, 'The fight to save battlegrounds from invasion of metal detectors', in *The Independent*, 22 September 2003
Kishlansky, Mark A., *The Rise of the New Model Army* (Cambridge: Cambridge University Press, 1979)
Leadman, Alex. D. H., *Battles Fought in Yorkshire* (London: Bradbury, Agnew, 1891)
Lynch, John, *For King and Parliament: Bristol and the Civil War* (Stroud: Alan Sutton, Ltd, 1999)
McIntyre, Lauren and Graham Bruce, 'Excavating All Saints, a Medieval Church Rediscovered', in *Current Archaeology* (August 2010)
Marsh, Simon, 'The Disarmed Multitude: The impact of the Lostwithal Campaign on the Earl of Essex's Army and its Reconstitution for the Second Newbury Campaign', in Serena Jones (ed.) *Home and Away, the British Experience of War, 1618–1721* (Helion & Co. 2018)
Money, Walter, *The First and Second Battles of Newbury and the Siege of Donnington Castle during the Civil War* (London: Simkin, Marshal & Co. 1884)
Murdoch and Grossjean, *Alexander Leslie and the Scottish Generals of the Thirty Years War, 1618–1648* (London: Pickering and Chatto, 2014)

Newman, Dr Peter, 'Marston Moor, 1644–1979, a study of a battlefield', in *Journal of Society of Army Historical Research* (Society of Army Historical Research, 1979)

Newman, Dr Peter, *The Battle of Marston Moor, 1644* (Chichester: Antony Bird, 1981)

Newman, Dr Peter and P. R. Roberts, *Marston Moor, 1644, the Battle of Five Armies* (Pickering; Blackthorn Press, 2003) with CD-ROM

Norman, A. V. B. Wallace, *Wallace Collection Catalogue, European arms and armour supplement*

Ordnance Survey 6″ to 1 mile maps

Ordnance Survey 25″ to 1 mile maps

Scott, Chris and Alan Turton, *Hey for Old Robin! The Campaigns and Armies of the Earl of Essex During the First Civil War, 1642–1646* (Solihull: Helion and Co., 2017)

Scott, Chris, *The Battles of Newbury* (Barnsley: Pen and Sword, 2008)

Smith, Lesley, *The Making of Britain, the Age of Expansion* (Oxford: Macmillan, 1986)

Spring, Laurence, *The Army of the Eastern Association* (Romford: The Pike and Shot Society, 2016)

Spring, Laurence, *The Campaigns of Sir William Waller* (Solihull: Helion and Co., 2019)

Sutherland, Tim (ed.), *Battlefield Archaeology: A Guide to the Archaeology of Conflict, Guide 8* (BAJR Practical Guide Series)

Temple, Robert K. G., 'The Original Officer List of the New Model Army', in *Historical Research*, vol. 59, Issue 139, May 1986, pp.50–77

Terry, Charles S., *Life of and Campaigns of Alexander Leslie, First Earl of Leven* (Longmans, Green and Co., 1899)

Terry, Charles S., *Papers Relating to the Army of the Solemn League and Covenant, 1643–1647* (Edinburgh, 1917)

Thurham, John, 'Description of an Ancient Tumular cemetery, probably of the Anglo Saxon Period at Lamel Hill, near York' in *Archaeological Journal*, vol.VI (1849)

Torr, James, *The Antiquities of York City and the civil government thereof... collected from the papers of Christopher Hildyard* (London: G White, 1719)

Varley, F. J., *Cambridge During the Civil War* (Cambridge: W. Heffer and Sons Ltd, 1935)

Wanklyn, Malcolm, *Decisive Battles of the English Civil War* (Barnsley: Pen and Sword, 2006)

Wenham, Peter, *The Great and Close Siege of York* (York: Session Book Trust, 1994)

Young, Brigadier Peter, *Edgehill 1642: The Campaign and the Battle* (Kineton: The Roundwood Press, 1967)

Young, Brigadier Peter, *Marston Moor 1644: The Campaign and the Battle* (Kineton: The Roundwood Press, 1970)

Newspapers

Leeds Intelligencer

Newbury Weekly News

Newcastle Courant

The Telegraph

Windsor and Eton Express

Yorkshire Gazette

Websites

British History Online (requires subscription for some material), <https://www.british-history.ac.uk/>

British Newspapers Archive (requires subscription), <https://www.britishnewspaperarchive.co.uk/>

Civil War Petitions <https://www.civilwarpetitions.ac.uk/>

Oxford Dictionary of National Biography online (requires subscription) <https://www.oxforddnb.com>

Youtube BBC series Cold Case, series 2, 'The York 113'